Chicken Soup for the Soul.

Raising Kids on the Spectrum

Chicken Soup for the Soul: Raising Kids on the Spectrum
101 Inspirational Stories for Parents of Children with Autism and Asperger's
Dr. Rebecca Landa, Mary Beth Marsden, Nancy Burrows, and Amy Newmark

Published by Chicken Soup for the Soul Publishing, LLC www.chickensoup.com
Copyright © 2013 by Chicken Soup for the Soul Publishing, LLC. All Rights Reserved.

The publisher gratefully acknowledges the many publishers and individuals who granted Chicken Soup for the Soul permission to reprint the cited material.

Front cover and interior photo courtesy of GettyImages.com/Photographer's Choice, ©Charly Franklin. Back cover photo courtesy of iStockphoto.com/gradyreese.

Cover and Interior Design & Layout by Pneuma Books, LLC

Distributed to the booktrade by Simon & Schuster. SAN: 200-2442

Publisher's Cataloging-in-Publication Data
(Prepared by The Donohue Group)

Chicken soup for the soul : raising kids on the spectrum : 101 inspirational
  stories for parents of children with autism and Asperger's / [compiled by]
  Rebecca Landa ... [et al.] ; [introduction by Rebecca Landa].

    p. ; cm.

  ISBN: 978-1-61159-908-4

    1. Parents of autistic children--Literary collections. 2. Children with autism spectrum disorders--Literary collections. 3. Asperger's syndrome in children--Literary collections. 4. Parenting--Literary collections. 5. Parents of autistic children--Anecdotes. 6. Children with autism spectrum disorders--Anecdotes. 7. Asperger's syndrome in children--Anecdotes. 8. Parenting--Anecdotes. 9. Anecdotes. I. Landa, Rebecca, 1955- II. Title: Raising kids on the spectrum : 101 inspirational stories for parents of children with autism and Asperger's

PN6071.P28 C453 2013
810.8/02/03525   2013930922

PRINTED IN THE UNITED STATES OF AMERICA
on acid ∞ free paper
22 21 20 19 18 17 16 15 14 13   01 02 03 04 05 06 07 08 09 10

Chicken Soup for the Soul

Raising Kids on the Spectrum

101 Inspirational Stories for Parents of
Children with **Autism** and **Asperger's**

Dr. Rebecca Landa
of the **Kennedy Krieger Institute,**
Mary Beth Marsden, Nancy Burrows,
and Amy Newmark

Chicken Soup for the Soul Publishing, LLC
Cos Cob, CT

www.chickensoup.com

Contents

Introduction, *Dr. Rebecca Landa* xi

❶
~The "A" Word~

1. This Is What It's Like, *Leigh Merryday* 1
2. I'll Take the Special, *Jessica Adam* 6
3. The Diagnosis, *Katherine Briccetti* 9
4. Autism Does Not Define Me, *Karen Krejcha* 13
5. First Talk, *Lana Clifton* 16
6. What's in a Label? *Jennifer Doelle Young* 20
7. The Boy Who Drew a Face, *Shari Cohen Forsythe* 23
8. The Seven-Year Twitch, *Amy Giles* 26
9. Your Own Dance, *Melinda Coppola* 29
10. The Eccentric Side of Normal, *Sarah Darer Littman* 31
11. For Jacob, *Sarah Mitchell* 35
12. Being Quiet, *Lava Mueller* 39

❷
~The Amazing Brain~

13. How Stuff Works, *Trey Brown* 45
14. The Art of Hope, *Jennifer Froelich* 48
15. Fun Facts, *Peggy Robbins Janousky* 52
16. We Love Vermont, *Beth Cato* 54
17. Look Up, *Jayne Thurber-Smith* 58
18. Sam, *Allison Hermann Craigie* 60
19. Convenient Care, *Tyann Sheldon Rouw* 64

20. James 101, *Nancy Burrows* 68
21. Jay's Odyssey Tales, *Sharon Fuentes* 73
22. The Rainbow, *Florence Strang* 76
23. Walk On, *Michelle Rubin* 78

❸

~Challenges~

24. I Hit the Roof, *Shelley Stolaroff Segal* 85
25. Obsession, *Michael D. Gingerich* 87
26. Bridging the Gap, *Caroline Saul* 90
27. What I Didn't Expect, *D.M. Rosner* 94
28. Peace, *Amy McMunn Schindler* 98
29. The Right Kind of Kick, *René Zimbelman* 101
30. Lost, *Jennifer Bush* 105
31. Don't Stop Believing, *Liane Kupferberg Carter* 108
32. Room Repair, *Kathy Labosh* 111
33. The Red Shirt, *Shelley Stolaroff Segal* 113
34. Always Learning, *Sue Jeantheau* 117

❹

~Friends and Strangers~

35. My Village, *Christine Coleman* 123
36. The Cardinal Rule, *Hope Maven* 126
37. A Loving World, *Joyce Rohe* 130
38. A Friendly Reminder, *Tina Dula* 132
39. Friendships, *Dawn Hentrich* 136
40. Trains and Angels, *Jean Marino* 140
41. Reconnect, *Anne Moore Burnett* 144
42. My Trip to Home Depot, *Stephanie Carmel* 146
43. Parting the Waters, *Robin J. Silverman* 149
44. The Birth of Camp Awesome, *Bonnie Monroe* 153
45. The Market, *Jean McAllister Brooks* 157

❺
~Finding the Funny~

46. Oliver Wears the Pants, *Kate Coveny Hood* 163
47. The Little Man Inside, *D'Ann Renner* 167
48. Return of the Prodigal Son, *Lorri Benedik* 172
49. Don't Call My Daughter "Normal" *Sarah Maizes* 174
50. Funeral Fun, *Angela Benam* 176
51. Scared or Angry? *Lori Odhner* 180
52. Dressing Up, *Michele Bissonnette Robbins* 182
53. Life Skills, *Carol Schmidt* 186
54. Womb Pact, *Sharon L. Martin* 189
55. It Is, Because I Said So, *Alisa Rock* 193

❻
~School~

56. The Most Popular Girl, *Cynthia J. Patton* 199
57. Yes or No? *Amy McMunn Schindler* 203
58. He's Not Even Wrong, *Jean Winegardner* 207
59. Seeing Eye to I, *Julie Casper Roth* 210
60. The Storm Before the Calm, *Jennifer Doelle Young* 214
61. Letter to My Child's First Teacher, *Leigh Merryday* 218
62. Let Me Tell You About Jake, *Jean Ferratier* 221
63. Field Day, *Adrienne B. Paradis* 224
64. Student Teacher, *René Thompson* 227
65. Never Giving Up Hope, *Kym Grosso* 229
66. Thank You, Diane, *Alison Dyer* 232

❼
~All in the Family~

67. The Salutation of Slapping Palms, *Jeneil Palmer Russell* 239
68. Do Dogs Have Autism? *Kathleen Leopold* 241

69. Back and Forth, *Seth Fowler*.................................244
70. Don't Sweat the Stimmies, *Joyce Rohe*.................................246
71. Rocky Road, *Eric Tor* 249
72. Finding My Inner Spectrum, *J. Vetter*.................................251
73. Our Passover Story, *Jennifer Berger*.................................255
74. Joseph's Wish, *Terri Manzione* 259
75. Thank You, Las Vegas, *Steve Spilde*.................................263
76. Beacons of Hope, *Christine Bakter*.................................266
77. The Boy from My Dreams, *Gwen Navarrete*.................................270
78. The Biggest Losers Win Big, *Phil Parham* 274

❽

~Snapshots~

79. Sound of a Sunset, *F. Lewis "Big Daddy" Stark*.................................281
80. The Blister, *Faith Paulsen* 283
81. Just for This Day, *Sally Meyer*.................................287
82. Tuesday Morning, *Douglas E. Baker*.................................290
83. They Think He's Dancing, *Maura Klopfenstein-Oprisko*.................................294
84. Twirl with Me, Mommy! *Amy L. Stout*.................................297
85. The Island, *D. Alison Watt*.................................300
86. Flying the Friendly Skies, *Michelle Landrum* 303
87. Because Night Turns into Day, *Janoah M. White*.................................305
88. Transformation on the Trail, *Kathleen Deyer Bolduc*.................................307

❾

~Hope and Expectations~

89. Ma Tovu, *Alison Singer* 313
90. When Ladybugs Roar, *Wendy Sparrow* 316
91. The Poem in My Nightstand Drawer, *Mary Roth*.................................320
92. Two Worlds, *Aspen Teresa Nolette* 323
93. The Other Side of Hope, *Janet Amorello* 327
94. Softness in the Vast Blue Sky, *Galen Pearl*.................................329

95. A Hug with No Arms, *Carrie Malinowski*............................332
96. Just Joey, *Luisa R. Fortunato* 335
97. Feeling Judged, *Laura Shumaker*...339
98. Bedtime Routine, *Nancy Burrows* 341
99. We're All a Little Spectrum, *Laura Cichoracki*....................343
100. Traditions, *Maura Klopfenstein-Oprisko*............................346
101. Learning to Iron, *Ann Kilter* 349

Afterword: Real Look Autism, *Mary Beth Marsden* 351

Glossary 354
Meet Our Contributors..359
Meet Our Authors 376
Thank You..379

Introduction

My first experience with autism spectrum disorder (ASD) was with a five-year-old nonverbal little girl. Her mother sat face-to-face with me and explained that all her hopes for her child were in my hands—her expectation was that I would teach this precious little girl to talk.

As a speech-language pathologist just out of school, at a time when very little about autism was known, I felt the weight of the world on my shoulders. I accepted the challenge that this mother set before me. I began to go through an all-systems check. Did the little one have enough understanding of objects, events, and relationships to communicate about them? Did her speech musculature work properly? Was she socially motivated to communicate? How did she think about the world, how much information could she process at once, and how could I find the answers to all these questions?

Slowly but surely, the strategies that I used during our intervention sessions began to show results. We started with playful routines that she enjoyed, with built-in motivating temptations for her to communicate. At first, I taught her a means to communicate nonverbally through gestures, signs, and simple pictures. All the while I provided simple speech models for her to imitate. She made tremendous gains, and yes, she did learn to talk, though not all children with ASD do.

As my relationship with this child and her family deepened, I knew that devoting my career to autism was inevitable. Fortunately for me, I came upon fantastic mentors who were international experts in autism, and I immersed myself in research and clinical work with children and adults with autism and their families.

One in eighty-eight children is diagnosed with an autism spectrum disorder (ASD). Every family that has been touched by ASD understands the challenges—and the joys—of raising a child on the autism spectrum. If you have a family member with ASD or have had an ASD diagnosis, you are not alone. There is a growing community of support for you, as is shown in the story "A Friendly Reminder" by Tina Dula, about her encounter with a generous woman at a restaurant, who happened to be another mother of a child with autism. If you have not knowingly interacted with someone with ASD, this book may compel you to reconsider encounters with strangers, or even with someone familiar, whose behavior is awkward or perhaps even off-putting.

This book's potential for impacting the world's understanding of, and compassion for, individuals with ASD and their family members motivated me to participate in bringing it to fruition. In my role as a clinician, researcher, and friend of many individuals with ASD and their families, I have walked alongside families experiencing the types of challenges and triumphs shared in this book. My life has been deeply enriched as a result. I love watching how children with ASD cultivate beautiful and caring hearts in their neighbors and schoolmates who learn to support them and cheer them on at special moments—moments like when they are upset because their usual spot at the lunch table isn't available, and moments when they learn to coordinate their eyes and hands to hit a ping pong ball with a paddle. I am inspired by people with ASD and their families, who steadfastly endeavor to achieve what many people think is impossible.

As a researcher, I tackle complex questions about ASD with the aim of getting answers that will improve lives. My research has shown that the earliest signs of ASD can be subtle, appearing in the first year or two of life, a finding that opens the door to the benefits of early intervention. We have developed early intervention models (such as "Early Achievements") and shown that very early intervention and education enables children with ASD to make big developmental strides, increasing their ability to connect with others in meaningful and rewarding ways. Another priority of my work is to translate research into effective and practical strategies that can be used by parents and teachers in the community. Some of these strategies are applicable to children with other developmental challenges or even children with typical development, helping them to achieve their greatest potential.

Through research, scientists also are learning more about the causes of ASD. Most of the improvements in healthcare, accurate diagnosis, and treatment for ASD have occurred because of the dedication of researchers and individuals with ASD and their family members. By participating in the research effort, families can help increase the pace at which researchers make life-changing discoveries for individuals with ASD. Participating in research may come in the form of answering confidential online questionnaires, donating small amounts of blood, completing tests of language or motor skills, or some other activity. Usually the time commitment for research is minimal, and you can rest assured that you have "paid it forward" to help someone else in ways you can't even imagine. Sometimes research about ASD seems irrelevant to everyday life. Yet nothing could be farther from the truth. Much of what is learned in research about ASD leads to new discoveries that help to promote healthy development and life experiences for children and adults in general. So whether you have a family member with ASD or not, I hope that you will seek out opportunities to participate in autism research as a member of a comparison (non-ASD) group or a group with ASD.

On a more personal note, many stories in this book explain how life changes when parents learn that their child has an ASD. And the changes that result often are not understood or envied by others. Many parents of children with ASD step off the beaten path of life as they strive to understand their child's idiosyncrasies, then create a new and uncharted world of possibilities for their dearly loved child. Things that most people take for granted, such as getting a full night's sleep or going out for an occasional meal, become rare and cherished events for parents of children with ASD. The complexities of ASD can challenge even the most competent and caring parent, as explained by Hope Maven in her story "The Cardinal Rule"—her son wandered away in the blink of an eye, only to be found in a store parking lot. As the symptoms of ASD emerge in a child, parents have to learn how to explain their own and their child's behaviors to others.

Stress and depression are common in parents of children with ASD, as many parents in this book openly share. Seeking support and tips from other parents of children with autism and from professionals trained to treat these problems can be a lifesaver and prevent lots of heartache. As Shari Cohen Forsythe advises in her story "The Boy Who Drew a Face," seeking out "autism angels" for support and taking a little time for pampering can help parents find hope when the going gets tough.

If you do not have a child with ASD and are not well acquainted with this neurodevelopmental disorder, here is a brief explanation about it. Historically, ASD was a broad label for individuals diagnosed with autism, pervasive developmental disorder not otherwise specified (PDD-NOS), or Asperger syndrome. Autism and PDD-NOS differed primarily in the number of symptoms present. To be diagnosed with Asperger syndrome, an individual had to meet additional criteria: demonstrate no delay in language development and have intellectual abilities of at least average levels. With recent changes in professional diagnostic guidelines, these labels will no longer be used. Rather, the diagnosis that will be given to all who qualify will be "autism spectrum disorder." To receive a diagnosis of ASD, an individual must show impairment in social and communication learning and behavior. Most individuals with ASD refer to themselves as "being on the spectrum."

ASD is a medical diagnosis, but there is not yet a medical test or cure. The diagnosis is based on developmental history, current behavioral features, and responses to specialized tests of thinking and behavior. In individuals with ASD, brain development is altered. This is not because of an injury to the head or a disease or "bad parenting," but because of genetic differences, and possible environmental exposures early in life to substances or viruses that alter brain development. Differences in brain development begin in prenatal life or shortly thereafter even though the signs of delayed or atypical development may not be noticed until the preschool years.

As you will see when you read the stories in this book, the diagnosis of ASD may be given to individuals representing a wide spectrum, or range, of characteristics. Individuals with ASD may have severe intellectual disability, or may fall within the gifted range. Some never learn to speak, while others are loquacious. Some have extreme sensitivity to sounds, sights, smells, tastes, or touch, while others have no unusual experiences of this type. The one thing that all people with ASD share is difficulty navigating interactions with others. That is, they have difficulty understanding others' intentions, facial expressions, body language, and perspectives. In addition, they have difficulty learning social conventions, or the unwritten social rules that most people learn simply by being exposed to everyday events within their culture. For this reason, they often say or do unusual things and become the target of others' teasing, ridicule, or bullying. Yet they often lack insight into the source of others' rejection and are at a loss as to how to remedy the situation. Their social missteps are innocent, not calculated. They are well-intentioned and loving individuals.

One characteristic that may cause a person with ASD to stand out like a sore thumb is the presence of strong preferences and restricted interests in topics or objects that seem inconsequential to others. Sometimes their need for sameness and predictability is overwhelming, and they need special help preparing for new experiences. Without such preparation, they may become quite upset. Many parents in this book tell about the meltdowns, or tantrums, that their child with ASD had during the early years of life, and for some, these continue into adulthood. These meltdowns are not happening because a child is misbehaving or is a discipline challenge.

Rather, they happen because children with ASD have tunnel vision and inflexible ways of thinking, and they have difficulty with the neurobiological regulation of their emotions. Individuals with ASD are most comfortable when they know what will happen next, so when their routines are changed, the world becomes unpredictable and scary for them. Caregivers and teachers can learn effective strategies for helping individuals with ASD learn to cope with unexpected events, and how to prepare for changes in routine.

Individuals with ASD often have better visuo-spatial than verbal reasoning abilities, and often develop a memory for information that is impressive given their other abilities. For example, a child with ASD may learn to recite the alphabet before being able to call "mommy" or "daddy" when in need. Another example involves hyperlexia, the ability to read the text in a book but not understand what is read. It is not uncommon to hear about children with ASD who teach themselves to read before they start school, but who have great difficulty getting the gist of stories when they get to school. You will see many other examples of special skills and insights that some individuals with ASD demonstrate as you read this book.

My hope is that this book provides you a deeper understanding of ASD while it dispels some myths. I hope that the stories give people on the spectrum an increased sense of value and of belonging. If you are a family member, may you find comfort in knowing that you are not alone in the unique blessings and experiences that result from adjusting your life to the parameters of ASD. If you are not directly affected by ASD, I hope that you have the opportunity to extend your hand to someone who is. And for all of us, I hope that the stories in *Chicken Soup for the Soul: Raising Kids on the Spectrum* lead us to help more and judge less, and to have a greater measure of patience next time we encounter someone who challenges our expectations. May this collection of stories inspire all of us to look upon others in a new light, appreciating that a soul is more than what meets the eye. After reading this book, perhaps we will be more inclined to align ourselves, rather than distance ourselves, from those whom we do not readily understand. Doing so might just be the "chicken soup for the soul" that sparks a new sense of confidence, hope, or courage for someone to keep trying against big odds.

~Rebecca Landa, PhD
Director of Kennedy Krieger Institute's Center for Autism

For more information and resources about ASD,
visit www.autism.kennedykrieger.org.

Chapter 1

Raising Kids on the Spectrum

The "A" Word

This Is What It's Like

We must be willing to get rid of the life we've planned
so as to have the life that's waiting for us.
~Joseph Campbell

Earlier this summer at a birthday party, a well-meaning acquaintance asked me an honest question: "What's it like to be the mom of an autistic child?" She wasn't being nosy. I happen to like her and know that she was genuinely interested in my experience. But what I saw in her eyes was pity. She even teared up while we were talking.

Those of us with special needs children know that look. I call it "The Look of Tragedy." Again, she meant no harm. So, I got to thinking: What is it like to have an autistic child? After all, they come in all shapes and varieties. Some of our children will be self-sufficient. Some will live with us or in a group facility for the rest of their lives. I cannot answer that question for everyone. But I can answer for me. And, in that answer, I will likely be speaking for other parents of other very special children.

So, this is what it's like:

1. To begin with, it's a kind of death. No matter how much you plan to give your children the freedom to achieve their dreams, quite naturally you have a few dreams for them as well. You dream of birthdays and holidays. Santa and presents. Playing dress-up, doing arts and crafts, playing *Candy*

Land, dance classes, Boy Scouts, sleepovers, team sports, high school graduation, getting married, and watching them have their own children to love. And, though many of our kids with autism will grow up and do just those things, more than half of them won't. So, you mourn for what might not be. You mourn for what you and they are missing now. And, later, you may mourn for what will never be.

2. Despite the death of the dream child you envisioned, you are deeply in love with the child you have. He still does adorable things you want to share with others. He loves you too, but the rest of world won't always get to see it. Because when he is away from home, he is not himself. He is not the happy, affectionate child who holds your hand, snuggles, and gazes at you adoringly while pulling your hand to scratch and rub his back. The world won't get to see him at his most charming and you will see pity in people's faces. They won't ever understand the very real, profound joy this child brings into your life every day. Part of being a parent is pride in your children. People won't see what you are so proud of. And that can be a lonely feeling.

3. Guilt assails you from all directions. You want to throw a beautiful birthday party for your child. But he may not notice. He may not be the least bit interested in the presents, and you fear disappointing the guests. He may struggle to get out of your arms during the party, and you may have to see the sadness just beneath friends' and family's smiles. So you consider not having a party. You consider not taking him to others' parties. You want more than anything to give your child the experiences typical children have and feel guilty when you don't. But sometimes it is simply too overwhelming for you to try. Therapists want you to spend hours doing activities to help him, but you also have a job, perhaps other children who need you, and you need some

downtime on occasion or you'll go insane. So it seems you can't ever do enough for him. The guilt is a killer.

4. You live in a constant state of uncertainty about the future. Yes, of course none of us knows our future. But, if you have a typical child, you can be reasonably confident he will have friends, self-sufficiency, and love. You know who to leave things to when you die. But if you have a child with autism, you don't know how to plan your estate. Do you set up a special needs trust? Do you leave it all now to the one typical child who can use it? Because lifetime care for your autistic child will just drain it. And what if he grows to do well and is able to care for himself? Because you can't yet guess what will be, every option seems wrong. Uncertainty can affect every part of your life. Should you settle down where you are or should you relocate to a city with more intensive care for his needs? Will he ever talk? Will he ever be toilet trained? You just won't know until it happens or it doesn't. And you live with the fear that one day your then-elderly, vulnerable child will lie sick or dying without the comfort of someone who truly loves him. Anxiety runneth over.

5. Spontaneity is a thing of the past. You can't just get up and go. You have to determine whether there is an escape route from any new activity or location. You have to pack things to distract him if he becomes upset. You have to determine if foods he will eat will be present or if you will need to pack his meal. If he isn't potty trained, you will worry about where you can take him to change that will afford you both some dignity. Everything must be planned and considered.

6. You begin to grow thicker skin. Because people stare. They stare in disgust, thinking he is simply badly behaved. They stare because they are curious. They stare in horror or pity, because "there but for the grace of God go I." People stare.

And the thing that will come back to haunt you are memories of when you, also, made a judgment about another person in public. Righteous indignation mixes with humility and all you want to do is get out of wherever you are as soon as possible. But you can't escape everyday life.

7. You grow weary of everyone else's opinion. Because there are so many of them. There are those who are certain they know how "this" happened. There are those who are certain they know how to "fix" him. There are those who don't think you do enough. There are those who believe you to be a saint. There are those who believe your child's very visible difficulties allow them to have an opinion over your finances, his education, your marriage, and even your decision to bear another child or not. Opinions abound, but your patience may not.

8. But mostly it's like love. A love that you, if you are a parent, can probably imagine. And a love that you can't imagine if you don't have a child born with a bulls-eye in a big, bad world. Unconditional doesn't begin to cover it. Limitless. Earth-moving. Making you question everything you know to be true about God and man. And that kind of love will haunt you every moment of every day. You can see it just behind the eyes of every special needs parent on the planet. We are filled with a love we never could have predicted. We are filled with fears we never could have imagined. We are, quite simply, at capacity most every day. And, yet, when inevitably called for, we find that capacity expands. We aren't better parents than you. We aren't saints. And our children aren't lucky to have us. We are lucky to have them. Because, despite all of the very challenging aspects of having a child with autism, none of us will walk away from this life without having grown—merely from having loved them. Having become more than we thought we could be.

No, this—like many challenges one never asks for—isn't easy. But, I assure you, these children are worth it.

~Leigh Merryday

I'll Take the Special

Normal is nothing more than a cycle on a washing machine.
~Whoopi Goldberg

Picture a lunch counter at the midday rush. The stools are all filled with patrons and newspapers are strewn over lunch plates and soup bowls. Down on the end, a hand is raised. "Excuse me miss, I'll have the special."

The image makes me smile as I think to myself, "Yes, I most certainly will! Line them up! I'll take them all!" And I am not talking food.

I am the mom of a special needs child. Maybe you are like me, maybe you're not, but when you get right down to it, don't all children have "special" needs?

Some children need extra help with homework. Some children need a night light. Some children need speech therapy. Some children need encouragement to speak in front of a group. Some children need that backpack of food over the weekend. Some children need to be picked back up when they get walked on. Some children need a voice. Some children need wheelchairs. Some children need a pat on the back.

The common denominator is the word "need." It's the word that ties us together and puts us in the same boat.

Life on the spectrum can be a lonely road at times. We don't wear our special needs like a coat. Just looking at us, you can't see the spectrum flashing around us in neon lights.

However, when you take the spectrum down to bare bones, you get the words "language delay, sensory issues, eating difficulties, and social issues." Those are the things people notice.

Some people are nice about it, others not so much. I remember going to a department store one time with my son when he was three years old. While a department store in general is a sensory overload for him, he was doing well. I had him on my hip and we were having fun looking at a jewelry rack. A woman walked right up to us, looked right at him and said, "You are too big to be held. You need to get down!" To say I was furious is an understatement, but I bit my lip and moved to a different rack.

Her comment made me realize our symptoms are somewhat invisible. Yet, at other times, we stand out in a crowd. I will never forget going to the art show at my son's elementary school. He has auditory issues, so I put his headphones on him so he could enjoy the show. He was tickled pink to be there, and was so happy as we roamed the halls looking at all the artwork.

Well, I had my first taste of what is must be like to physically wear your differences. Ironically, the kids looked right at him. The parents were another story. They would look at him and then quickly look away. No parent would even look my way. Even people I knew from businesses around town wouldn't look at me. It was surprising to me how differently we were treated just because of a pair of headphones.

But I am here to tell you it doesn't matter. That boy is the best gift I have ever received. It doesn't matter to me what the road and journey is like as long as I have that boy in my life exactly the way he is. I would never, ever change anything about him, headphones and all.

His whole being radiates light. It's as if he is walking around with God's hand on his shoulder. He has no worries. He is the happiest person I have ever known. For five years and four months he woke up singing every day! Who does that? He seems to be protected by a grace no human can touch. He doesn't notice the looks or hear the comments. He just IS.

That kid is the joy of my life. My cousin and I have a saying: "Jump with both feet." It means stop standing on the edge of life, take a chance, take a deep breath and jump, for crying out loud!

He is not afraid to take a chance or to be brave. In his presence I have stopped living on the sidelines. Would I have ever thought I'd go down the waterslide at the pool in my hometown? Heck, no. I did it twice! Would I have ever stepped off the trail? No way, yet there we were, walking on the rock cliff around the river.

Do I get down sometimes? You bet I do. Do I worry about him and if people will be kind to him even though he is different? Lord knows I do. Sometimes I worry way too much! I worried about him starting kindergarten for seven months before it even started! And guess what: He loves kindergarten! We must have gotten the best teachers and classmates ever, because he gets his backpack on in the morning before he puts on his pants!

The lesson I have learned is to be brave and live out loud. I don't take one second with that boy for granted. The next time you imagine a lunch counter at midday, I will be the person on the end with my arm up saying, "Excuse me, Miss, I'll take the special," and you'll know what the "special" really means.

~Jessica Adam

The Diagnosis

Turn your face to the sun and the shadows fall behind you.
~Maori Proverb

n the child psychiatrist's office, I introduced my eleven-year-old son. "This is a wonderful boy," I said to the doctor, who looked no more than twenty, but had diplomas from Stanford and the University of California on the wall behind him. I wondered whether he knew what he was doing. I was aware we were about to spend the good part of an hour talking about Ben's behavior problems in front of Ben and that there wouldn't be time for listing all of his joyful qualities. "He's smart; he's a whiz at math; he's good at sharing." I smiled at Ben. "Well, most of the time."

Ben was picking at his nails and looked stricken, as if he was about to be carted off to jail.

"And he's honest," I said, laughing.

Dr. A's smile looked forced. "I'm sure he is a wonderful boy," he said. He was building rapport with us; I'd learned how to do that in my psychology-training program, too. "So why have you come to see me?"

My partner and I described the most recent meltdown, which ended with a broken toe for me, and then Dr. A guided us in a lengthy history taking. I recognized many of the questions designed to ferret out a diagnosis.

Were there any repetitive motions, any hand-flapping? No. He didn't have those signs of autism.

Did he line up objects, count things excessively? No. It's not OCD.

Inability to focus? Lots of excess energy? No. It's not ADHD.

Limited interests? Lack of friends? No, he has a handful of friends, the brainy boys from elementary school. He's a little obsessed with the Giants, but aren't lots of boys? I'm not sure what we're ruling out here.

Lack of empathy? No, he hugs me when I cry.

Difficulties learning? No, he's a whiz at math, we say again. And he likes to read. He doesn't have a learning disability.

Dr. A listened to our descriptions of Ben's development, his getting "stuck" on ideas and questions, his need for black-and-white answers to questions, his extreme frustration when he hears "maybe" and "I don't know," his raging when his routine changes. The meltdowns. How his best friend had stopped calling this year.

Finally, the doctor had heard enough, and he sent Ben to the waiting room. "Let me get right to it," he said. "First of all," he directed to me, "you are a psychologist, right?"

"Yes."

"Ph.D.?"

"Yes." I shot a look at Pam. "Pam is his other mother," I said.

"I taught special education for thirty-three years," she said.

He glanced at Pam and then spoke to me again. "What do you think it is?"

I shrugged. "I think it's sensory integration dysfunction with a lot of emotional overlay." But for the first time I was no longer sure.

"Let me tell you what I think it is," he said. "I think your son has Asperger syndrome."

It had never occurred to me that my son might be showing signs of Asperger's, and I immediately felt ashamed. I should have known. What kind of psychologist was I, if I didn't keep up with all the syndromes, if I couldn't even figure out what was going on with my own son? What kind of mother?

I rubbed the hard plastic arm of the chair. "I never thought of that."

"I see at least one autistic child or adolescent every day. Sometimes two or three." He was smiling again, as if proud of his experience, his diagnostic acumen.

But I didn't understand why he was telling us about autistic patients. What did autism have to do with Ben?

Autistic meant the kids I'd worked with back in the eighties, the kids who flapped their hands and echoed what I said to them. Even while I was thinking this, I knew I was wrong. I'd read about the autism spectrum; I knew there were milder forms. I knew that the number of people diagnosed with Asperger's had been rising. The rest of the appointment began to blur. My son was on the autism spectrum. He was barely on the autism spectrum, I needed to believe. AUTISTIC sounded too serious, like CANCER. Way too scary.

• • •

On the drive home from Dr. A's office, the three of us were quiet. I'd known only a couple of children diagnosed with Asperger's, like the third grader the previous year who at recess walked on tiptoes around the perimeter of the school yard, running his fingers over the chain link fence. The children I remembered from the playground were much more impaired than Ben. I wondered if Dr. A was wrong.

After we dropped Ben back at school, I e-mailed two friends about the diagnosis, using the words "weird, in shock, disturbing, freaking out." It was easier to write it than say it. I wanted both the instant connection of e-mail and the safety of hiding behind it. If I'd picked up the phone or told someone in person, I wouldn't have been able to get the words out past my sobs.

I didn't tell my mother, to whom I had just given a book on sensory integration disorder. I could have said, yes I'll pick you up from the airport, and let's go to the symphony this month, and, by the way, your grandson has Asperger's.

I couldn't tell people yet. I was ashamed, scared. I didn't know what to say.

Before the kids got home from school, I raced to the bookstore and pulled books about Asperger's off the shelves. I read half of one sitting on the cement floor, and within two minutes I knew that Dr. A was right.

Extreme reactions (e.g., tantrums) to minor upsets.

Difficulty being flexible, changing plans. Gets stuck on topics.

Upset by ambiguous language. Interprets language literally.

Concrete and literal thinker. Prefers things to be black and white.

Difficulty making and keeping friends.

Poor coordination.

I stuck Post-its on the pages I wanted to copy for his sixth grade teachers. Staying busy kept me from weeping.

The next morning, before work, I found the website of a woman whose father, brother, and two sons had Asperger's. She had made a long list of the positive qualities of "Aspies." I was blown away by her enthusiasm, her cheerleading for Asperger's, but I was not in the cheerleading frame of mind. Mostly, I still wanted to play on the team that would trounce the Asperger's. At that point, I thought of it as a disease, one that could be cured.

As I read more about Asperger's, I understood it was not going to go away. From the books I'd skimmed in the store, I knew we'd have to learn new ways to deal with him, and he'd have to be taught directly the skills he'd need to make and keep friends, to understand body language and idioms and sarcasm. But he would always have Asperger's, and we would always be teaching him. Little did I know how much he would teach us too.

~Katherine Briccetti

Autism Does Not Define Me

To be nobody but yourself in a world which is doing its best night and day to make you like everybody else means to fight the hardest battle any human being can fight.
~e.e. cummings

Accept me for who I am.
Understand that I may not always get what you're saying.
Trust that God has me here for a reason.
I am an amazing human being.
Socially, I might not fit in with society's expectations.
Mentoring can help me along the way.

Don't forget that I have feelings even if I don't express them.
Opportunities for my happiness are indeed possible.
Educate and encourage me without prejudice.
Show patience and kindness along the way.

Never give up trying to "get" me.
Ostracizing me will just shut me down.
Take time to try and come into my world.

Defining me as my diagnosis ignores my essence and best qualities.
Emerging talents may arise when you least expect them.
Friendship and honesty is valued to me more than you can imagine.
I am in need of love and tenderness too.
Never let me give up, especially when you see my mood shift.
Expect the unexpected and watch me enrich your life.

Many people will read this and I pray millions will act.
Embrace and empower someone with autism today.

I originally wrote this poem on April 8th, 2010. My sons Justin and Ryan were ten and three at the time, both having been diagnosed on the autism spectrum in 2008.

Ryan was diagnosed first with autism when he stopped speaking around eighteen months old and a variety of behaviors changed. We did a tremendous amount of research about autism and Asperger syndrome and realized that our older son, although he didn't have the speech challenges of our younger son, had his own set of issues. Both children also had many sensory processing challenges. Justin was diagnosed a couple of months later with Asperger syndrome. Later, at an autism conference, I met some adults on the spectrum, including a couple of women (who present differently) and a light bulb went off in my head. I had been living for over forty years as an undiagnosed Aspie.

At the time I wrote "Autism Does Not Define Me" I was fulfilling a pledge to blog once each day during Autism Awareness Month in April. That particular day I felt an overwhelming connection with both Justin and Ryan. I wanted them to know that they have my full support in being who they are and I wanted to remind them that who they are is not defined by a word.

It wasn't long after I wrote the poem that I founded a non-profit public charity called Autism Empowerment, which launched in June 2011. Our four foundational pillars are Accept, Enrich, Inspire and Empower and we share a message of positivity and support locally, regionally and around the world through Autism Empowerment Radio and the development of inspirational programs and services.

~Karen Krejcha

First Talk

Autism is part of my child, it's not everything he is.
My child is so much more than a diagnosis.
~S. L. Coelho

The crowd pressed against us in the line for the Lilo & Stitch attraction. The heat of Orlando in July made the closeness of human flesh even more uncomfortable. I felt a shift in the small hand I held and realized my son, Aaron, was trying to break free.

Oh, no, not in this crowd. "Hey! What are you doing?" I said.

"I can't do this." Still trying to free his hand, Aaron looked up at me, his brown eyes wild, mouth clenched into a thin line. "Let me out!"

My husband, William, and daughter, Ann, turned to see what was going on. They tried to reason with Aaron by showing him the little kids in line and reminding him the ride was based on a favorite cartoon.

"I don't care!" Aaron shouted.

I was afraid he would bolt. "We'll wait outside."

Aaron led me against the flow of people pushing to get to the ride entrance. We emerged into the bright sunlight. After my eyes adjusted, I looked for a place to sit and wait. I found a bench, and we walked over and sat down. I dug in my backpack for water bottles, handed one to Aaron, and for a minute we just sat, drinking.

He let out a big sigh. "What's wrong with me, Mom? I mean, I wanted to do that so much, but I couldn't."

Please, God, give me the right words.

We were surrounded by people rushing to get to the next ride, enjoying the things I wanted so desperately for Aaron to experience. The shouts and murmurs of the crowd faded away as I focused on my boy. His red hair was damp, skin flushed with heat. He wanted answers, and even though he was only seven, he deserved them.

"Nothing is wrong with you."

I paused. He needed more than platitudes. "Everyone has strengths and weaknesses. We must use our strengths to overcome our weaknesses."

"I don't know what you mean. What's my weakness?"

Should I name it or just explain? "Remember two years ago when we went to a doctor's office and different people asked you questions?"

"Maybe." He crinkled his nose as he tried to remember.

"They were trying to understand why you seem sensitive to certain noises and clothes, can't stand to be thirsty, hungry or hot and don't always understand why people act a certain way toward you."

He frowned. "What does that have to do with Lilo & Stitch?"

I couldn't turn back after this. "When all those people at the doctor's office talked to you, they decided you have something called…" My throat closed, and I choked out the rest. "Asperger syndrome."

"What?"

"Asperger syndrome. It means you think differently than other people. You are really smart, but you have trouble processing your senses when you feel them too much. You know how when you are too hot you have trouble thinking and making good decisions? You feel panicked like you are in danger. When you feel like that, you react like you are being attacked and either get really mad, run away, or shut down."

"I felt like that just now. I felt like if I stayed in there, something bad would happen."

I glanced up at the giant comical faces of the Disney characters on the outside of the building, inviting everyone to step into their world for a few minutes. How could I explain why he was frightened?

"Maybe because you don't like surprises. You prefer things to be lined up and scheduled. When you walked into that tunnel and didn't know what to expect, your brain warned you of danger when there really wasn't any. Not all kids with Asperger's have that problem, but you do."

"But why am I like this?"

I looked down and fiddled with the straps on my backpack. I wanted him to know I didn't consider his Asperger syndrome to be something wrong with him. It was part of who he was. "This isn't all a bad thing, Aaron. You know how I call you my finder?"

Aaron nodded, and the corners of his mouth turned up just slightly. Progress.

"That's because you're so aware of the things you see."

He opened his eyes wider. "I am good at finding things."

"Or math and computer stuff. You're good at those because your brain likes to think of things in a way that makes those subjects easier. See? It's not something wrong with you—just different."

This was serious business, the discussion of a lifetime. I had to get it right. I wanted him to understand why he struggled sometimes, but not consider Asperger's a crutch or excuse.

I tried to relate his situation to someone with a different disability like the visually impaired, but the comparison was lost on him.

"I can see just fine," he said. Literal thinking at its best.

I decided to be more direct. "Sometimes you have to have a talk with yourself so you don't panic when there isn't a reason. Use brain power to see through the anxiety." I looked up and saw our family heading to meet us. "We'll keep working on it. Meanwhile, try new things, and remember life can't always be planned out." I smoothed a tendril of hair away from his forehead.

He drew back, but only a little. "Mom, will I always be this way? Will I get better?"

Since his diagnosis, well-meaning friends and family had told me so often he would grow out of it that this was a sore spot with me.

How could I explain without making him feel hopeless? "Asperger syndrome is not something you can cure, but you can learn things that will make life easier. Your dad and I will do whatever we can to help you."

Aaron put his head down, and drew a circle on the ground with his foot. "Now I understand why I have trouble with things other kids don't. I wish I didn't have this," he said.

"I know, but here's a secret. God made you this way for a reason. He has a plan for you like everyone else. I want to help you learn what you need to know to accomplish it, not change who you are. Asperger's is part of you, and it makes you pretty special. I love you."

I spread my arms, inviting him into a hug, and he snuggled in. I was glad he liked hugs. That was not always the case with Asperger syndrome.

William and Ann approached us. I looked at them through bleary eyes and smiled, thankful for so much in that moment: the chance to have this talk, Aaron's ability to understand, and the knowledge that we could all work together to help him. We were going to be okay.

Ann ran over. "You should have gone! It was so cool!"

"Maybe I'll try it later," he said. He looked at me and smiled. "I'll just have to talk to myself about it first."

~Lana Clifton

What's in a Label?

I see autism as having many different strands. All of these strands are beautiful... if you try and take away the autism by removing the strands you also take away parts of the child... they are what makes them who they are.

~J.M. Worgan

On the way to school this morning I was finally asked the question for which I've been preparing for years: "Mom, what's autism?"

I answered with a question of my own: "How do you know that term, honey?"

"I saw it on that paper. It said I had it."

Damn! I'm usually painstakingly careful about keeping any ASD-related information out of my nine-year-old son's sight. But then I thought back to last week and remembered the report with his assessment strewn across the kitchen table, carelessly left out for not even ten minutes and forgotten in the daily distraction of sorting through school-related paperwork.

I should have known he would spot it. No detail, no matter how tiny or seemingly insignificant, ever escapes his notice. This is a boy who, by age five, could tell you the make, model and year of any oncoming car, just by glancing at its headlights.

Now, he waited patiently for my answer, seemingly unconcerned as he studied the toy car in his hands. And I believe he wasn't concerned at all… just mildly curious. This word, this label, being yet another small detail to file away in his constantly humming brain.

But to me, it wasn't just a small detail. It was a life-altering diagnosis, a sentence to a lifetime of extraordinary challenges… and to me, as his mother, it embodied all manner of fears for his wellbeing, and threats against his happiness.

My son is on the autism spectrum, at a high enough level of functioning that he could potentially integrate completely into society but for a few communicative and behavioral quirks. These quirks, many of which I find incredibly endearing (his mature vocabulary, which makes him sound like a baby-faced professor, how he interjects completely unrelated snippets of obscure trivia into conversation, how he pumps his arms when he's excited) and others, not so much (the explosive tantrums and panic-fueled meltdowns) are all part of the Simon that I know and love, but may not be viewed as tolerantly by those who don't know him. Even worse, they might not see him at all, but only that word—autism—and use that label in ways that will define and limit and isolate him. My son is so much more than a label. And I wanted desperately for the whole world, and especially for him, to know that.

I knew the day would come when he would either realize he was somehow different from other kids, or he would overhear something to make him realize he has this thing, this condition that contributes to his uniqueness. And I both looked forward to—and dreaded—the day we would have that first conversation about it. I looked forward to it because I hated hiding his autism in the first place. Hiding implies shame or embarrassment… and that couldn't be further from the truth about how I feel. I am inexpressibly proud of how he handles his daily challenges with such perseverance and honesty. But I wanted to delay the burden of this knowledge until I felt he was ready to handle it. Not that autism itself is necessarily a burden; the burden is the weight of people's ignorance and intolerance towards anything or anyone outside of what's "normal."

And I dreaded this talk because of the sheer weight of its significance. In a few crucial moments, I would have the power to either reinforce everything I'd tried so hard to instill in him (tolerance of others' differences, empathy, and the three "selfs": self-confidence, self-respect, self-esteem), or, if I didn't handle it in just the right way, leave him with the alienating feeling that being different means being inadequate or defective.

So I rehearsed potential conversations in my head endlessly, and talked to other moms of autistic children about how they handled that particular turning point. And still I felt ill prepared to guide him into that moment of self-awareness, utterly afraid of messing it up... of messing him up.

So, how did I end up answering his question?

"Well, honey... it just means that your brain is wired a little differently from some other people. So you might not always think or see or feel the same way as others. It means you're unique... and very special. Do you understand?"

A pause... and a rapid hammering in my chest...

And then, "Yes." He spun the wheels on his toy car. He seemed content.

I asked him if he had any questions or concerns about what I just told him. "No." I encouraged him to come to me at any time in the future if he wants to talk about it further. "Okay, Mom." And then, "Did you know that the Bugatti Veyron has 1200 HP and can reach 267 mph?"

And just like that, the conversation was over... at least for that day.

And as I continued to watch in the rearview mirror, he resumed playing with his car, humming softly to himself. I was filled with a certainty that reached deep down into my bones... he would be just fine.

~Jennifer Doelle Young

The Boy Who Drew a Face

*I see people with Asperger syndrome as a bright thread
in the rich tapestry of life.*
~Tony Attwood

My husband and I have two wonderful sons. Our older son, Alex, is a handsome twenty-year-old who plays the piano and tennis, loves movies and music, traveling and the beach, and has a smile that can light up the world. He also has Asperger syndrome.

I remember vividly the moment when a capital "A" would forever describe his condition, not merely the first letter of his name. It was a day Alex and I visited the Head of Child Psychiatry at a large Chicago hospital. An OT and psychologist had been working with him. But, given his tender age, they hesitated to label him. She did not. She ushered me back into her office, just minutes after meeting with my son alone, and said, "I know that you already have concerns, so this diagnosis will not come as a shock."

It was most definitely a shock, as I struggled with the enormity and finality of the diagnosis. Even though he didn't relate to his peers in an age-appropriate way, even though he perseverated on words, actions, thoughts, and feelings, I wanted to believe, had to believe, that we all got it wrong. This had to be just a phase.

It wasn't just a phase and we began our Autism Journey that

day. It has had many pitfalls, but some triumphs as well. The road is bumpy and less traveled than most paths. But, if you keep your eyes on the vista ahead, you will learn things about your child, yourself, and the world that others, in the clamor and speed of daily life, cannot possibly comprehend.

The early years were about learning to navigate the world and we are grateful for the many dedicated teachers and professionals along the way. Alex had sensory integration issues galore, crying jags and tantrums, and many fears. He was like "Swiss cheese," one teacher told me. He had strengths, but large, gaping holes as well.

We learned, over time, that he didn't like a large painting we had hanging in our family room. It was a Modernist painting of a woman gazing downward. Eyes, as they say, are windows to the soul, and hers were closed.

I was perplexed when his kindergarten teacher called me in to tell me that Alex had defaced school property. That wasn't like him. I scanned the classroom and saw a busily decorated space all done up in red, white and blue. Nothing seemed amiss. When I inquired about the problem, the teacher held up a tiny peg of wood dressed up as Uncle Sam. On it, my sweet, young son had delicately added two dots for eyes and a thin straight line for a smile. He couldn't stand to look at the figurine without a face. It was his best artwork to date! I thanked her for making me aware of the infraction and left the room promptly before I said something I would regret. I had already learned to pick my battles.

At the end of the year, we changed schools and school districts. Our new school district welcomed us with open arms—even after we told them his diagnosis. It was a struggle at first, but by middle school, he was getting A's and B's—and we actually looked forward to meeting his teachers at Parent Night.

I would like to tell you that the last two decades have been easy and that we have solved the autism puzzle, but we have not. Yet, Alex has gone from a fearful, timid boy to a bright and sensitive young man who became a National Honor Society recipient in high school. When he received the JFK Award for Courage last year, given to one high school senior who has overcome great obstacles, he received a rousing, standing ovation from the packed auditorium. There was not a dry eye in sight.

Alex is now living and studying at a small, New England college. Just this morning, he locked himself out of his dorm room and called to tell me that he couldn't get back in. He did the same thing yesterday. He is still learning. I nag him, now over the phone, but I could not be more proud of him. Only his dad and I truly understand what a miracle this step toward independence is.

To the parents of newly diagnosed children on the spectrum, I would like to give you a collective hug, along with some words from the heart:

- Subdue self-doubt and recriminations—I spent too many nights crying myself to sleep and walking around like a zombie the next day.
- Find an Autism Angel to talk to—someone who has been there and that you can connect with. My friend, Sharon, is mine.
- Don't waste your time on people who don't care about you or your child, or who criticize either one of you.
- Look into respite care and find time for yourself—even if it is just an hour or two once or twice a week.
- Savor the precious moments when your child masters something new or has a good afternoon.
- Resist comparing your child to anyone else—it is an exercise in futility.
- Don't neglect your other children—they need you too.
- Chart a new path. Think outside the Neurotypical box.
- Most importantly, have faith—even when all reason shouts not to.

~Shari Cohen Forsythe

The Seven-Year Twitch

*Hope begins in the dark, the stubborn hope that if you just show up
and try to do the right thing the dawn will come.*
~Anne Lamott

"What color is this?" Maggie asks, holding the crayon in front of her face. I am frozen in suspended animation on the staircase, waiting.

Watery sunlight streams through the window, washing over my two girls, their legs folded beneath them in matching Ws on the kitchen floor. A kaleidoscopic bucket of broken, discarded crayons sits on the floor between them, as pixie dust swirls around their golden silhouettes.

"Purple," Julia answers.

I ease backwards down the stairs to erase my presence, careful not to make any sudden noise that might break the fragile truce unfolding, where an older sister has taken it upon herself to pull her younger sister out of her dark spell. A five-year-old, who in just a few short weeks has learned the principles of Applied Behavior Analysis (ABA) and is applying them in her own kitchen-floor play therapy with her baby sister, who was recently diagnosed with an autism spectrum disorder.

The ink is not yet dry on Julia's reams of paperwork. A parade of evaluators, therapists, doctors, and a full committee have all weighed in and unanimously agreed: Julia is officially a preschooler with a disability, squashing any last hopes we may have held that she was simply delayed and would eventually come around. I still haven't grasped the full impact of this diagnosis. Will she go to college? Will she get married? Is she even capable of sustaining any kind of relationship? Will I ever have a meaningful conversation with my daughter? Instead, I ask all of them, "What will become of my child?" My eyes plead with them for a shred of hope, but they cannot answer me. "No one has a crystal ball," they tell me with a sympathetic shrug.

The heartache of her diagnosis is so debilitating I believe the gaping wound will never heal. Every time I see Julia trapped within, lost internally, unable and seemingly unwilling to communicate, every time I see her stimming (self-stimulatory behavior) around the house, humming and grunting and thrashing into furniture to self-soothe, every time she explodes in frustration because no one, not even her own mother, can understand her, I feel that wound is torn open, again and again, all day long. I develop a persistent nervous twitch under my left eye, branding me so my anguish is both internal and external for the world to see.

I grieve, day and night. I mourn for Maggie, who should have had a playmate in her sister. Instead, my sensitive firstborn tries to protect me by shouldering more responsibility for her sister. She has a preternatural ability to look deeply into my soul and feel my pain viscerally, as if it were her own. I mourn for our family and the new uncertainty of our future. But mostly, I mourn for Julia who may never know a life where everything is possible. I rock my second born in my arms at night, staring at the stars and the moon outside her window, and ask out loud to God, my ancestors, the universe, anyone who will listen, "What will become of my child?"

We enroll Julia in a special education class over the summer. The principal is not sure this is the appropriate placement for her; Julia doesn't even respond to her name. She may need something even more restrictive than a self-contained class with a one-on-one aide, but we will review her progress at the end of the summer. Julia spends two and a half hours a day at school, five days a week, and is pulled out for speech therapy, occupational therapy, and physical therapy. But it's not enough and the district agrees to an additional fifteen hours a week of ABA therapy at home. At three years old, Julia is working from seven in the morning to as late as five in the afternoon.

My husband and I sit in with the ABA therapists and learn to emulate their words, their strategies, even their intonations. They have given us the special education manual to our child. We're learning a new language and are slowly cracking the code to break through to Julia. Where before she had only looked past me, through me, or around me, we now begin to see flashes of eye contact, those beautiful orbs the color of the Aegean Sea that now glance at me hesitantly, for only a heartbeat at a time, but with new clarity and awareness. Her tantrums decrease from hours to minutes. Her speech therapist tells me Julia has blown her away; she never thought she'd see such significant gains so quickly. I cry in response, heaving sobs, because it's the first time I'm allowed to feel hope.

•••

That was seven years ago. Today, Julia is in a mainstream class. Her IQ and language skills are in the high average to superior range. Her diagnosis has evolved from PDD-NOS to Asperger's. She was accepted into her school's enrichment program designed specifically for students who are identified as academically talented. Julia sits next to Maggie at the dinner table, sweeping away her sister's long strands of hair so she can whisper—loudly—in her ear. Maggie's shoulders shake with laugher, possibly even relief. The girls are making up for those lost early years. Julia's teachers are working on her "calling out" without first raising her hand. I can't help but smile with pride. My greatest fear—Julia not communicating—has been turned completely on its head. Now, we can't get her to *stop* talking.

My seven-year twitch is all but forgotten.

~Amy Giles

Your Own Dance

I am different, not less.
~Temple Grandin

It's the little ones who unnerve me.
Small bodies flexible and strong.
They seem to leap to the top of the jungle gym, swinging
By one hand, they jump and land on two feet, laughing.
Their words weave simultaneously stories,
Negotiations, insults and shared delight.
They size each other up
Quickly and adjust accordingly,
The bully, the smart one, the prima donna.
Roles that shape them for the rest of their lives.

Around the perimeter of that same play yard
You stride, little alien, measuring
The meters with the rulers of your legs.
Your gaze is on the treetops, where leaves
Dance in the air and speak a fascinating language
Only you can hear. You stop to fling your hands
Wide, first one and then the other,
Flicking your fingers quickly in a rhythm
That must soothe your ruffled senses, must
Make sense.

In a world where making sense means making cents
The children on the play yard, the others,
Other people's children,
Are already matriculating,
And you don't even know
You're left in the dust, and if you did
Know this, you would have only odd delight,
The way the fine dirt particles shimmer
In the translucent air,
The way the leaves
Dance to meet
Your frantic fingers.

~Melinda Coppola

The Eccentric Side of Normal

What fun is there in being normal?
~Cristina Marrero

Normal, I've learned, is in the eye of the beholder. Shortly after my cousin Beth's son Ethan was diagnosed with pervasive developmental disorder (a catchall diagnosis for high-functioning autism that's not Asperger syndrome and doesn't fit other diagnostic boxes), I came to the United States on a business trip and paid her a visit. I knew of Ethan's diagnosis, but my knowledge of autism back then consisted of Dustin Hoffman's performance in the movie *Rain Man*.

When I met Ethan, he was an exceptionally bright, talkative child. Okay, maybe the things he said were a bit repetitive, and he flapped his hands around a bit, but hey, at age four, the kid could already read.

We went out to a local kid-friendly restaurant for dinner, and later, after Ethan was in bed, I told Beth that although I knew her son had been diagnosed with autism, he seemed pretty normal to me. I asked her how the autism manifested itself, what symptoms should have clued me in.

"Did you notice how he freaked out when we took a different route than we normally do to get to the restaurant?" Beth asked.

"Well, yeah," I said. "But that's normal. Joshua does that."

Back home in England, if I took a different route than usual when driving Joshua to nursery school, he'd have a conniption in the back of the car. "NO! Mummy! Not *that* Way! The *other* Way!" This would be accompanied by kicking the back of my seat, waving arms and various ear-splitting sound effects.

Joshua was my first child. He freaked out. So to me, it was normal for kids to freak out if you went a different way than usual. Although I had worries about Joshua's socialization at Parent and Toddler Group and his extreme reaction to balloons bursting and other loud noises, it didn't cross my mind for a nanosecond that perhaps *Joshua does it, so it's normal* wasn't the correct conclusion.

Oh, the irony! About six months later, in response to the concerns we expressed at a parent-teacher conference, our son's Pre-K teacher handed us a leaflet about a condition I'd never heard of: Asperger syndrome, an autistic spectrum disorder. Reading it was a revelation; it was as if someone put a framework on those niggling worries that everyone had been poo-poohing as the neuroses of an overanxious first-time mother.

I went straight to our general practitioner, and listing Joshua's traits, asked that she refer him to the Autism Assessment Unit. She agreed, reluctantly, but then commented, "You know, Sarah, he might not have Asperger's, he might just be on the *eccentric side of normal*."

At the time, I was incensed by my GP's comment, because it felt like another of a long line of fob offs to my very real concerns. But in retrospect, and I suspect without meaning to, she hit the nail right on the head. For what better description of Asperger's than "the eccentric side of normal"? Long before 1944, when the Austrian pediatrician Hans Asperger published his paper on "autistic psychopathy," describing the condition that would become known as Asperger syndrome, many families had their eccentric relatives. Mine certainly did.

Back in 2006, Josh, who was twelve at the time, interviewed me at the StoryCorps booth in Manhattan. A short three-minute clip from our interview aired on NPR's *Morning Edition* and had a huge response, and it was subsequently made into an award-winning short by Rauch Brothers Animation, which has had over 891,000 hits on

YouTube. Josh asked me this question: "Did I turn out to be the son you wanted when I was born? Like did I meet your expectations?"

Even now it makes me tear up, because it goes straight to the heart of what every child wants to know, but most would never come straight out and ask: *Do you, Mom, Dad, love me the way I am, not the way you expected or hoped I would be when I was born, but the way I actually turned out?*

In Joshua's case, though, it was even more meaningful, because as elementary school progressed he became more aware of his differences and at the time of the interview he was experiencing isolation and bullying in middle school. He was aware that certain things—particularly the social aspects of life—didn't come as easily for him as they did for his sister, and the question revealed his anxiety that I might not love him as much because of it.

Nothing could be further from the truth. I told him that he had exceeded my expectations and that because he thought differently than I did and from what I read in parenting books, I really had to learn to think outside of the box with him. That had forced me to become more creative as a parent and as a person, and I will always thank him and be grateful for that.

Having Josh as my son has also taught me to trust my instincts. Even before his diagnosis, I noticed he had problems with transitions—particularly if he was playing his favorite computer game, Richard Scarry's *Busytown*, and I told him it was time to go upstairs for his bath. He would have a complete meltdown.

Without advice from doctors or therapists, just mother's instinct and common sense, I had the idea to give him a five-minute warning by setting a kitchen timer. He knew that when the bell rang, it was time to go upstairs without fuss. It worked. As long as he had the warning and the auditory cue, the transition was tantrum-free. I also created visual calendars using laminated poster board and Velcro, with pictures of people and activities. We had "This Week" and "Next Week," so if he was perseverating about when an activity was going to happen, I could show him in visual form.

When Josh was finally diagnosed, these tricks I'd figured out by instinct were amongst the strategies recommended by therapists.

So my advice to parents is to learn everything you can possibly glean from experts, but to trust in yourself. No one else is paying the same level of attention, and no one loves your child the way you do.

With the increasing and incredibly misguided emphasis on standardized testing, we need to rethink our definition of "normal," and broaden our acceptance of those who don't quite fit the mold. Looking at history, it's people like Josh, the ones who think outside of the box, who have made the world a more interesting and infinitely richer place.

In the words of philosopher John Stuart Mill: "Eccentricity has always abounded when and where strength of character has abounded; and the amount of eccentricity in a society has generally been proportional to the amount of genius, mental vigor and moral courage it contained. That so few dare to be eccentric marks the chief danger of the time."

~Sarah Darer Littman

For Jacob

We cannot direct the wind, but we can adjust the sails.
~Author Unknown

"Something is wrong! He won't talk; he won't look at me. I don't know what he wants," I said to my son's doctor. She reminded me I was a first-time mom, and boys develop slower than girls. When they sent me home the fourth time with my two-year-old, I called the children's hospital and made an appointment with the Developmental Unit, but it wasn't for six months.

Our daycare center suggested we call Early Intervention and get Jacob evaluated. A speech therapist went to daycare twice a week to work with him.

I got home from work a few weeks later to find my husband, Ian, standing on the front porch, wide-eyed and pale. "Babe, something happened. I don't know what, but he won't step on carpet. He just screams." I rushed inside to find Jacob playing on the kitchen tile.

For a week, my heart ached as Jacob moved blankets, towels, even toys around the carpet to shield his body. "This is his home. His safe place," Ian said, as he and I cut, pulled and tossed cream-colored carpet out the front door. We were scared. What was wrong with our baby? We had friends with kids the same age, and they didn't act like this. After a long night and with sore hands, Ian left for work, and I held my breath as Jacob touched his toes to the now exposed plywood, then exhaled slowly as he walked. We met with his daycare;

they agreed to put plastic runners around their center. Jacob stuck to his path and we carried on.

A few months later, Jacob was playing silently in the bathtub when he suddenly started to scream. I grabbed him out of the water, searching him. "What is wrong? Are you hurt?" I said, fighting back the panic in my voice. He just screamed and rocked his wet body, then pointed at a fly in the water. For about a month Jacob refused to get in the bathtub. Every night, after Ian showered, I handed him Jacob, we soaped him, rinsed him, and got him out. No fun. No toys. Just tears.

Jacob would eat only four things and wear only sweatpants and soft shirts. He screamed and head-butted the cart at stores. Walmart was like pulling teeth and the grocery store... oh, the grocery store.

One day, on my way home from shopping, I called Ian. "People were staring at me like I was a horrible mom. This is my fault. I didn't hug him enough. I went back to work too soon," I cried. Ian reminded me that we would have help in two weeks. At that moment, I decided that I couldn't wait for some stranger to help him; I had to do it myself. That night I watched him sleep and wondered if I had messed up somehow. Do you know what it is like to not understand what your child is feeling?

Saturday morning Jacob and I took photos of everything inside and outside our house. I filled my memory card with 275 photos of stores, DVDs, toys, parks, friends, family, and food.

I printed all the photos and glued them to 3x5 cards. I gave every photo a one-word name, laminated them, and organized them in three plastic boxes.

I took the next week off from work, and woke to a hand pushing on my shoulder. "Good morning, Jacob." I smiled, and he looked at my cheek. "Are you hungry?" I asked. He walked towards the kitchen. I closed my eyes. "God, help us today," I whispered.

He ate his breakfast and got dressed for daycare. When I told him we were staying home, he frowned. "Do you want a cookie?" I asked. I had bought his favorite cookies, and it was time to get to work. He ran to the kitchen and pointed to the cupboard. I got down on my knees in front of Jacob, showing him the 3x5 card and the cookie. "Say cookie," I said. He stared, tears streamed out of his eyes, and then he walked away. I hung my head. Why wouldn't my son talk to me? We did this three times that day until I heard him whisper, "ookie." I handed him his Oreo and hugged him. He went to eat it and I slid down to sit on the floor, hands over my face and elbows on my knees as I cried.

That night I felt renewed. Once he was showered and in bed, I ran to Walmart and bought all four scuba Ninja Turtles. The next day, I ran a bath.

He watched as the tub filled and I pulled out one of the turtles. His eyes shifted to the turtle, and he reached for it. I tossed it in the clean, clear water. He tried to get it. I pushed it out of his reach and said, "He's for the bath only, buddy. You have to get in." He refused. The turtle went on the top shelf. I felt mean and harsh but knew this is what I had to do. After two days of filling and emptying the tub a few times, he finally climbed in, grabbed his turtle, and held him tight while I ran water over his back. Then he got out. I put the turtle up and reminded him, "Bath only." Friday morning, I tossed the turtle in and smiled as Jacob followed, playing with the Ninja Turtle. Success!

"Mrs. Mitchell, Jacob is autistic," the specialist informed me. I looked at my son stacking blocks. "He lacks the ability to show compassion. He might never talk, make friends or go to school," she said calmly. I wanted to yell, scream, maybe cry but instead I smiled at Jacob. He got up and climbed onto my lap, putting his hand on my cheek. No, I had to be strong, for him.

I quit my job that day.

Jacob will be eleven in January. He attends a typical school with the help of an aide and visits to the sensory room. He doesn't understand emotions or his body, but he tries. Jacob will always be different, but he has friends. He speaks at a nine-year-old level and loves his cat, Jerry. We have an eighty-acre hobby farm and there is nothing on this farm he can't do. The animals are drawn to him. Jacob's two little sisters, Abigail and Mackenzie, both have his back. Jacob is an amazing Wii player. He plays on a typical, and a special needs, ice hockey team. When Jacob is on the ice, all the stress leaves his body, and he is at peace.

We spent seven years juggling twenty hours a week of TSS, equine, aquatic, speech, physical, and occupational therapies a week.

We have more good days than bad, and as long as I prep him correctly, Jacob can go anywhere. I thank God every day for Jacob. While teaching him to be a little boy, he taught me to be a better mom.

~Sarah Mitchell

Being Quiet

Just as when a child is still in its mother's womb, the child's cravings are
reflected in the mother and become her desires.
~Tukaram Maharaj

When I was pregnant with my first child I eagerly joined birthing groups, and I enjoyed sharing pregnancy stories, maternity clothes and hearty laughs. My husband and I continued to host weekly potlucks, staying up late playing music with our friends. I worked until my due date as the director for an afterschool program surrounded by the loud activity of enthusiastic children. I was out in the world, smiling and ready for anything, with an abundance of good friends always at my side. Once my daughter was born she joined in the fun. The best way to soothe her when she was fussy was to bring her to the park or a party. She loved a social gathering.

When our daughter was still a baby, I became pregnant again. Many months before we thought we were ready, our next child began his amazing journey. Surprised, but delighted, I researched a prenatal yoga class, but as I dialed the number I felt a strong need to hang up the phone. Against my instincts I made the call and attended the first session. Women with bulging bellies and loose yoga clothes chatted with each other before class. I began to approach them, eager to join in on the chatting, but again, something pulled me away. Instead of laughing with them, I stretched quietly on a yoga mat in the corner, focusing on my breath until the instructor began the class. It was lovely and relaxing, yet I never returned.

Each week I made excuses to cancel our Friday night potlucks. I stopped taking my daughter to playgroups and instead invited the quietest child and her shy mother to our house. I enjoyed the social interaction, but I just wanted it to be quieter. One night my favorite band was playing a free concert in the park, but the thought of the crowds and the noise made me feel sick. On hot days I put on the sprinkler for my toddler rather than going to the local pond with our friends. My husband did the grocery shopping, as he understood my strange need to stay home and be quiet.

As the due date approached I refused to have a baby shower. We had all we needed, I argued, but really I sensed the baby wouldn't like it. My daughter, husband and I settled into a sweet time of closeness, excited—though quietly—about the new baby's arrival. Meanwhile I had a feeling, call it mother's intuition that the new baby was getting ready for a tremendously challenging transition—not that I anticipated a difficult birth—but more likely, a difficult life for this little guy who I thought might not like crowds or noise.

Sure enough the birth was fine, he was adorable and our love for him was beyond words, and still I had the strong urge to protect him. We allowed few visitors into our quiet home, and when I had to take him out, I bundled him tightly and kept him close to my chest. When the first signs of "trouble" arose, I was heartbroken, but not surprised. As a toddler he often struck out at children, especially when there was a lot of noise and chaos. Fortunately his father's kind and gentle voice could calm him down.

After the first day of kindergarten his teacher angrily approached me and said that when it was time to say his name at their morning circle he picked up the brand new box of crayons she has just given him and broke every one, with a great big smile on his face. She was livid. I was sad and confused. His reading and math scores soared while he continued to alienate his peers. By the time he was in third grade I had gotten the message from the school: Your child is a problem; it's your fault: fix it!

When he was nine we moved to a new community. His new doctor said to me, "Have you ever considered that your son might have Asperger's?" His new school tested him right away when they realized he could not be placed in a regular classroom because he was too disruptive. He was definitely on the spectrum, and also had an anxiety disorder. The school took actions that his old school never considered. With a strong support system in place they worked respectfully with him. By fifth grade he was able to rejoin the classroom full time. By sixth grade he was able to go without an aide, a big step for him.

As he is entering his teen years I see a boy who loves computers, math and doing projects with his dad. He has an amazing mind and a kind heart. We have inspiring conversations about God and the healing power of love. He does not care for sports, parties or crowds. He has a few good friends who are able to overlook his "quirkiness" and who love him as he is—especially because he can show them things on the computer they could never figure out on their own! He still turns to his dad when the anxiety is high and he needs to be held.

His therapist told us that we can't imagine how he feels in social gatherings. The tools we were born with for shielding ourselves from unwanted pressure and stimulation are absent for him. Stimuli come at him all at once, bombarding him with terrifying force. "He has to work much harder than most of us just to survive socially," she told us, "and at times it's going to be too much." She assured us that it's fine for him to spend a whole day isolated in his room after spending days at school working tremendously hard to control himself.

Recently I was telling him about my pregnancy thirteen years ago. "I had this strange urge to stay away from people," I said. "I wouldn't even let friends come over."

"Yeah, that makes sense," he said. "I hate people." And we both laughed, because although it is true, it's also not true. I know this because I experience this boy's love and kindness each day and I thank God for the gifts I have learned from my quirky little guy, especially the gift of knowing how to be quiet.

~Lava Mueller

Raising Kids on the Spectrum

The Amazing Brain

How Stuff Works

If you were to get rid of all the autism genetics,
there would be no more Silicon Valley.
~Temple Grandin

Just after his sixth birthday, Benjamin began to explore how stuff works. He'd always had a mind for putting things together, making bridges over bridges in complex Thomas the Tank Engine train tracks when he was four, but his sixth birthday closely followed his entry into kindergarten, and kindergarten came with school bus rides. And it was the bus rides that started his obsession.

The driver of Bus 64 recognized that Benjamin was different, and she tolerated his eccentricities and the delays they caused. And so Benjamin made it a habit to stick his head under the bus and look around before boarding. He'd snap a picture in his mind and save it until late afternoon when he could get paper and crayons, colored pencils, or markers. Benjamin began coming home from his after-school care with detailed schematics: tires, axels, driveshaft, linkages, engine, transmission, pipes, wires, lines I couldn't decipher but knew were there.

On weekends, he asked me to pop the hood on my car, and his smile spread as he took in the compartment. What's that? The engine. What's that? The coolant. What's that? Oil filter. What's that? What's that?

He went back and drew it all.

Walking back to the car from swimming class or shopping was a half-hour ordeal. He poked his head under every car along the way and held his hand out to stop cars that slowed to stalk our parking spot.

And when the visible became mundane, he drew the inside of the engine, as best as he could imagine: spark plugs with lightning bolts, pipes with crazy-angled joints, cables wrapping around and extending out to nowhere.

He combined styles, the underside of his bus connecting to a cut-away of the engine compartment, details filling large sheets of poster board and easel paper.

In his autism-focus class, he spent large amounts of time in the bathroom, practicing skills that he didn't really care to learn. But he observed everything in the bathroom, and brought home complex drawings of the anatomy of a toilet. He put someone on the toilet and drew the plumbing in the wall and beneath the floor, how the water came in, where waste products went, what happened when they got stuck.

Then everything changed with his first human body book.

His mouth literally hung open when he turned the pages: body system after system revealed in full-color overlays. He stopped with circulatory and stared at the pattern from the heart, the thickest arteries to the smallest capillaries branching out until the shape of the body was recognizable in the flowing, pumping blood.

He drew the systems. Circulatory and nervous systems filled the body. When he drew others, he'd bring home strangely beautiful hybrids. The esophagus, stomach, small intestines, and large intestines filled the middle of the body, and pipes, cables, and gears extended out into the joints, serving the purpose of filling the shape and of providing working designs for the coolest Human/Bus 64 cyborg ever imagined.

He thumbed the book every night. What's that? The liver. What's that? Kidneys. What's that? I don't know; let me read it. He learned all the names I had to read, until the questions became a quiz. What's that? I don't know. It's the duodenum.

As amazing as all of this continues to be, neither his art nor his understanding of how things work is savant ability. His knowledge and talents draw from intense focus. The question "How does that work?" must be answered immediately and with an understanding of every specific detail.

For Valentine's Day, his kindergarten class drew hearts. His heart included arteries, veins, ventricles, and an aortic arch. Someday, some girl will get a Valentine's heart and will ask him, "What's that?" And Benjamin will fall in love.

~Trey Brown

The Art of Hope

If nothing ever changed there'd be no butterflies.
~Author Unknown

The old church building is charming, though almost obscured by trees, in the middle of a small farming town. As we climb the steps, my teenage son cranes his head to look up at the tilting steeple, taking in every detail. Visitors at a special service, we enter quietly and sit close together on an oak pew, waiting with open hymnals in our laps.

Andrew is still looking around, measuring the architecture, I suspect. He has done this since he was little. Any new place is examined—room-by-room, if allowed. He used to draw pictures afterward—floor plans even. I saved stacks of them. Sitting beside him now, I squeeze my songbook, resisting the urge to hand him a notebook and pen from my purse.

Andrew has been drawing since he was two. He couldn't press hard enough to make pencil mark paper, so we bought him a magnetic drawing board instead.

"Draw," he would say, putting it in my lap. I would draw a picture while he watched, and then he would reach over and pull the lever to erase it. "Draw," he would say again. Before long, he started drawing his own pictures. He drew things he loved—power poles and fountains, elevators and Steve's chair from *Blue's Clues*. Before he turned three, he drew that chair from an angle—his first three-dimensional drawing. My husband and I gaped and then failed to stop him from erasing it. We learned to take pictures of Andrew's drawing board.

Andrew spent his childhood drawing—first on his drawing board, and then on reams of paper or with the computer's paint program. He drew hotels, playgrounds, malls, maps and swimming pools. He drew Willy Wonka's factory, Captain Hook's ship and Darth Vader's Death Star. When his speech therapist asked, "Can you draw me a house?" he replied, "I can draw you all the houses in Whoville."

With his first box of blocks, Andrew began to build what he drew. A fire station, perfectly housing his Tonka fire truck, and a pedestal sink including an actual basin—with a red block to turn on the hot water and a blue one to turn on the cold.

We marveled. His grandmothers bragged. His aunts said, "Isn't he amazing?" And I comforted myself—I clung to his gift. Because my son had trouble holding a conversation, making eye contact, adjusting to change. He had insomnia and anxiety and auditory processing dysfunction. My son had autism.

They say autism affects each person differently, each family differently. But spectrum parents all share one trait—worry. Our minds leap forward as we lie awake at night, riddled with questions. What will the future hold for my son? Who will be there for him when I'm gone? What kind of career can he expect? Will people be fair? Will they look past their presumptions and see his true worth?

When questions like these threatened to overwhelm me, I would look at what Andrew built or drew, and I would feel better. This was a talent—a gift from God that my son could depend on. There were so many options in his future—so many possible uses for his talent. If only we fed it, fostered it, and let it bloom, my son would be an artist one day.

But then adolescence hit and something happened that almost broke my heart. Andrew stopped drawing. Not altogether, but almost. He still drew in art class, but not at home. His art became a private thing—I was not allowed to share it with family anymore. No

Facebook posts, no holiday cards designed by Andrew. His drawing pads sat half empty—those he did use were labeled, "KEEP OUT."

"I'm not that good," he would say, and no amount of encouragement convinced him otherwise.

I reacted badly. To me, drawing was inseparable from Andrew's character. I tried to reboot his interest. I bought him quality markers and a drawing tablet for the computer. I downloaded better software. He played around with them, but it wasn't the same. I wouldn't let up. I resented those things he now loved: Nintendo and YouTube. Whenever he said, "I'm bored," I would say, "Why don't you draw something?"

His negative responses began to take on a worried tone. It took me too long to realize what it meant.

Andrew thought I was disappointed in him.

I was stunned. I had been wrong—as wrong as I could possibly be. My son was doing what teenagers do, after all. He was changing, maturing, making choices that were different than mine. And I was being stubborn about it, thinking that his tendency toward constancy and his limited scope of interest would at least serve him in this one way—to keep him focused on his art. Now I was guilty of leaning on a stereotype about autism itself, and pasting a label on my child that no longer fit.

Would it upset me when my typical daughter stopped playing with dolls? Of course not. Or would I assume that, because she stopped playing with dolls, her future would not include the nurturing of children? How absurd.

Shouldn't I be encouraging his exploration? His vital, youthful humanity—his independent thought? Wouldn't that freedom foster rather than stifle his creativity?

I apologized to Andrew. I hope he took it to heart. I took a lot of deep breaths and my prayers became more focused and fervent. My role as a mother was not to raise an artist; it was to raise a decent human being. I miss seeing Andrew's head bent over a drawing tablet, yes. But I am proud to see his compassion, his gentleness, his honesty and his sense of humor. I love the way he asks me how I am, every single day. I love how he chooses random moments to ask thoughtful questions — so much more caring than I was at his age. These are the qualities I need to foster, the traits I need to praise.

When I learned to let go, I realized something else. Andrew may not draw much anymore, but his creativity remains. He plays *Minecraft* a lot these days, building cities — even worlds on his computer. He designs video games too, listing each level, making diagrams. After a trip to Disneyland, Andrew began imagining new attractions, plotting them in his head, jotting down features. He's now taking a drafting/engineering class at school.

So what was I so worried about?

Back in the little church building, Andrew is leaning toward me, his brow drawn together in concern. "Mom?" he whispers. I wonder if the crowd is bothering him, or the unfamiliar faces and smells.

"What is it?"

"I think it must be hard to be a husband," he says. "You have to make sure your wife is happy. Then you have to make sure your kids are happy too."

I'm stunned. For a moment, I'm mute as well. I will answer him eventually, but first, my heart melts and soars. I know now what my son wants to be when he grows up. He wants to be a good man. And that's the most wonderful thing he can be.

~Jennifer Froelich

15

Fun Facts

Reality leaves a lot to the imagination.
~John Lennon

There are 300 lights on the ceiling.
There are 900 tiles on this floor.
Did you know aloe plants are quite healing,
And a wild angry pig is a boar?

There are 6,000 words on this web page.
There are 23 fleas on the dog.
Oh I told all your friends 'bout your real age,
Then I posted it here on your blog.

There are 88 stitches on softballs.
There are 13 small hairs on your chin.
Did you know that you sound like a moose call,
When your sinuses start to kick in?

Did you know that your mouth looks quite scary?
And your indoor voice seems rather loud.
I know thousands of facts on canaries.
All this info must make you quite proud.

I am sure that my teachers love fun facts,
Cause their faces all look like yours do.

By the way there's a note in my backpack.
My school must be proud of me too!

~Peggy Robbins Janousky

16

We Love Vermont

Each day comes bearing its own gifts. Untie the ribbons.
~Ruth Ann Schabacker

I just wanted my son to talk. I wanted some affirmation that I was a decent mom, that my kid knew he was loved. At age two, Nicholas spent so much time in his own little world. If we took him around other kids, he would lie face down on the carpet, giggling to himself, and stay there for an hour until we left. At home, he flicked through book pages to a steady rhythm for entire afternoons. He had to be coaxed to point at things. He spoke only a few words—the basics, like "no," "juice," "milk"—and not any sentences.

Receiving a diagnosis of high-functioning autism was vindication for me. Nicholas's slow development wasn't my fault; he simply thought in a different way. This was something we could work with, and work through. As a psychologist told us, he was very bright. Nicholas knew the alphabet and could count past one hundred, even if he didn't say "hi" or look anyone in the face. He was making progress, albeit slowly. There was hope. We just needed to find a way to open his eyes to a wider world.

Our miracle came in an unexpected form: a lap-sized wooden puzzle of the good old United States of America.

When I set that puzzle in front of him, his eyes went wide in an immediate reaction. I sucked in a breath. It was unusual for him to connect with a toy that fast. At age two and a half, he already had a strong preference for books instead.

"This is Texas," I said, holding up the biggest piece in the set.

"Texas," repeated my little parrot. He reached for the state's northern neighbor.

"That's Oklahoma."

"O-ka-hom-a," he said. We went through the rest of the states one by one. Concerned that he might lose the smaller pieces, I reassembled the puzzle and put it away out of his reach.

The next day, I found him staring up at his armoire. He didn't point, he didn't use words, but I could tell he wanted that puzzle again. When I placed it before him, he grinned wide and reached for Texas.

"Texas!" he announced. "O-ka-hom-a!"

Not only did he repeat most of the states back to me, but he picked up all the pieces in the exact same order I had the previous day. My mind was boggled. This time I left the pieces out for him. He stroked the edges and studied the names, chanting beneath his breath.

Puzzle time became a daily ritual. For two hours straight in the morning, he would sit there and ponder his puzzle and fit pieces into the larger map. Over the baby monitor, I heard him recite the names in a singsong. When it was time to put the puzzle away, I named each state as I put them in their places, and he echoed me, always watching.

The next week I had the news on in the background as I made supper. Nicholas began to squeal excitedly.

"Look," my husband said, his voice soft in awe.

I glanced towards the television, expecting Nicholas to be ecstatic about some commercial. Instead, the weather map was on the screen showing the western United States, and Nicholas was engaged in a bouncy dance that would put Tigger to shame.

"Arizona! Cal-fornia!" he yelled, arms over his head as he boogied. He made the connection. The United States didn't just exist as a puzzle in his bedroom. The states were everywhere. They were something other people talked about, too.

Nicholas's favorite puzzle states began to make tours of the house. I would find them lined up in front of the TV, or framing his placemat at the dining table. For some incomprehensible reason, Vermont became his very favorite. He carried it everywhere, whispering beneath his breath, "Vermont, Vermont, Vermont."

No matter where I was in the house, I could expect him to run up to me with that Vermont-New Hampshire piece in his hand. He stared at me, waiting, the piece thrust into my face.

"Yep, that's Vermont," I said.

He squealed and ran away again, the identity of his favorite state confirmed for the twelfth time that day.

I went through his book collection and found a lift-the-flap book on the states that we had bought months before. Nicholas didn't care for it at the time, but now the moment was ripe. He squealed with glee when he saw his states in book form. Within days, I had to bring out the tape to reinforce the pages and flaps.

Nicholas began to understand more abstract things about the states, too. "What state were you born in?" I asked him.

"Washington," said Nicholas, pointing to the state.

"Where do we live?"

"Arizona! Cap-tal, Phoenix."

He would do the same thing using the world map on his shower curtain, or an atlas, or a random map we would find in a store. When other people mentioned state names, he perked up in understanding and looked them in the eye, grinning. When I read the morning newspaper, he shouted out the state names he recognized in the headlines.

Nicholas was still developmentally delayed, there was no question, but by recognizing the places in the world, his personal world became larger. Maps were a language he could understand. Through those places and names, he could connect to other people, too.

On one particular day, Nicholas had been everywhere, into everything. It was one of the days that gave the "Terrible Twos" its name. I was a frazzled wreck by the time my husband got home from work. He wanted to cheer me up somehow, so he took Nicholas on his lap and asked him, "Isn't Mommy pretty? Don't we love Mommy?"

Nicholas looked me square in the eye, his smile blinding. "I love Vermont!" he said, bouncing at the words.

I took that as a yes.

~Beth Cato

Look Up

If a little dreaming is dangerous, the cure for it is not to dream less but to dream more, to dream all the time.
~Marcel Proust

y crafty child (crafty as in "artsy," not "manipulative") was driving me crazy the other day. I was frantically getting ready for a house full of company to arrive. I walked across our open foyer to find bits of folded paper scattered over the recently-swept tile.

"Paul must have been trying to carry his scrap paper from the living room to the garbage can and dropped a few pieces." I sighed, picking them up.

Moments later I passed through the foyer again to find more paper strewn over the tile. No quiet sighing this time. I called out, "Who is throwing garbage around the entrance?"

No answer. Instead, I saw more bits of paper silently floating down from the upstairs hallway. Looking up, I saw my seven-year-old, Paul, hanging over the rail.

"Paul!" I groaned tiredly. "Stop making a mess."

Paul stared fixatedly at the paper bits falling softly to the floor.

"It's not a mess."

"Yes it is, and I'm tired of picking it up."

"It's butterflies."

"Sorry, what did you say?" I hadn't heard him clearly.

He didn't answer. Paul has autism and rarely answers a question unless I'm right in front of him, gently holding his head in my hands, saying softly, "Eyes to me, Paul." He is high functioning, and while occupational and applied behavioral therapies have brought him a long way, verbal communication is an effort for him. Especially when he's focused intently on something else.

He ran down the stairs to retrieve his papers.

"Where are my other butterflies?" he asked, looking around.

Every time Paul puts five or more words together my heart says a prayer of thanks. For the first three years of his life there were no words, the next three years he barely put two words together, but lately he seems to realize that the benefits of forming complete sentences when communicating are worth the effort.

Butterflies. Of course. I rushed into the kitchen to rescue them from the garbage, dusted them off and handed them to my young craftsman.

"Wanna see them fly again?" he asked with a shy smile.

"Oh yes! They're beautiful, Paul," I whispered.

He ran back upstairs to float his masterpieces down again. I watched them gently fly down towards me. They really did look like beautiful little butterflies.

That day Paul reminded me to look up at beauty instead of down at garbage. How many other masterpieces do I miss because I'm too caught up in Paul's therapies or my housework or dinner preparations to take time to appreciate what's right in front of me? Life is not what happens to us, it's how we look at it. Now, I look up.

~Jayne Thurber-Smith

18

Sam

We have a voice if you're willing to listen to us.
~Chase Johnson

Ever since I was a little girl there was nothing I wanted more than being a mother. After several miscarriages, I finally had my son. We named him Samuel, which in Hebrew means "to be heard."

Sam was a baby who treated my insides like his own personal jungle gym, a toddler who repeatedly hid all of his Hot Wheels in the refrigerators, and a three-year-old who almost didn't make it to four because he dumped his dad's collection of 500 alphabetically organized CDs all over the floor.

As a baby, Sam didn't make eye contact when nursing, and he was quite reactive to any sound. He fussed when there were too many people around him and cried if there were competing noises, like a TV and radio playing simultaneously. Everyone thought I was just a nervous new mother as I tried to shield him from these triggers, but I knew it was something else. I just didn't know what.

In preschool his teachers had behavior charts to help regulate his impulses. He tried hard to sit in circle time without rearranging the weather charts. Unaware that Sam was reading independently, the teachers didn't realize why he knocked over the bookcases, frustrated because he had read every book on the shelves. At the end of gym class, an expert in the routine, Sam would start picking up the purple rubber sitting spots because he knew the teacher was about to collect them. The problem was that the kids were still sitting on them.

Sensory Integration Disorder arrived when Sam was exactly eighteen months old. His fear of toothpaste, shampoo and lotion made mundane tasks a nightmare. Every day, I held Sam on my lap, facing forward, his legs wedged between my thighs, my left arm wrapped around his chest holding both of his arms tight, and pried his mouth open with an Elmo toothbrush. It's amazing our neighbors never called the police, his screaming was that loud and lasted that long. He used the color blue exclusively until he was six. He only wore blue clothing, had a blue bedroom and when given a seventy-two pack of crayons, picked out the seven shades of blue and threw the rest away. His fear of paint meant that we were the only kindergarten parents who had a lovely blue outline of our child's hand instead of the usual handprint.

When Sam was three, we hired a developmental pediatrician who shadowed him at home, school and on play dates for three days. Thousands of dollars and a seventeen-page report later, we learned the word autism.

No one is ever ready to hear that word and certainly, not everyone is willing to accept that diagnosis, as was our case. Sam's father and I divorced two years later due to parenting differences. I thought that love, medication and therapy would change his behaviors. His dad felt stricter parenting was the answer. Neither of us was willing to compromise, so I took my kids and set out to follow all of the instructions the diagnosing pediatrician had given me.

We tackled every issue as it arose, with therapies, specialists and medications. His perseverations shifted from blue to baseball. By fifth grade, Sam knew the entire history of baseball back to the 1800s. It was at that time he decided to surreptitiously read books about baseball under his desk rather than listen to the teacher. After all, as he pointed out to one, they were using outdated maps and he couldn't be expected to learn from those old things. Social skills training began the next day.

Sam's hand was always raised in class and his teachers loved him because of his enthusiasm for learning, to say nothing of his innate intelligence. I think they also enjoyed that he not only provided definitions on vocabulary tests, but illustrations as well. He had an intense drawing perseveration that was now in full swing.

Eventually, Sam adjusted to school life and we got him to lower his hand as well as the height at which he wore his pants. It only took a year of CBT to get his belt buckle loosened so his pants weren't up in his armpits!

Sam worked hard at making friends, being more typical and learning the differences between being serious and sarcastic. We role-played a lot, practicing give and take conversations. He now realizes that though he can recite every fact about baseball, not everyone wants to hear those facts.

Never once did Sam question my strategies. When he was twelve, when many kids are calling their parents idiots, he said to me, "You always do what's best for me." The few times he disagreed and I had to summon help from his dad, Sam listened, knowing that his dad always wanted the very best for him too; and due to their mutual love of baseball and debate, he and his dad formed a bond that I know will never break.

Over the years Sam has worked hard to see outside his world. He was a little boy who gave away his racecar bed to a child he didn't know, but heard had no bed; a boy who, in Israel, packed boxes of food for the hungry, even though he was starving due to an intense dislike of hummus; and a teen who is the first to say hello and the last to back down.

Sam is now fifteen and has made more transitions than most people make in a lifetime. Some have been made with confidence and aplomb and some, more recently, have set him back years. He has adjusted to many moves, living in three different states and changing schools. He has been bullied and befriended. He has accepted a plethora of unexpected change and has experienced some extraordinarily painful losses.

The doctors who told me there was nothing we could do—they should see Sam now.

The therapists who said that's all they could do—they should see Sam now.

The teachers who refused to see past his issues—they should see Sam now.

The kids who didn't "get" him—they should see Sam now.

They couldn't see what we always saw—a gentle, sweet, kind, loving boy who just wanted to be accepted for who he was—a perfectly great kid.

Sam now speaks nationally about his Asperger's, with hopes of raising awareness so it will lead to tolerance, patience and friendship. His message is that Aspies make very good friends because they know what a gift a good friend can be.

I already know what a gift he is as my son.

~Allison Hermann Craigie

19

Convenient Care

*It is not until you become a mother that your judgment
slowly turns to compassion and understanding.*
~Erma Bombeck

After a few weeks of listening to my nine-year-old son's
cough, I decided it was time for Noah to see a doctor.
I no longer rush to the doctor's office the moment I
notice a sniffle. I'm the mother of three boys, and I've
seen my share of illness. When I decide to make an appointment, it's
the real deal.

I called our pediatrician's office, but due to cold and flu season, she was booked the rest of the week. Our only option was to
go to the Convenient Care Clinic after hours. No appointment was
necessary.

Snow fell as we drove to the clinic. We were bundled in our
heaviest winter gear. As we wiped off our boots after getting inside, I
heard the coughing, wheezing, and sneezing coming from the waiting room. It was a full house, packed with kids and adults, all who
seemed to have a similar ailment.

"Don't touch anything!" I said to Noah as we checked in. I pulled
out my disinfectant wipes from my purse. "I think my son might have
bronchitis. How long can we expect to wait?"

"I really have no idea," the receptionist said. Her eyes were warm
and kind. She pointed to the few open chairs in the waiting area.

Noah, who has autism, couldn't understand that we had no appointment and therefore no idea how long we might be there.

"It's called Convenient Care because we come here when we are ill, without an appointment, when it's convenient for us," I explained. He wasn't convinced.

It wasn't long until Noah was absorbed in his books. As we waited, he read *Bill Nye the Science Guy's Big Blast of Science*. Between coughing spells, he talked to me about gravity, protons, and electrons. He also read through much of the *Encyclopedia of Dinosaurs: And Other Prehistoric Creatures*.

As we sat and waited, I thought about how far Noah has come in the past seven years since his autism diagnosis. When he was younger, he had few play skills. Change was difficult. Strangers frightened him. He loved books but only because his eyes preferred the sight of the turning pages as they swept across his field of vision. His speech was scripted and repetitive. He entered kindergarten wearing diapers.

Now he is a fourth grader who excels academically with minimal special education support. He's potty trained. He tells jokes every year at the school variety show. He plays flag football and enjoys horseback riding. His memory is remarkable. He sings with the sweetest voice. He's polite and sensitive. He is a creative thinker who has a positive attitude. He understands adversity.

"Do you care if I go to the bathroom, Mom?" Noah's words interrupted my thoughts.

"Just be sure to lock the door, and wash your hands with soap."

After a few minutes, Noah sat down beside me. "It felt like absolute zero in there, which is -459.67 degrees Fahrenheit or -273 degrees Celsius!" He shivered and walked over to look at the sports section of the local newspaper.

When Noah's name was called, we marched into an exam room. A nurse spoke with us about our concerns, and we waited a few more minutes.

The doctor walked in. She had never before met Noah and

didn't have his medical records. As far as I knew, we would never see her again. I didn't feel the need to mention his autism diagnosis. Although he knows about his diagnosis, sometimes I don't like to talk to professionals about it while he is present. During this appointment, there were no explanations. For once, I wanted a doctor to see him as a "typical" kid.

"What seems to be the trouble?" asked the doctor.

"Well, I'll give you a hint," Noah explained. "I think the problem is in my respiratory system."

She looked at the notes the nurse had left for her. "How long have you had this horrible cough?" the doctor asked.

"Two weeks plus the hour I was in the waiting room," Noah replied.

I didn't know whether to laugh or cry. I said nothing.

"I am the only doctor here treating all of these patients, you know," she snapped.

I mumbled something about it being a long day, as she listened to Noah's lungs. The doctor concluded Noah had a respiratory infection and prescribed the antibiotic, azithromycin.

"That's one I'm not familiar with," I said.

"Well, Mom," Noah interrupted, "that's because you're not a doctor AND you didn't research this like you did the bronchitis that I don't have."

My face turned bright red.

The doctor handed me the prescription, and we all stood up. I gathered our coats and other winter gear. On the way out, Noah noticed two huge anatomy posters that covered most of the wall.

"Wow, look at those charts of the muscular system! I'd like to ask for those for my birthday coming up!" Noah shouted. "Do you know that your blood pumps through 60,000 miles of your veins every day?"

Out of the corner of my eye, I saw the doctor in the hallway, watching us leave. She was shaking her head.

"Well, Noah," I said, "we got the answer we were looking for today. Once you get some medicine, you'll feel much better."

"Let's get out of here," Noah said. We held hands and walked outside to the winter wonderland.

I couldn't have said it better myself.

~Tyann Sheldon Rouw

James 101

… autism… is as much about what is abundant
as what is missing, an over-expression of the very traits
that make our species unique.
~Paul Collins

Time Matters

James has a tag hanging on his backpack that says "Time Doesn't Matter!"

This is a lie. For James, time doesn't just matter, it matters more than anything. The tag, an attempt at thought shifting by James's behavior therapist, hasn't made a dent in my son's all-consuming obsession with time. It's a nice goal to have dangling there, though.

From the moment James learned about numbers (at a precociously early age), he has been fixated on them. The perseveration has taken on many different forms over the years — counting, calendars, computation, and the one that has lasted longest — clocks. As James's fascination with time has persisted, and even grown, so has his anxiety about it. Deviations from planned arrival and departure times create meltdowns. Affinity for particular times on the digital clock dictate when he will enter or leave a room — or the house. It used to be "wish times" — 11:11, 1:11, 2:22 etc. Now it's :41 after any hour—but only on our microwave—he likes the way the space between the 4 and the 1 looks on that particular digital readout. It is exasperating—and exhausting.

The flip side of this time obsession is that it can be helpful, and sometimes nothing short of extraordinary. James knows exactly what time it is at any given moment—a skill that has assisted many adults, including his teachers. He notices and remembers the exact moment we leave somewhere. You'd be surprised how useful this can be. He is also able to predict, with astonishing accuracy, what time we will arrive at a destination—sometimes one that is hours away. This past Thanksgiving, we set off on an excursion with my nieces. We all made a guess as to what time we would get where we were going. It appeared that James had come in a minute early on his prediction, when, just as the car rolled into the gates of our destination, the clock flipped—James was exactly right! Mayhem followed in the car, as his cousins shrieked in amazement. James just laughed and said "What? I always do that!"

I know that James will always feel a draw to the clock—and that his frantic attention to it will eventually give way to something else. When? I guess, when the time is right.

Frankfurter Frenzy

Saturday night, November 8th. Eight-year-old James and I are deciding what book to read before bed. He picks one up and starts flipping through it, again and again, like he's looking for something. "Where's that word, Mommy?"

"What word?"

"Frankfurter—that means hot dog."

"I don't know."

Slightly agitated. "We read a book on September 16th. It was a

Tuesday. And it said 'frankfurter' and you told me that was another word for hot dog. I thought it was this book."

It wasn't.

We spend the next twenty minutes trying to figure out what book it was. These are the kinds of things that produce great anxiety in James. The lip goes out, the eyes well up, the voice becomes shaky.

"It had a town in it, Mommy, and the word frankfurter. It was on September 16th."

Did I mention it's November? He not only remembers what day we read it, he knows what day of the week it was. Chances are he knows exactly what time it was too. Why the hell can't he remember the name of the book?

I rack my brain, thinking about everything we read, because I know no one will be going to sleep until we figure this out. There's no "we'll keep looking tomorrow" for James. No "oh well, it'll turn up!" The word "frankfurter" WILL be found—no matter how long it takes.

Do you know how many stories use the word "frankfurter?" Not too many. The books pile up on the floor, as James's anxiety builds. He starts crying—and I'm starting to sweat.

My frantically darting eye lands on an anthology of stories that we've read from exactly once in our lives. I grab it, remembering a story about a town that had lots of food in it.

I flip through—YES I'm right! It's *Cloudy With a Chance of Meatballs* I declare triumphantly! James starts laughing. He grabs the book—and there it is: "frankfurter."

"Mommy—you found it!" Pure glee. I breathe a sigh of relief as we settle in to read. It's 9:40—at least an hour past James's bedtime. But at least he'll be going to sleep! And thankfully, so will I.

Perfect Pitch

At fourteen months, James would wake up in his crib humming a note. When I carried him downstairs and put him down in front of our keyboard, he would play whatever note he was humming—go right to it, without hunting around for it.

At two, I taught him the names of all the notes on the keyboard. The world became one big tonal universe… leaf blowers were B flats, elevator dings were Fs, the ring of phone was a C….

At three, James was listening to a group of live musicians tuning up their instruments at a restaurant, and called out "I like that A! Nice C sharp!"

We bought a piano.

James was four when our piano was tuned for the first time. He was out of sight in the kitchen and began calling out the names of the notes along with their numeric location relative to the eighty-eight keys. The piano tuner almost fell off the bench. When the tuning session was complete, he said, "I've tuned over 20,000 pianos—including Stevie Wonder's—and I have never experienced anything like what I've just seen in the past hour!" Maybe he'd never tuned a piano for a kid with autism.

Over the years, James's musical fixation has brought him—and those around him—great pleasure. It has also been the cause of intense perseveration, distraction and isolation. Overall, it has been more of a blessing than a curse. Music has served as a source of bonding and amazement wherever James goes. I sit down at the piano and struggle to figure out a song by ear. James wanders in and casually remarks, "You're playing that in the wrong key, Mom, there's an F sharp in that song!" At school, where he generally remains on the fringes of the social fabric, James is famous for his musical gifts. He is placed front and center during school shows, to keep the other kids in tune. Top 40 radio hits serve as a lunchtime conversation topic in his class. In third grade, at the end-of-the-year awards assembly, James was given a framed mock-up of a futuristic magazine cover with his photo and the headline:

"HOW JAMES BURROWS IS CHANGING THE FACE OF POPULAR MUSIC!"

They just might be right about that.

~Nancy Burrows

Jay's Odyssey Tales

Each man delights in the work that suits him best.
~Homer, The Odyssey

The term "odyssey" has come to mean any challenging journey. My ten-year-old son Jay however refers to *The Odyssey* ... as in Homer. My son reads for enjoyment many of the books that are dreaded by high school students. Where other children his age are collecting baseball cards, my boy collects mythological facts. He loves to share his knowledge with everyone too, whether you want to hear about it or not.

Every morning he spends fifteen minutes retelling a tale to his little sister Grace. I am not sure if it is Jay's amazing storytelling talent that makes her listen or if it is just her way of showing her big brother with Asperger's that she cares. Nonetheless she sits there and lets Jay weave a web of god and goddesses, mythical creatures and mere mortals. It actually has become the highlight of my mornings. I listen from downstairs and let them have their special time. Of course I have to eventually put an end to it or else they both would be late for school because Jay can go on and on and on. But for those fifteen minutes... it is Jay and Grace and together they travel back in time to ancient Greece.

The other morning was a repeat performance of the *Cyclops Cave*. Grace sweetly listened to the tale as if it was her first time hearing it. In many ways it is, because each time Jay tells the story a little differently.

"Odysseus and his men had been traveling for a very long time and they needed more food and supplies so they landed on shore and they found a cave full of sheep. They cooked the sheep and ate them. What they did not know was that the sheep belonged to a Cyclops, a huge one-eyed monster!" Jay excitedly told her. He then went on to tell her how the Cyclops got upset and started to eat the humans. The next part of the story was his favorite part because it involved trickery, outsmarting an opponent. He told Grace how Odysseus got the Cyclops drunk, blinded him with a stick and then hid among the sheep making bah-bah sounds while he crawled away to safety. After a quick session of Q&A I reluctantly stopped story time before Jay started another tale. "We'll do the next part tomorrow," he told his sister and then they both disappeared into their own rooms to get ready.

The amazing thing is that special exchange is so quickly forgotten. By the time they come down to breakfast they are fighting over who gets the orange vitamin and who gets the red. They are pushing and shoving while putting on their jackets. I am not complaining, well maybe a little bit, but mostly I don't complain because I love this sense of normalcy. I love this regular sibling bickering and interaction, because many days Jay isolates himself or withdraws. But still how is it possible for them to have had such a fantastic fifteen minutes together and then just as quickly drop it?

I understand why Jay enjoys the *Odyssey* tales so much. In many ways his life is an odyssey, a challenging journey. Every day Jay faces his own Cyclops. It may not come in the form of a giant one-eyed monster. More likely it will look like a five-paragraph writing assignment or sitting through a loud assembly. Every day, Jay, like Odysseus, will need to use trickery. Jay needs to trick his brain, which is wired differently than ours, to do what is considered normal. He will seek ways to hide until he can crawl away to safety. This is what my baby faces every day.

I understand why Jay loves stories about how the gods come down and help special chosen mortals. Homer's *Odyssey* tells of the troubles that Odysseus and his men faced over the years as they traveled to find their way back home. I am sure that Jay can relate to these stories in ways I will never be able to totally understand.

I am not sure that I like the idea that a famous Greek poet who lived over 2,700 years ago may understand my son better than I do. But I am happy that at least my son has chosen something with which he can identify. What mother wouldn't want her son, be he special needs or typical, to identify with a hero?

~Sharon Fuentes

The Rainbow

We all have spiritual DNA; wisdom and truth are part of our genetic structure even if we don't always access it.
~Lama Surya Das

When I was diagnosed with breast cancer at the age of forty-four, my biggest concern was how my teens, Kaitlyn and Donovan, would take the news, and how they would adapt to having a sick mom around the house. I was not so much concerned about my six-year-old, Ben, who has autism. With his very weak verbal skills, I reasoned that Ben would not really understand what was happening. Even if he did comprehend my illness, I figured that being "in a world of his own," he wouldn't really be bothered by my plight. I couldn't have been more wrong!

While he says very little, Ben recently learned to use the computer to express himself. Several times during my illness, he surprised me by bringing me typewritten notes (done without prompting) with messages like: "Dear Mom, you are nice" and "Dear Mom, I love you." Sometimes I would find his notes lying around the house, with messages such as, "Mom is sick," or "Mom is hurt."

On a rare occasion, Ben will catch me off guard by speaking a full, meaningful sentence. Never was I more surprised than one night while putting him to bed, when he said to me, "Good night. Guardian angels watch over you and protect you." Some might say he was just echoing something he had heard me say a hundred times before. True. But the miraculous part is that it is the one and only time I ever heard him speak those words, and it happened to be on the day I was diagnosed with breast cancer.

While Ben is not an affectionate child by nature, he seemed to relax his rules a little during my illness. On days that I was confined to the bed or the couch, he would often come to me with his stuffed dog, Scruffy, looking for a cuddle. One day, shortly after my diagnosis, Ben and I were alone in the house when a freak spring snowstorm hit. The blizzard outside seemed to mirror the storm of emotion that was happening inside me as I wondered what lay ahead and whether I would even be around to see another spring. Ben, sensing my sadness, came to me with Scruffy for one of our rare cuddle sessions. As we lay on the couch, looking through the window at the blowing snow, Ben pointed to the sky and said, "Look, a rainbow." This took me by surprise, as Ben, like many children with autism, is not one to use his imagination in this way. I asked, "Where is the rainbow?" Again, he pointed to the sky and said, "A rainbow." I suddenly felt a sense of peace, as I took this as a sign that everything would be okay and there would be a rainbow at the end of my storm.

Ben may look like he is "in a world of his own," but these gestures prove to me that he is a sensitive boy who is very much aware of what is happening in my world. After a very difficult year of cancer treatments, I am happy to say that I am now cancer-free, and as I reflect on the experience I can say that seeing this new side of Ben has certainly been one of the "perks" of having cancer.

~Florence Strang

Walk On

There is something about the outside of a horse
that is good for the inside of a man.
~Winston Churchill

wanted my son to talk to me. I wanted him to express himself in the ways that my other children always could. Scott is the oldest of our three boys. Watching how easily life moved along for our other two sons made Scott's struggles seem even more difficult. We were exhausting every resource we could to bring our autistic son into our world. I had an overwhelming desire to hear his voice, and I decided to try animal therapy, specifically horses.

I enrolled Scott, at age four, in a therapeutic horseback-riding program in Broward County called Horses and the Handicapped of South Florida, Inc. I am by no means a "horse girl," but I had heard about their uncanny intuition with special needs children. I had been told that riding a horse could help individuals with autism conquer their sensory defenses and increase communication skills and cognitive reasoning. I wanted Scott to achieve all of these things, but most of all I wanted him to experience some sense of normalcy. I thought that if these horseback-riding lessons could bring him that feeling of accomplishment and belonging, then I would be sold!

Scott's first time on the horse gave me a view of my son I had never experienced before; he was sitting quietly. This gave me a glimmer of hope that he was indeed able to focus, to listen to direction, to experience something outside of himself. The horse seemed to accomplish all this and more.

Scott is a natural sportsman. He has always enjoyed anything that gets him moving—skiing, basketball, running. You name it, Scott will try it. Horseback riding would simply be another experience to add to Scott's long athletic résumé. Over the years, I watched the instructors and volunteers work patiently with Scott, encouraging him, reminding him of the riding cues. The instructor gave him basic direction: pick up your reins; steer to the left; steer to the right; say "whoa" to tell your horse to stop; say "walk on" to tell your horse to go.

Suddenly, after nearly fourteen years of life, Scott spoke his first words, and they were on a horse! He told the horse to "walk on." This sudden onset of speech came as a complete shock to our family and everyone who knew Scott, including his medical team. His time on the horse suddenly took on a new meaning. He had made the connection that when the command "walk on" was given, his horse would move.

There was my formerly silent son, on top of a 900-pound animal, speaking clearly and confidently, as if he had been doing it his entire life. Soon this connection spread to other activities and Scott quickly joined the social circle of our family, his school and the community.

Scott has been riding for sixteen years now, and I have seen tremendous improvements in not only his speech, but also in his confidence. He began riding with a horse handler and sidewalkers, helping him find his balance. Today, Scott is one of the ten fully independent riders. Not only does Scott say "walk on," he is able to use all of the proper verbal commands to direct his horse fearlessly at the walk, trot and canter! He is the official "barn greeter," asking volunteers and staff alike the most important question: "What did you have for lunch today?" Hearing Scott talk is music to my ears, as he confidently relates to his peers. When people forget what they have had for lunch, Scott keeps them on their toes. Scott will pry it out, and no matter what you have had to eat, Scott's lunch was always better than yours!

Scott and his classmate Stephanie partner up each week to canter around the arena, something that would scare most people. It is an absolute thrill for Scott. He has ridden in the Broward County Special Olympics Games and is always called upon to help at special events for Horses and the Handicapped, where he delivers a short toast to the crowd with ease, and mingles with guests like it is his job!

Scott has given me, his dad, and two brothers a life we would never have known—one filled with empathy, patience and caring. I know it goes against the grain to say that in many ways we are grateful for Scott's autism. I often remark to families dealing with the grief of initial diagnosis that "it's not as bad as you think" and I really mean it.

~Michelle Rubin

Chapter
3

Raising
Kids on the
Spectrum

Challenges

I Hit the Roof

We feel free when we escape — even if it be from the frying pan to the fire.
~Eric Hoffer

My autistic son, Josh, climbed out on the roof when he was four years old. What a clever child. When I turned my back in the upstairs hallway he quickly figured out how to unlock the window in his bedroom and crawl out onto the flat part of the roof. And then he scurried up the angled part that overlooked the brick patio. (Who said he was low-functioning?) He just wanted to get a better view of the neighbor's pool.

"Watoh, Watoh," I heard him squeal when I quickly discovered he was missing. Of course, on pure instinct I shimmied out the window and flew after him. Before I knew it I was halfway up the roof yelling, "SIT PLEASE!' in my best ABA voice, slipping in my sandals. My fatal mistake was looking down. It makes my hands sweat just thinking about it. In my panic I'd forgotten about my fear of heights, so when I spotted the brick below I froze in terror.

Josh was thrilled about having company. He oohed and aahed over the glittery water in the distance, blissfully unaware of my altered state. There we were, both planted at an uncomfortable angle on the roof — one of us content, the other hysterical — in total lockdown. "SARAH!!" I screamed at the top of my lungs. My lungs must have been pumped with adrenaline because they were the only part of my body that wasn't frozen. "SARAH! COME HERE, COME HERE!"

Lovely Sarah was new to our therapy team. She was very sweet and had superb hearing. When she heard my cries from downstairs she ran up to my son's open window. I couldn't turn in her direction because I was scared stiff. "GET JEFF! GET JEFF!" And Sarah was off.

It was unusual that my husband was home when it was still daylight outside. He typically returns from a bike ride or from the office after dusk. At that particular moment he was in the dungeon below the house working. After a few moments I heard him yelling in Josh's bedroom. "SHELL?" By that time my left hand, the one that was gripping Josh's leg, was starting to slide down from perspiration. It was getting difficult for me to contain my enthusiastic son and keep him on his perch.

I could hear Jeff's heavy dress shoes clambering up behind me. By this time I'm sure the three of us made a pretty scene. Jeff and I would've snickered together if the situation hadn't been so dire. Sarah was getting an early taste of my family life. (And was probably thinking that climbing was not in her job description.) Jeff dragged me down to safety undone but intact. And bless him, I don't know how he managed to reach Josh in those slippery leather shoes, but he "rescued" him immediately. Josh didn't want to be rescued. He wanted to go over to the house next door and swim. We all just looked at each other, sighing, sweating, feeling yet another storm cloud pass over us. Another autistic adventure. Another narrow escape. At least we found Josh this time instead of our neighbors.

I called the handyman the next day. We screwed all the windows shut upstairs except for one. If Josh could speak I'm sure he would implore us to reconsider. He would swear to never climb on the roof again. Especially if we built a pool. Yeah, right. That's all I need.

~Shelley Stolaroff Segal

Obsession

It's hard for me to put into words why I like the beach so much.
Everything about it is renewing for me, almost like therapy.
~Amy Dykens

t's my favorite moment of the year, early each Father's Day. I enter our son Matthew's room to help him out of bed and to get him dressed. And then it is my joy to say, "Matthew, guess where we're going today!"

He knows what's coming next. A huge smile breaks on his face. His steel blue eyes twinkle and brighten. His hands start flapping. His legs begin twitching...."To the beach!"

It is a wonderful Father's Day gift to myself.

His loud squeals pierce the room, alternately hurting my ears and filling me with enchantment. His entire body quivers, coiling with elation and anticipation. He claps his hands eagerly, unable to contain his absolute joy and delight. He can't focus on anything else now. He can neither eat nor drink. He's too excited, absolutely thrilled. Our annual weeklong trip to the beach is finally here. After a year of not so patiently waiting, it's time to go back again!

Matthew is obsessed with the beach—absolutely fixated on going there, on being there, on anticipating being there. He has other obsessions too. But the beach is his most constant and intense. He cannot speak. But he can clearly communicate, strongly and well, his desires about the beach. When we so often struggle to understand what he may want or need, there is no question about his feelings on that place. Because every day of the year, he indicates that he wants to go to the beach—by pointing at the photos of him there that can be found all around our house. There are photos of past vacations—of him with his mother, of him with me, of him with his brothers, of him with his grandparents, and of him alone. In each one Matthew's joy is unmistakable—in his body language, in his broad, squinty-eyed grin. His excitement is unambiguous.

When it comes to the possibility of going to the beach, Matthew is eternally optimistic, perpetually hopeful, and infinitely expectant. He is relentless and unyielding. His badgering is constant, and it can wear pretty thin some days. I'll be honest about that. His insistence can be frustrating and it can fray our nerves.

He packs constantly. There are a lot of things he does not understand, a lot that he appears not to grasp. But he absolutely knows what he believes he needs for the beach. He is obsessed about gathering tubes of sunscreen, swimsuits and T-shirts, Reese's Peanut Butter Cups, a towel, cups of pudding and a water bottle, and the Pull-Ups he wears because of his incontinence. If he can drag a beach umbrella up from the basement, he will insist on that being included too. He presents them to us and won't rest until as many of those necessities as possible are stuffed into a bag or backpack and set by the front door. Some days we pack those bags over and over again. Most days we are forever tripping over the bags and "necessities" by the door.

Matthew also wears a swimsuit and T-shirt twenty-four hours a day, 365 days a year. No matter how hot or cold it is. No matter where he goes or what the occasion he is wearing a swimsuit. He wore one to both his older brothers' weddings, under his suit and tie, and to his high school graduation ceremony, under his gown. He wears one to church each Sunday, to his activities program each day and to bed each night. He has two dozen of them, in the bright, patterned colors he loves. There are extra swimsuits and T-shirts stowed in each of our cars and in the backpack he takes to his program each day. He has one packed in a bag that hangs on the back of the transport chair he uses when he is out in public. The red ones are his favorites. His Spider-Man suits come next in the pecking order.

Some of his swimsuits are threadbare and worn through, patched again and again to make them wearable as long as possible. When it's warm outside, a suit and T-shirt will be all he wears wherever he goes. But when it's cold, they are always on underneath another, warmer shirt and a pair of long pants. When he had surgery and an eight-day hospital stay this past summer he wore them instead of the standard-issue hospital gown.

Matthew is twenty-four years old, long past the age when wearing a swimsuit and T-shirt everywhere he goes and for everything he does is normally cute or acceptable. But in his childlike innocence, in his autism, they are simply part of who he is. His obsession is his joy. When he is on the beach, sitting on a low chair at the water's edge, he is as calm and as contented as he can possibly be. Matthew rarely sits still — ever. He is always in motion, pulsing with frenetic energy, even in bed, even through the night. But when he is at the beach, with the waves washing up to his feet, sometimes washing up over him, occasionally crashing into him and knocking him and his chair over as he howls with laughter and glee, he is tranquil, serene, supremely contented — at peace. The packing has stopped. The obsession has paid off. He is finally at the beach.

And when he is, for at least this one week out of the year, his mother and I can find tranquility, serenity, contentment — blessed peace — as well.

~Michael D. Gingerich

Bridging the Gap

In the depth of winter, I finally learned that
within me there lay an invincible summer.
~Albert Camus

glanced in the rearview mirror; my son had balanced his book and his beloved dictionary on his knees, allowing him to look up any new words as he sped through yet another paperback. As we drove towards the surgery, I wondered how to word my son's latest crisis to our family doctor, who has journeyed with us and our son's high-functioning autism for many years.

"What will you tell him?" my husband had asked me earlier.

"I don't know. Maybe I'll just tell him that our son has an appetite for paper, playing cards and workbooks instead of cereal and toast!"

"At least this time he picked something fibrous," he replied cautiously, unsure if I was ready yet to find humor in the reality that our son was again eating things he shouldn't be.

Sensory issues weave a pattern around my son, affecting the choice of materials, length and color of clothing he'll wear and his ability to cope with noise and visual triggers. I can't pretend to understand his inflexibility about certain foods: why cheese is his enemy but pizza is his friend, why ice cream must always be brown and only eaten in a cone, or why sleeping on a tiled floor is more comfortable than a bed. For him, it seems painful to live like this. For me, it's exhausting.

The list of his sensitivities is lengthy and ever-evolving, but after many years I have at least stopped asking him "Why?" on a daily basis. The answer simply is "Because." We work hard on these issues, doing our best to understand him without allowing his obsessions to rule us. Sometimes his inflexibilities pass—a passionate hatred of buttons one year was barely remembered the next—but it's a complicated balance and one that often ends in frustration.

Since his toddler years, our son has struggled with strong cravings for inedible things. His list of favorite snacks has included mud and licking the soles of dirty shoes. Still, his latest obsession had caught me by surprise.

"Why do you have all these torn pages in your school books?"

He looked up. "Oh, those are my teethmarks, from where I took bites." He gave me a small, kind smile, as if to say, "Wow, I can't believe you didn't already know that."

My son explained that he couldn't help it (a recurrent theme), his body just wanted to swallow paper. And, as you would expect, the school was full of the stuff. So like a kid in a candy shop, he was consuming copious fiber goodies every day.

We alerted the school and tried many tactics to help him stop. We talked it out, threatened punishments and bought an expensive chewy stick recommended by the occupational therapist. But despite our valiant efforts, the problem escalated and I started getting calls from the teacher.

"We did cutting in art today, and I found him eating the strips of paper that were meant to be thrown in the bin!"

The teacher was shocked by his behavior and I did my best to feign despair, though I wasn't really feeling frantic. We had dealt with worse over the years and I hoped it would resolve itself. But within a few days of her call, I caught him carefully peeling and eating the shiny colored covering on a pencil and began to doubt myself.

Now, sitting with the doctor, I shared this background information with him, humbled by my need to ask for help yet again. We spoke in the code language of adults, although we could have talked freely. My son was distracted, having already climbed onto the examination table and pulled the curtain closed in order to check his own blood pressure—a game he played at every appointment. As we chatted, we could hear him wrap the cuff around his arm, pumping away vigorously. Our doctor was kind enough to let him, until it became obvious that either my son or his blood pressure machine were about to explode, at which point he moved quietly behind the curtain and helped my son release it without any rebuke.

We encouraged my son to sit down and join us but he wasn't finished playing. He walked over the weighing scales, and stood heavily on them proudly yelling out his weight—loud enough for the whole waiting room to hear.

"This week, he graduated from paper products to playing cards. I found him in his room with a decapitated Jack of Spades. When I asked him why he'd eaten the card, he told me not to worry: there were three more Jacks in the pack!"

The doctor glanced over at my son and then back at me, and we shared a small smile that acknowledged the thread of humor that runs lightly through these conversations. Our doctor has a very special relationship with my son. He recognizes his inner spark as a strength that is greater than his oddities. The few others that I'd told about the card eating incident had been horrified. Reactions ranged from concerns about the toxicity of the plastic coating to less-than-subtle judgment calls. I wasn't sure how the doctor would handle my son today, but I knew it would be gently.

My son was very open with him about his desire and inability to stop eating stationery supplies. Their dialog made it sound so natural, as if this was a common complaint in family medicine.

"You know," the doctor told him, "we all battle with things that our body wants us to do but we know we shouldn't. You're not alone on that one. It happens to me too." At this, my son stopped fiddling and looked in his direction.

"I also want to eat things sometimes that I know I shouldn't. So I tell myself, 'No.' You want it, but you can't have it. It's not easy, but I really think you can do it." The doctor let his words settle in my son's mind and then together they discussed tactics for winning the war of willpower.

I thought of my own food battles—with cappuccinos and cheese buns and wondered how different my son's demons were from mine. I'd been struggling to relate to my son's behavior. I knew that cognitively we could blame sensory issues but I felt angry, embarrassed even, about his lack of control. But the doctor was telling my son that his challenges were not so different from other people's—we all struggle with something.

Since that visit, the packs of playing cards have remained intact. The problem is not fully solved, and probably never will be, but when my patience with my son wanes, I try to remember that he sits on a spectrum—of autism and sensory issues. A curve where no one can say with certainty where the so-called "acceptable behavior" begins and where it ends. If my son and I were to step towards each other, we might find that we're not as far apart as I sometimes believe.

~Caroline Saul

What I Didn't Expect

The cyclone derives its power from a calm center.
So does a person.
~Norman Vincent Peale

"This isn't what I signed up for," I thought, struggling to hold onto a five-foot nine-inch thirteen-year-old. I had my training as a red belt in Tang Soo Do and determination on my side. He had four inches more height, plus rage, working to his advantage. It was an even match, but it wasn't on the dojang floor, and it wasn't about winning points. This was my son, in my living room, and if I let go he would hurt himself or me. I kept a safe hold on him, and cried.

Fifteen years before, when my first son was born, I read all of the "what to expect" books. They never seemed quite accurate to me, because Nicky hit all of the milestones well ahead of what was considered typical. Without another child for comparison, I had no way to know whether the books were wrong or if I had a precocious child.

I pulled those same books off the shelf when I had Kyle two years later. Again, the books missed their mark for us, but this time it was different. Kyle fell far behind all of the developmental milestones, and by the time he was two years old, we knew why—Kyle had autism.

Autism wasn't in those books, or if it was, it was only a passing mention. It wasn't something I was supposed to expect.

Nowhere did they say anything about an endless stream of doctors and therapists, specialized classrooms in school, or an array of unusual behaviors. The books didn't tell me my child might kick out the window screens and run away, or laugh uncontrollably for no apparent reason, or become hysterical if something didn't go as planned. They certainly never warned me my child would try to hurt me or cause himself harm.

By the time Kyle was six or seven, I had learned a great deal about autism. I read a lot, spoke to doctors and parents, and had a pretty good idea of what was typical for a child like mine. I had come to terms with this new concept of what would pass for "normal" in my household, and I thought I finally knew what to expect.

Then one evening, during a meltdown, Kyle put his fist through a window. Fortunately, the result was only a few minor cuts, a lot of tears, and a rare complete sentence. "I'm sorry, Mommy."

A good cleaning and some Band-Aids were all the medical treatment Kyle needed, but the next time we visited the pediatrician's office, I mentioned the incident to one of the doctors there.

She nodded and said, "It seems most children with autism do that at some point."

The books told me when Kyle should smile, walk, and talk, but somehow they overlooked the part about putting his fist through a window.

Meltdowns had long been an issue, but visual aids and schedules helped with some of the problem behaviors. Even so, unexpected frustration could launch him into sudden bouts of aggression. Walls were his first target, and it wasn't long before I became exceedingly good at drywall repair.

It also didn't take me long to realize aggressive meltdowns were about to present a very real danger. While Kyle missed significant cognitive milestones, he was above average height for his age. He was also heading for the hormonal roller coaster of puberty. Teaching him self-control would take time — more time than we had left before his size and aggression could overpower me.

Soon, I had a sweet, loving giant who occasionally exploded

into a rage, and, as a divorced mom, I had to manage him mainly on my own.

Seeking assistance, I found classes designed to help parents deal with many aspects of autism — potty training, getting their children to eat better, basic behavior management strategies — but not one that taught parents how to keep themselves safe and prevent their children from hurting others or self-injuring. Teachers received formal training on this, but parents were on their own.

I sought other options, and ended up studying the Korean martial art of Tang Soo Do. My instructor helped me modify techniques to contain my son during an aggressive meltdown without hurting him or allowing him to hurt me. I learned to block his strikes when he tried to hit, how to escape when he would grab my arm and dig in with his fingernails, and how to use safe holds when necessary, like the one I used that day in my living room. I discovered that applying these techniques also helped me calm Kyle more quickly. My goal was still to help him learn to overcome this behavior, but in the meantime, this allowed me to keep both of us, and anyone else around us, safe.

I never expected Tang Soo Do to be a useful parenting skill.

People who spoke openly about therapies and special diets tended to avoid the subject of aggressive meltdowns, and it makes me wonder why parents are left to learn the hard way about something so important. Why are we unprepared for that gap between the start of aggressive behavior and the glorious day our children learn self-control?

Maybe we're afraid that mentioning it will give our children with autism a poor public image. Maybe we feel bad about the idea of putting our children into safe holds, or we're afraid of what people will think about us. Perhaps we just don't want to admit to ourselves that our beautiful, wonderful, sweet children can have moments of violence, lashing out at the people who love them most. So we struggle and cry and keep our silence, and other parents never learn what to expect.

Just like with those books I read, not everything can be predicted.

Every child is different, and I hope yours will never be aggressive… but it could happen. So what should you expect?

Expect broken windows, bad days, lots of stress, and Tang Soo Do lessons. Expect challenges that change from day to day and year to year. Then expect all of the joys, happiness, and unconditional love those books did mention, along with triumphs big and small.

Expect to grow as a person and as a parent, and to find strength you never knew you had to deal with problems you never could have anticipated. Expect to have your own stories, good and bad, and that eventually you'll be able to look back at most of them with a sense of humor you couldn't have imagined at the time. Then share your stories with the rest of us, even the ones that seem hard to tell, because all of us, as parents of children on the spectrum, need to know we're not alone.

Most of all, know that if your child is anything like mine, you can expect far more hugs and smiles than meltdowns and broken windows.

~D.M. Rosner

Peace

Adversity is the first path to truth.
~Lord Byron

can hear the echo of his steps as he slaps his shoes against the hard tile floor. Slap. Slap. Slap. Slap.

His pace is quick. He stares intently at the ground. Slap. Slap. Slap. Slap.

He walks along the perimeter of the common areas where the white tiles change to color, a path that he set in entirety even before he started. Slap. Slap. Slap. Slap.

If people are in that path, if they do not keep up with his pace, he simply pushes through them. Fingers in his ears, humming nothing specific and tuning out the world, today, this is how our older son is finding peace. Here, at the mall.

In these final days of August, when our special kids are on break from their summer services and awaiting the start of the new school year, just coping with the day can be a struggle for us all.

This break, our son recovered from a seizure while he had a colitis flare. We gave him a new medication to which he is apparently allergic.

He developed a swollen, itchy rash right when the air conditioner broke in the house.

Suddenly, he found loud, buzzing fans everywhere, fans that other people kept turning on every time he tried to turn them off.

It made people angry when he turned off the fans. But, those fans hurt his ears. They hurt his head. They disturbed his sleep. Yes, life for our son during this break from services has been pretty darned uncomfortable.

So, by day, he searches for peace in the mall, even before the shops are open. He walks. He retreats within himself, fingers in his ears and unresponsive to communication.

He escapes inside his body that itches and twitches, jerks and stomps its hurried way up and down each and every corridor. He becomes lost inside his own mind, that place of peace inside him that has helped him cope with the outside world.

Our world.

Day after day, I dutifully follow behind him. I keep him from harm's way, from injuring people he doesn't care to see in his path. Admittedly, I sometimes find it hard to scrape together the patience to work with an unresponsive shell of a child when I, too, am feeling stretched.

Often defeated, I let my mind wander. I think of other things or I think of nothing at all. When we stop for a rare break along our path, I'll pull out my phone to make contact with people who don't live this life, to talk about anything other than autism.

Or, maybe I do talk about autism. Maybe I curse it, depending upon the day.

Either way, disconnected and with a blank stare, my nose often pointed down toward my phone, I realize that my place and posture of peace during this break are not all that different from our son's.

I know that I could socialize with him or with anyone else around us for that matter. But I just don't want to. I'm tired. I haven't slept well. I'm prickly and sensitive. I'd rather shove my nose in my phone or zone out and plow through the day.

Life is just more peaceful that way.

I love our son. I don't want him to be a shell of a child. Yet, it is along our path today that I have become more protective of his right to sink inside himself and to shut out the world—at least temporarily—in order to establish his peace.

We all do it.

Maybe we don't pace the floors of the mall. Maybe we don't shove our fingers in our ears and hum some strange sound. Maybe we don't twitch loose our muscles.

For what it is worth, our older son doesn't happen to use a phone.

I do. To each his own.

~Amy McMunn Schindler

29

The Right Kind of Kick

*The central struggle of parenthood is to
let our hopes for our children outweigh our fears.*
~Ellen Goodman

"**C**atch it!" my husband and I yelled. Our shoulders sagged in unison as we watched the ball hit the grass near our four-year-old's feet as he continued to kick at the dirt. It was midseason, but he wasn't any closer to becoming engaged in his tee ball game. We called his name and then said, "Pick it up! The ball!" He turned his head with a blank stare, in time to see the first baseman snatch up the ball and lob it toward home plate. Then he went back to kicking the dirt.

It was obvious, as the games rolled by, the coach didn't want our son to play. We practiced with him and I hunched over the bat and said, "Place your hands here." My husband added, "Throw the ball like this," and he demonstrated a solid overhand. Our son never did grasp the concept of running the bases or the other things we tried to teach him.

At the end of that season, our son was once again rewarded with a "Most Improved" medal, a medal he'd received before in other sports. My husband and I looked at each other, and I said, "Well, at least he's improving," but it reminded me of other sympathetic gestures from coaches or teachers. By now I was used to this feeling, of our son being different, unable to assimilate into activities.

"He's not paying attention," his preschool teacher told me that same year. "He fiddles with his hands in class, lies under the playscape at recess and stares at the sky." This isn't what any parent wants to hear, but I knew it was true. As a stay-at-home mom, I was exhausted from having to repeat my instructions to him. But in the beginning, I wasn't sure how much of it was typical, because he was our first child. We decided to have him assessed, but it was basically a guessing game regarding what was going on with him until he turned six, when finally, we were able to have a professional evaluation done, and it was determined he has Asperger syndrome.

"He'll be okay," my husband said. "He'll go on to have a family and work in the real world." And it's true. Our son is blessed with good looks, intelligence, and an aloof nature that is perceived as shyness. There are no obvious signs he has Asperger's, aside from frequent lack of eye contact; it's more of an ever-moving undercurrent, perceptible only to those who know him best. Especially during moments like homework, what to fix him for dinner, or still, repeating instructions.

"I'd like to invite your son to my son's birthday party," a friend of mine said after his diagnosis. I was excited until I learned it was a dirt-bike party and my now-six-year-old couldn't ride a regular bike. I flat out told her he wasn't ready for that. She was a preschool teacher like me, and she understood that all kinds of developmental delays occur in children, and that the sooner you tackle it, the better off the child will be. Not everyone is so understanding.

He didn't go to the party, but at least it prompted us to get our son back out there on his bike. The training wheels were removed and he begrudgingly wobbled down the hill, trying desperately to keep his balance. The more runs he did, the more frustrated he became. Why couldn't this experience be like those home movies where the father is running alongside the bike and the child is smiling ear to ear? Just once, couldn't something be easy?

"Place your hands here on the handlebars," my husband said, pointing.

"Try not to lean so far forward," I added.

"I hate this," he said, finally, and kicked, with all his might, the spokes on his front wheel. It wasn't until we put the bike away for the winter that he cracked half a smile.

The next summer, we were giving our son tips on how to score a soccer goal. By the end of that summer, our son was finally blazing down the soccer field with the ball, about to kick a goal, when a parent accidentally stepped over the boundary line and caused him to lose the ball. The look on my husband's face could have broken ten thousand hearts. His boy's only chance to score a goal that season, and it was snatched away. He wanted to yell at the parent, to make him understand the magnitude of his actions, but he managed to keep it in. After all, how could anyone really understand how important one goal could be unless they've waited six years?

There are moments when our son is brilliant. Wicked smart. So intuitive it's unnerving. But those moments are random, like slices of sunlight let in by a dancing curtain.

That is, until he was seven, and he was taking swimming lessons. He'd had lessons the summer before, and he did all right, but I wanted him to really learn how to swim. So back we went.

I was surprised when I peered at him over the pool and he was beaming a smile so wide my heart leapt to my throat. He waved at me, grinned, and bobbed up and down in the water. I'd never seen him so excited. Something about swimming that time around "took."

So again, this last summer, when he turned eight, we were back again. He learned the front stroke, the backstroke, and finally, the butterfly. It was inspiring to watch his strong legs kick and his arms move, as he made his way across the pool.

I've always wished I could swim, something beside the dog-paddle, so I slipped into the pool after one of his lessons, and immediately he asked, "Okay, Mom, do you know how to do the butterfly stroke?"

I shook my head.

His eyes flashed with understanding. "Let's start with floating," he answered. "Here's what I want you to do for me," he continued, and placed his hand beneath me to support me while he helped me ease onto my back. For the first time, it was him giving the instructions. It was him saying, "You can do it." He sounded like an instructor, and I pictured him as a young adult, teaching a class of his own one day. It made me smile.

I left the pool that day happy, and I realized he really isn't so different from anyone else. Just give him something he's passionate about, something he's good at, and he can shine like the rest.

~René Zimbelman

30

Chicken Soup for the Soul

Lost

*The test of a first-rate intelligence is the ability to hold two opposed ideas in
the mind at the same time, and still be able to function.*
~F. Scott Fitzgerald

The bracelet arrived in the mail, small and shiny. I put it on
my four-year-old son's wrist, fumbling with the clasp. For
a few days, we both were acutely aware of its presence.
When I tried to put it on him in the morning, Wesley would
squirm. I'd curse under my breath as I struggled to take it off at bath
time. His wrist was pink where he tried to bite it.

I thought of the kids who wore this type of medical jewelry when
I was young. The kid with the peanut allergy. "You can't even use the
same spoon as the batch with the nuts," my mom would tell me, "or
he could die." The diabetic kid at camp—the one I pretended not to
stare at whenever he took out his kit. My friend with epilepsy.

But Wesley doesn't have any of those things. In fact, Wesley
doesn't have anything. My son wears a bracelet because of what he is,
and what he might do.

Wesley is autistic.

Wesley doesn't speak. He is unlikely to respond to his name.
And he loves to run.

Like many kids on the autism spectrum, Wesley attends a spe-
cial-education day class. My husband drops him off in the morning,
and six hours later, I pick him up, chatting with the other moms as
we wait for the teachers to bring out our kids.

Every day, I spy my little Wesley, with his blue eyes and curly blond hair, walking hand in hand with one of the people I entrust with his education and his care. Every day they bring him back to me.

Except one day, when they didn't.

I wasn't worried at first. Wesley's class is often last to appear, as they are the smallest bunch, preschoolers slowed down by oversized backpacks and the frequent need to investigate some bug or crack in the sidewalk. But when the rest of the class had arrived and I signaled to his teacher, she made an excuse about a forgotten backpack. I saw her run back toward the classroom, and I knew.

They had lost my little boy.

For a few minutes, I waited there, the still center of a time-lapse photo. The other parents left. Teachers went back to their classrooms. The bus came and went. And I stood there waiting.

During those seven or eight minutes, I thought of Wesley's brace-let—the one that had finally become part of his morning routine, the one he still fiddled with but no longer fought against. Why had I put so much faith in that thin piece of metal? It couldn't keep him safe from the creek running behind the school, or getting hit by a car, or lost in the sea of children leaving school.

I still don't know who found Wesley, who had slipped into an empty classroom. His teacher brought him to me like nothing had happened. I cried on the drive home.

Later that day, Wesley was wild. He ran maniacally around the house, screeching and crashing into the walls. I dodged his attempts to bite me as I wrestled him to the floor for a diaper change. His nails, overgrown because he refused to let me cut them, scratched red marks into my neck.

No more than an hour before, I thought my sweet boy was in danger. I thought I would never take another moment for granted, no matter how challenging his behavior. And yet, there I was, red-faced and bursting with rage. Why couldn't Wesley just control himself? Why did everything have to be so difficult? And why wasn't I strong enough to handle it with grace and good humor?

Perhaps I was the one who was truly lost. Or maybe just human.

F. Scott Fitzgerald wrote that the test of a first-rate intelligence is the ability to hold two opposed ideas at the same time, yet still retain the ability to function. To be able to see, for example, that things are hopeless and yet be determined to make them otherwise.

By that definition, I must be a genius.

We parents of special needs kids face overwhelming joy and sadness, intense love and frustration, breathtaking wonder and fear—often in the course of a single day. We work tirelessly to help our kids succeed in the world, even when we have no idea what that success will look like. We are given so much reason to be hopeless, and yet, sometimes hope alone propels us forward.

And so it is that I send Wesley out into the world every day, offering the only protection I can give him: hope, a hug, and a small silver bracelet.

~Jennifer Bush

31

Don't Stop Believing

If you can imagine it, you can achieve it.
If you can dream it, you can become it.
~William A. Ward

Two days before our nineteen-year-old son Mickey leaves for sleep-away camp, he asks to get a haircut. No big deal, right? But fifteen years ago this would have been unthinkable.

Back then, the barbershop was the scene of some of our worst parenting moments. By 8:00 a.m. of the Dreaded Haircut Day, my husband Marc would already be muttering, "I need a Scotch before I can do this"—and he doesn't even drink Scotch. Bracing himself in the barber chair, Marc would clench Mickey in a bear hug and scissor-lock him with his legs. Mickey would flail frantically, head-butting his father and screaming like someone undergoing surgery without anesthesia. Customers gawked. One old man snarled, "Rotten spoiled brat." Marc sweated through his shirt. When the barber declared he was done, I'd take Mickey into my arms. Sobbing and spent, he'd collapse against my shoulder, smearing us both with snot and hair. We tipped big. Very big.

Unable to face a repeat performance, we'd let long months go between haircuts. Mickey's great-uncle Jack liked to tease him. "You look like a girl, buddy!" he'd say. Some days when we'd walk by that barbershop on our way to the deli, I could swear that as soon as the barbers saw us passing, they'd quickly pull down the white shade that said "Closed for Lunch."

But today when we enter the barbershop Mickey sings out a cheery "Hi Dom!" as he plops into the chair. Dom drapes him in a maroon cape, and picks up a shaver. A screen splits in my head: I can still picture that terrified little boy, even as I watch my son, nearly a man, sitting solemnly watching his reflection in the mirror.

I wait quietly, soaking in the sounds of barbershop banter, the sports talk, the sharing of summer plans. It is all so completely ordinary. A radio is tuned to a Lite FM station; the song playing is "Don't Stop Believin'" by Journey. I reflect how anyone who'd seen my son all those years ago would never have believed that Mickey would one day request—*insist*—we take him for a haircut. Yet here we are.

"How's this?" Dom asks. I stand beside Mickey and glance down; the cape is feathered in a field of light brown hairs, as covered as a forest floor.

"Let's take it down a bit more," I suggest. "Is that okay with you, Mick?"

"Yeah, Mom," he says.

I remember how we used to sneak into his bedroom at night with a pair of shears to give him a trim as he slept. I think of the time he was five and we took him to a local performance by the Paperbag Players; we hadn't known that they were going to perform a new skit called the "The Horrible, Horrendous, Hideous Haircut." "NO!" Mickey shrieked, and every head in the audience swiveled our way.

Nowadays, Autism Speaks' Family Services division offers a *Haircutting Training Guide* for families and stylists on how to make the experience more positive, but back then there was nothing. Fortunately, one of our behavioral therapists offered to tackle the challenge. Mickey was seven years old. She took him to the next town over—too many negative associations with our local barber—where they simply practiced strolling by a barbershop. The following week, they stood in the doorway. Eventually they progressed to sitting in the waiting area, watching other people get haircuts, then having Mickey sit in the barber chair. Eventually they introduced the cape, the shaver, the scissors. It took months, but by the time Kathy was done, Mickey was able to—miracle of miracles—tolerate a haircut.

"This feels better," Mickey tells me. His hair is crew cut short; I can see scalp. I think he's more handsome with a little more hair. But Mickey is happy with how he looks, and that's all that matters.

"Thanks Dom," Mickey says softly. Dom dusts a brush with talcum powder, sweeps it across the back of Mickey's neck. Mickey stands, turns to me and asks, "Can I have a dollar?"

I give him a twenty-dollar bill. He hands it to Dom. "Keep the change," he says breezily. A man of the world.

"Is Dom proud of me?" Mickey asks.

"Very proud," I say. "You know what? We're all very proud of you."

This whole visit to the barbershop has lasted fifteen minutes. But it took us years to get here.

~Liane Kupferberg Carter

Room Repair

Every day may not be good,
but there's something good in every day.
~Author Unknown

ost teenagers' rooms are messy, but my son Nicky's looked like a demolition zone. There were soft spots in the carpet where the floor underneath was giving way. It was especially bad just in front of the mirror where Nicky would jump up and down repeatedly in his excitement at seeing his reflection. Parts of the wall were missing behind his bed. He had a habit of lying on his stomach and drumming his feet against the wall. When the wall finally gave way, he was intrigued and removed large parts of the drywall, exposing the studs and electrical wires. Those wall pockets were a great place to hide trash and DVDs. Lastly, the curtains were down on the floor again. Nick's obsession with sticks made the curtain rods a constant target. I needed help.

I called a friend who just happened to be a handyman extraordinaire. He came over, assessed the situation and came up with a plan to Nick-proof the room. First he took up the carpet and removed the damaged floorboards. He put horizontal two-by-fours between the studs to brace them and then covered the floor with the thickest plywood he could find. He did something similar with the walls, removing all the damaged areas, cleaning out the junk and bracing the studs with horizontal two-by-fours. Then, instead of the drywall he put up smooth-sided plywood that he spackled over and sanded until it was flush with the wall. The entire room was then repainted the same color as before. Lastly, he put a translucent film on the bottom half of all the windows, taking care of privacy concerns.

Nick's room looked normal and whole. I was so pleased. The next morning I was woken up by a loud banging noise and a slow smile spread over my face. I walked into Nicky's room and there he was on the bed, trying every spot to kick through the wall. No success! I looked at him and said, "Ah, do your feet hurt?" He looked at me and started jumping up and down on the bed instead. That I can live with!

~Kathy Labosh

The Red Shirt

The sea, once it casts its spell, holds one in its net of wonder forever.
~Jacques Cousteau

ichelle had been my autistic son Josh's therapist for five years when she suggested we take a family vacation and join her at her mother's beach house for a week. Josh and his twin sister, Jordan, were seven at the time. I hesitated because I knew I'd be exhausted from watching Josh around the clock, but the guilt won and I agreed.

When my husband, Jeff, called me during the week I was grumpy and half-delirious from fatigue and stress. The beach house was crowded with visitors and Michelle's friends were laid out in hallways, floors, and couches. It wasn't a great environment for a low-functioning child with autism, but I felt obligated to spend "quality" time with my family.

Josh and I were fortunate to have our own room. The problem was that he refused to sleep. It didn't matter that the radio and noise-makers were on. When he started jumping around and squealing at 5:00 a.m. I had to usher him out of the house so he wouldn't wake anyone. We'd drive around the island searching for a twenty-four-hour market where we could kill time. When the sun rose we went back.

When Jeff arrived that Friday, things were better. Josh was a good swimmer and loved the ocean. He reminded me of my late father. He wasn't afraid to smash into the waves and venture out into the deep.

I was lukewarm about the water. That day I was especially aware of my environment. The strong riptide worried me, and I'd heard about a shark attack the day before at a nearby beach.

But all was well. We couldn't get our gleeful son out of the ocean. Josh allowed me to sleep five hours that night. Saturday was okay, too. My husband couldn't understand why I'd been so edgy on the phone. Sunday morning I dressed Josh in his favorite red shirt with the blue train. I waited to make breakfast because Jeff and I were discussing an impending medical trip.

While we were talking, Josh was out on the balcony in front of a sliding glass window. Jordan was watching cartoons and glancing at her brother through the glass. Michelle told me that Josh was very good about staying on the balcony. After about ten minutes I went downstairs to feed everyone. But when I went outside to get Josh he wasn't there. I frantically searched the house and property but he had vanished.

We flew out the door and Jeff ran to the beach, which was about five minutes away and hard to find. I jumped in the van and started searching the narrow streets. At some point, I abandoned the van and ran to the ocean. The waves were thunderous, but the beach was tranquil and empty. I scanned both directions and saw nothing but my husband in the distance waving and pointing. All I could see was a towel. As I got closer to the water I could see it wasn't a towel—it was Josh's red shirt, lying in front of the waves. I ran along the water searching for a body. I saw a woman approaching and screamed, "Get a lifeguard, get a lifeguard, my son's in the water! I've killed him! I've killed him!"

She said, "But there aren't any lifeguards!"

I begged her. "Get a helicopter—please. I've killed him!" I kept running and in my nightmare I started thinking bizarrely. "I'll have to plan my second funeral this year. A second funeral." I'd just buried my father in the fall.

Jeff searched the other end of the beach and I kept sprinting. After about half a mile I noticed one family in the distance sitting under a striped umbrella. They had neon-colored beach balls, which no doubt attracted the tiny figure approaching them from the sea. Josh was obsessed with balloons. I ran like a mad woman and grabbed the shirtless child who was soaked head to toe. "Josh! I was worried about you! You're okay! You're okay!" I can't remember what else I said. I just remember squeezing him and whispering how much I loved him. Josh couldn't understand why I was so upset; he just wanted a balloon.

We found Jeff near a bridge. I'd never seen him cry before. He grabbed us hard and didn't let go. It still hurts. We collapsed with relief over our near-loss. I grieved over my stupidity and irresponsibility. And even though I yelled at both Michelle and Jordan, I knew it was my fault for not protecting Josh, for ignoring my instincts.

We cut our vacation short and left that day. The car's silence broke when the kids fell asleep. And then, the questions. How did he find his way to the beach? Why didn't he drown? He was alone and under the water and the waves were huge, and there was that riptide!

Finally Jeff turned to me and asked me the fateful question, "If you had it to do all over again would you have our son?" I don't remember what I said. If Jeff asked me today I wouldn't hesitate saying yes, but those were the dark days. And even though Josh was an amazing child—sweet-spirited and beautiful—when the autism took over he was gut-wrenchingly difficult. I do remember discussing how deeply we loved him, and how we'd been tested that morning. My husband said, "We almost lost our son today." Yes, but we needed the test; it sustained us during the times when Jeff and I and Josh were unlovable.

Three years later we returned to the scene of the crime for a celebration of life—Michelle's wedding. We walked the long stretch of beach leading to the wedding site and Josh screamed the whole way. His behavior had improved so much over the years that I was saddened at the outburst. He now refused to swim anywhere but a pool. He clung to me as we trudged through the sand. Sometimes he would let go and run up to the dunes to distance himself from the water. We were in a hurry and I couldn't soothe him. Finally we reached our destination, camera-laden and sweaty. As the drums began to beat and the bride started her glide down the sandy aisle, Josh calmed himself down, sat in one of the ribboned chairs and was quiet. After the couple expressed their love for each other and the ceremony was over, he got up and ran into the ocean. And we couldn't get him out.

~Shelley Stolaroff Segal

Always Learning

Learn from yesterday, live for today, hope for tomorrow.
~Albert Einstein

My daughter turned seven the year her special education teacher suggested the park district's summer camp as an extension of her social skills training. An inclusive day camp to be held at her school, the program offered therapeutic aides for campers who needed them. Rebecca would be attending "extended school year" in the morning, so lunch and camp would round out her afternoon. I continued to think through the possibilities: new counselors and helpers, meeting new kids, and staying at her school. If there's one thing I do know about Rebecca's autism, it's the kind that doesn't like change. School was familiar ground; this would be a new, fun framework. Not lost on me either was camp's two-week time frame, which meant built-in respite for me.

I sent an application to the camp's therapeutic aide director. As a follow-up, he came to the school to observe Rebecca to see if she was a candidate. At day's end, he said yes. I then received word that he would have an aide for her. There was a meet-and-greet night at which Rebecca "interviewed" her new helper by making her play "Follow the Leader" and sing various songs. Senior therapeutic recreation major. Past camp counselor. The young woman even wanted to design objectives for Rebecca at camp and observe her in her school time. It all sounded wonderful. And, on paper, it was.

First day of camp, I got a call from an on-site camp director that Rebecca had hurt another camper and was in violation of camp policy. I immediately drove to the school, arrived at the room in which they were keeping Rebecca and found her aide in a completely exasperated and defeated state, while another camp director spoke of kicking, hitting and generally reckless behavior. I was expecting a rough first day—because even with the safeguards, it was still new—but nothing like what I was hearing.

Any attempts to do camp activities were met with resistance by Rebecca. The aide's interventions didn't work. Another camp aide, who also worked as an aide at the school, called Rebecca's special education teacher at home for advice. Later that night, the therapeutic aide director left a phone message suggesting that maybe camp wasn't the best fit for Rebecca. But he added: "By the way, tomorrow's field trip day. Can you please go to make sure everything goes okay?"

The field trip was bowling. Had Rebecca ever been bowling? No. Would she walk into the bowling alley? It depended on the day. Before camp week, I had hoped this would be the opportunity to introduce Rebecca to an activity that we could then do as a family. Now I was worried and drove behind the camp bus all the way to the bowling alley to spy on my own kid. Rebecca never fussed, resisted or misbehaved. Peering from the café area about twenty lanes away, I could see that she was having the time of her life—bowling with help, and cheering on her teammates with high-fives! We were all smiles leaving the bowling alley.

After the trip, though, things went downhill. The staff asked me to pick her up at 3 p.m. instead of 5 p.m. "It seems like she's had enough of everything," they said.

Then, I was the one who resisted. One of the reasons for having Rebecca in camp was to push her limit of doing organized activity beyond the end-of-school-day hour. "It's only the second day! Can we please keep trying?" I thought. Then, Wednesday ended up being worse than Tuesday. Thursday would be the last day of camp that week, with one more week to go.

I decided—after hours of internal debate—to walk away. Not

run, just walk. Lots of people had made an investment in the week. Running away wouldn't be right. Rebecca finished out the camp week, with a visit to the ice cream truck, no less. She had had a pretty good last day, all things considered. But, the fast uphill learning curve for the camp staff, the anxiety, the lack of basic happiness on everyone's faces, even Rebecca's... we were losing more than we were gaining, and it was time to walk away.

What I know about my girl and autism continues to change. So, I read a little more, talk with the experts a little more, pray a little more, and study up on ways to improve my approach. We'll give it time and try again.

~Sue Jeantheau

Raising Kids on the Spectrum

Friends and Strangers

My Village

How we interact with each other in our lives — whether we are centers of peace, oases of compassion — makes a difference. The sum total of these interactions determines nothing less than the nature of life on our planet.
~Desmond Tutu

At pick-up Tuesday after school, Cuyler had what I can only describe as a meltdown of epic proportions. It hasn't happened in a very long time.

He has meltdowns and temper tantrums. But this one was a doozy.

Something very minor set him off right before the bell rang and his anger and inability to manage got ahead of him. He took off. I had to chase him down and stop him, then figure out how to safely restrain him so I could get him back to the van. He was flailing and screaming as loud as he could for several minutes.

I was sweating, shaking, and very embarrassed. Not because of his behavior, but because I didn't know what to do. The last time I had to deal with a meltdown like this he was smaller, lighter and weaker. Every time I thought I had a good hold, he'd flip out of my grip. Then he flipped out of his jacket. Kicking, flailing, screaming.

Finally I was able to flip him upside down, wrapping my arms around his waist with his legs hanging over my back. He was still kicking and screaming but I was in control. I forced him into his seat and belted him in.

As I drove home all I could think about was how ridiculous I must have looked trying to get the situation under control in front of all those kids and parents at dismissal. I felt inept and incompetent and could only imagine what the other parents thought.

When I got home I told my husband Sean what happened and was so proud of myself that I didn't cry. I thought I was about to at one point, but I didn't. I stayed strong!

After an hour or so, Cuyler was settling down.

I checked my e-mail and found things like this written on my Facebook wall and in my messages from parents:

Hugs to you. I know it wasn't easy. I know how impressed I was with how calm you were (on the outside at least). I'm not sure I would have been.

Been thinking of you since I got home. How's it going?

You handled that amazingly well. I saw the look in your eyes and couldn't help but think of you all afternoon.

Everything settle down now? He ok? YOU ok?

[hugs] hope he's ok now.

That's my village. That's what people were thinking as they watched. That's what made me cry. People who care. No judgment against me or Cuyler. Simply concern and worry. Asking how they can help the next time it happens.

The comments, encouragement and cyberhugs made all the worry I had about my ability as his mother disappear. So I didn't look like an idiot trying to parent this unpredictable little boy. I didn't appear too rough with him. I kept my cool.

I'm not sure if they know how their positive words helped. How much they are appreciated. I am so lucky to live in the community I do. Cuyler is very lucky to have this village surrounding him.

Once Cuyler had finally settled down, he curled up in my lap, snuggling like a sick baby. He's not a cuddler by any means but I think it was his way of saying he was sorry.

And the kisses I smattered all over his head were my way of saying "I love you no matter what."

~Christine Coleman

The Cardinal Rule

The path I travel is lit by those who came before me,
and it will shine brighter for those who follow me.
~Author Unknown

My son Ryan's diagnosis of autism spectrum disorder at eighteen months brought about a dramatic paradigm shift. Without hesitation, I accepted the diagnosis and moved forward with intensive early intervention. Time previously spent on my marriage, friendships, and career was reallocated to attending appointments, completing paperwork, researching, and acquiring funding for services. Any remaining energy was devoted to directly teaching Ryan new skills. The depth of unconditional motherly love I devoted to him was awe-inspiring, even to myself.

Three years into our early intervention journey with Ryan, my younger son William, at nineteen months, was also diagnosed with autism. The persistent demands on my time, finances, social life, self-care, and the amount of energy required to implement evidence-based behavioral strategies in our daily lives were beginning to take their toll. By the time William was diagnosed I was growing weary and hadn't quite learned how to respond to the judgment of others.

Not long after his diagnosis, I stopped by a mini-mall with William in tow. Until this day he had no history of escape attempts. I believed I could complete the errand while keeping him safe. I was wrong.

When we entered the store, I buckled William into a shopping cart and provided him a lollipop to keep him busy while I shopped. When the sucker was gone he began thrashing violently in the cart. This is where I made my first mistake. I did not yet understand that bringing my son shopping comes with the risk that I may not finish before we need to leave. I was stubbornly determined to finish my shopping despite William's growing discontentment.

As my son's tantrum became louder, a nearby shopper lowered her chin and looked at us with disapproval. I felt pressured to quiet him. This led to my second mistake. Instead of using my behavioral training, I was more concerned about the impression of the other customers. So, I unbuckled William and set him down in an aisle between two rows of clothing. I reached back into the shopping cart to retrieve my purse and when I looked down, he was gone.

I peeked under the rack of clothes directly in front of me. No William.

I turned around to check under the rack behind me. No William.

I called his name. Silence.

I rushed out from the clothing racks to the main aisle but he was nowhere in sight. My son had disappeared.

I scurried toward the back of the store, shouting, "William? William! Where are you?" All of my shouting was to no avail; he did not answer me.

Then it hit me.

My child could not speak. William was not going to respond. As I surveyed the scene I continued calling his name, each attempt more desperate than the last. There was no time to stop for help but maybe if someone heard me they would join my search.

After systematically combing through the store I headed back toward the front door. I looked up and standing before me was a woman with beautifully styled hair, carefully applied make-up, and neatly pressed clothing. She was practically perfect. On her hip sat William. What a relief.

William's face was calm but hers was bright red, with narrowed eyebrows, a lowered chin and a stern glare. She was fuming. I ran to her and took him tightly into my arms. The woman said, "Do you know where I found your child? He was wandering around outside in the parking lot."

I peered over her shoulder at the front door. It was the kind that opens automatically. William must have run straight to that door and the door opened up for him to run outside.

I looked at the Good Samaritan who rescued William, my eyes pleading for understanding, and managed to eek out, "Thank you." By now I noticed a group of onlookers glaring and seemingly sharing in her disgust. The woman held her glare steady, then sucker-punched me with: "Some people were just not meant to be mothers."

Not meant to be a mother? Are you kidding me? Did she have any idea what I had been through in the last three years with Ryan? Thousands of hours dedicated to paperwork, appointments, therapy, school district, parent training, medical bills, marital strain, and now I was doing it all over again with William.

Despite everything I had endured in the name of motherly love, there I stood, the center of attention of a disapproving crowd questioning whether I was qualified to be a mother. Should I have told them he had autism? Would they have even understood how that related to what just happened?

At that moment I remembered that an experienced mother of a child with autism had given me information cards about autism. I retrieved the cards from my purse and handed one to each of the onlookers, including the Good Samaritan. It was empowering to educate the public who judged me so harshly. I smiled graciously and said, "Thank you for all of your help." I held my head high as I carried William to my car. We never did buy the items we needed that day, but my son was alive and safe.

Later that evening, I thought of the experienced mother who armed me with autism information cards. I wondered how she knew that I might one day need those cards.

Today, six years into our journey, there is more clarity about what is involved with raising children with autism. Our family has created a new dream. My husband and I have reclaimed our marriage. My sons have benefitted from an early diagnosis, educational services, funding for therapy, intensive early intervention, rehabilitative and alternative therapy. I am proud to say our family is strong and thriving.

Meanwhile, my perspective on raising children with autism has expanded from family-focused to community-focused. I appreciate the value of forming connections with other families so that we can encourage each other and build each other up. Thanks to the tenacity of experienced parents who are continually clearing pathways on behalf of all of us, my sons' futures are bright. These mentors, who have walked this path before us, lead by example in passing down the cardinal rule for parents of children with autism: We pay each other back by paying it forward.

~Hope Maven

A Loving World

*Each of us is a unique strand in the intricate web of life
and here to make a contribution.*
~Deepak Chopra

love Luke and Faith more than I thought possible prior to
becoming a mom. I love each of them in a unique way. I'd
imagine most mothers would express something similar
regarding their own children—the love for each is equal, but
different.

I've tried hard to always make sure Luke and Faith each feel
accepted and cherished for exactly who they are. I've often wondered
how God knew that I wanted precisely these two kids. Still, if I've ever
played favorites, the scales have leaned toward Luke—not because
I love him more, but because I feared the world would love him less.

I wanted to make up for the disappointment and rejection that I
thought would characterize his interactions with others—the bullying, the comments and stares. I knew I couldn't, but I'm his mom.
I had to try. Recently, Luke's program supervisor made some changes
to his therapy regimen that required him to go out in public to practice his newly acquired skills. There was a certain comfort in having
him in private home therapy. At home I could control who entered
his orbit, creating a giant love bubble of protection around him, but
I also knew that branching out was a positive step. So, a couple of
months ago, Luke began taking daily field trips with his therapists.

I was not prepared for what happened next.

Everywhere he went, I watched Luke turn people into the best versions of themselves. Normally indifferent employees broke into big smiles when Luke came through the door of their store or entered their checkout lane. Hurried customers waited patiently as Luke practiced giving and receiving money from the cashiers. Life slowed down and people took time out of their day to talk to Luke. He evoked feelings in them that made them want to be a part of his progress. They liked who they were with Luke. He made them better.

There was Russ, a gentleman in charge of pony rides at a local park. The rides were closed, but he saddled up a horse for Luke anyway. As we left, he gave us his phone number, encouraging us to call anytime Luke wanted to ride.

There was Joshua, a thirteen-year-old boy, and his brothers and sisters, who played soccer with Luke. I'll never forget the sound of him yelling, "Let's let Luke score the winning goal!"

There was Lauren, who took Luke swimming because he wanted to go in the pool and I didn't have a change of clothes for myself.

There was the young man at the pet store, whose name I didn't catch, who took animals out of the tanks for Luke to experience up close—all of them angels in human form, and the very few people who have lived down to my expectations have made me appreciate the acts of kindness from everyone else so much more.

So, to my precious son, I'm so sorry for doubting your superpowers, and to those who have embraced my son with love and compassion, thanks for proving me wrong, and loving him more.

~Joyce Rohe

A Friendly Reminder

In life you have a choice: Bitter or Better?
Choose better, forget bitter.
~Nick Vujicic

've become accustomed to stares. Strange looks because of the strange sounds my son makes. Jerky movements and high-pitched squeals draw looks of curiosity, sometimes censure, and worst of all, pity. Yes, autism tutored me well in the ways of self-consciousness, and then taught me to ignore it all.

Public places have been difficult minefields for my family to negotiate ever since Myles was diagnosed with autism at the age of two. He had quickly deteriorated from a bright, vibrant, ever-learning toddler, to a vacant-stared, silent child who seemed frozen in some alternative universe completely inaccessible to us. The strange behaviors were challenging but created some situations that make me laugh… in hindsight. Way hind.

Like the time at the park fountains when Myles ran naked through the water. Kids do the darndest things, right? Did I mention he was nine years old at the time?

Or the time he came downstairs to greet the friends we'd invited over for dinner... without any clothes on. Did I mention he was ten years old? Ah, the naked years.

Some incidents, though, even in the rearview mirror, will never make me laugh. One time, I had gotten up the courage to take Myles out to Golden Corral without my husband. Restaurants mean a lot of people and a lot of noise—two things that often spell sensory overload for my son. First came the screeching. Then the banging on his chest, which devolved into banging on the table. With my nerves stretched paper thin, I noticed a sweet old lady ambling my way. I prepared my "thanks, but no thanks" to the offer of assistance I was sure she was about to make.

"Can you keep him quiet?" she snapped. "I'm trying to eat! Is he on medication or anything? He should be!"

I held my tongue out of respect for my elders. I apologized if Myles had disturbed her meal, and with as much dignity as I could, hightailed it out of there. I didn't bother to look around for compassion or concern or more of what the old lady had given me. I had to escape the weight of the eyes around us. It was humiliating and disheartening.

After that incident, and others like it, I built a wall around my heart, a shell to protect my most vulnerable, tender parts from other people's opinions about my family. About my son. It hurt too much when they didn't understand, so I told myself it didn't matter. And really, in the larger scheme of things, it didn't. I still had the great privilege of raising this very special child. I still saw things in him only a mother would discern. I still felt compelled every morning to create a better reality for him, to imagine the best future I possibly could for him.

It didn't matter what anyone thought, but I had lost something. I no longer gave people the benefit of the doubt. I stopped giving them the chance to be compassionate, stopped looking for the opportunity to help them understand. I assumed the worst about them, and in many ways that was as bad as what that old lady had done to me that day.

So when I found myself back at Golden Corral with my son, who started screeching and banging the table again, I looked up with wary eyes at the middle-aged woman approaching. Her face was perfectly serene as she assessed the situation at the table with my son, my husband, and me. I readied my comeback. This was no little old lady, and if she had a complaint about my son's behavior, I was prepared to pull the trigger and give her the piece of my mind I had held onto before.

"Hi, how are you doing?" she asked, her tone kind, her eyes steady.

"I'm fine," I said curtly, furrowing my brow as a clear warning to her that she did not want to mess with me.

"I hope you don't mind me asking," she continued. "But does your son have autism?"

If I had a dollar for every time some perfect stranger had used that as their opening line to advise me on how to raise my kid, I'd be a rich woman and probably wouldn't be eating at Golden Corral.

I flicked a glance at my husband as he soothed my son, who was now less agitated, but still humming and rocking a little. I raised my brow at him, using my highly-developed nonverbals to say, "Here goes another one."

"Yeah, he has autism," I replied to the lady, who was waiting patiently.

"Well, I raised a child with autism," she began.

Great. Now she really felt like she could tell me how to raise my kid. The only thing worse than a clueless person telling you how to raise your special needs child, is someone who does know the deal telling you you're doing it all wrong.

"I know you don't know me, but my name is Pam," she said, reaching to touch Myles' shoulder. "Like I said, I raised a child with autism, my stepson, and if you ever need any help, please call me."

I looked at the hand she extended, holding a slip of paper with her name and number scribbled on it.

"I can offer references," she said into the silence. "My pastor. I also drive a bus for the public school system. There are several people who could vouch for me, if you ever want me to watch him for you. Give you guys a break."

My husband offered her a friendly, grateful smile. I couldn't speak for the lump clogging my throat. The smile she directed at me barreled through the walls I had erected. The pure compassion of her offer bulldozed my defenses. I blinked stubbornly at the tears threatening to spill over.

"I-I-don't-" I stammered, swiping at the renegade tear that had escaped and streaked its way down my cheek.

"It's hard," she cut in, saving me from blubbering. "I know how hard it is sometimes, and if you ever need help, please call me."

"Thank you," I managed to whisper.

"Call me," she reiterated, smiling at my husband and me, and saving a special, knowing grin for Myles before walking away.

I did call her, and she became as close as family. She often babysits for free. She had a lot to teach not only Myles, but to teach me. Lessons I couldn't have unearthed in any book, or at any seminar or conference. My experience with her became a master class on the depth and breadth of kindness. Humanity at its best, unfettered by selfish motives, unhampered by agenda. Kindness of the simplest and purest variety.

Somewhere along the way, under the weight of curious stares in restaurants, impatient looks in grocery stores, and horrified silences in too many places to name, I had forgotten what kindness looked like. How it felt brushing up against my cynicism. How it softened my world-weary edges. Pam helped me remember that it was worth taking the time to teach people about autism, because people enlightened about the challenges and rewards of autism are kinder. They are part of a better future for my son. These are the people who will have the chance to accept, to understand and appreciate a generation of kids like Myles.

I can huddle behind my old hurts, burrow into my self-pity, or I can engage. I can teach. I can learn. She reminded me that day, and a dozen times in a dozen ways thereafter. And for that, I am forever grateful.

~Tina Dula

Friendships

Silence makes the real conversations between friends.
Not the saying but the never needing to say is what counts.
~Margaret Lee Runbeck

One of the things you might find discussed *ad nauseum* in all the websites, books, etc. is how the impact of a special needs child can change your relationships. Usually, they are referring to marriages or romantic relationships. But I'm not here to talk about marriage. Sure, my husband and I have felt the impact of the label, and the recognition of what the future may or may not hold. But—oddly enough—facing the truth of the situation, and the acknowledgement that we really have to live in the "now" actually helped us. There was no more push to be "perfect" as we tried to get our son to "catch up." In accepting him as he is, we continued our promise to accept one another as we are.

Friends, however, can be a different story. Friends aren't bound by vows or joint checking accounts, even though they've seen you wild and crazy as much as your spouse has, maybe even more. I found that even before the diagnosis, when the differences became more obvious, friends began to fall into different categories.

First and foremost are the golden friends, the ones who've been there through thick and thin. They were the first ones to call when word got out that we had a diagnosis. They are the ones I can call in the middle of a serious problem to take my boy for the night. They are the ones who get up and do a happy dance every time my son does something awesome. In short, they are family—maybe not blood, but family nonetheless. These are the friends to be cherished—and rewarded, with pie and expensive bottles of wine.

On the other side, there are the friends with whom you completely lose touch—the ones who ran when they saw or heard that my son was "different" from their kids. I'm happy to say, they weren't many, and frankly—their absence is for the better. I mean, if they are freaked out by my kid, does my kid need to be around them?

You can recognize these friends by the repeated blow-offs. I'm not talking the "My kid is sick, can we meet next week?" typical blow-offs that happen to all of us. I'm talking the "My kid is sick, but not sick enough to do something fun with other parents that is then shared and bragged about on Facebook." And then maybe you see that person at the park from time to time, and you get the fake hug and the "Yeah, we should totally hang out." They don't really ask about your kid, or they do so with the cringe or stage whisper and pity look. And they are perfectly willing to tell you everything about their kids and every single milestone they have crushed.

Then there are the new mommy friends—the ones that "get it" because your life is their life, give or take a margarita. These are the mommies of kids who are in school with yours, dealing with the same tantrums, the same quirks, the same vocabulary, the same concerns. It's strange, but they are sort of "instant friendships"—maybe because we can relax around them—there's no explaining here. Sharing of new ideas maybe, but no apologies over your kid grabbing toys, or not wanting to play, or screaming in protest when hugged. We share those looks that say—yeah, it's that kind of day. And we share the joy of seeing our kids make eye contact and running together—because we know that's a huge step for them in the realm of play.

Then there are the friends that, well, maybe don't mean to blow you off, but do. Because they are confused. A golden friend reminded me of this the other day: sometimes, they just don't know what to say—to me. They don't know that they can just sit down, have a cup of coffee and talk about the junk we talked about before the diagnosis. Because, it turns out, my son and I are still the same people. Some of my vocabulary has changed, and my outlook has shifted slightly, but I'm still heavy handed with the liquor in my cocktails, and I still bake tasty whole-wheat banana/zucchini bread. And unless you come over and are mean to my kid, there really isn't anything you could say that would offend me. If you have questions, I can supply answers. And our kids might play together, although I wouldn't hold your breath.

Now, I can't talk about friendships without evaluating my own actions as well. Sometimes when you hear the diagnosis, when you get immersed in this new world, you hide. Heck, I was down for a good month—lucky to get my toilets scrubbed, let alone step out in public for anything other than a grocery run. And I was prepped—we had been in therapy for a few months, and I was ready to hear what was going to be said—and it still knocked me on my butt.

It is the tendency of new moms of special needs kids to hide—not that we're hiding our kids, but we are hiding ourselves. I didn't want to burden my friends with tears that showed up unexpectedly while I got my emotions under some semblance of control. And I didn't want to hear about their kids. I didn't want to have to hide my jealousy, my frustration, my anger.

But I'm not hiding anymore, even though I'll still cry at the drop of a hat. Usually it's over the sort of things I would normally cry about—soup commercials or greeting cards—like any other peri-menopausal woman, right?

There is an old belief that I've always cherished: when you make friends with someone—a child is born. Each friendship is a child to be nurtured and cherished. This would explain why I'm not the social butterfly: I take the "raising" of these "children" very seriously. The relationships that truly matter to me are precious, and must be cared for—for each is its own individual gift.

So, if you've been hesitant to call, feel free to pick up the phone.

And if you called me yesterday, you can call me again today. I just put some banana bread in the oven, and I would love a good chat....

~Dawn Hentrich

Trains and Angels

You can't live a perfect day without doing something for someone who will never be able to repay you.

~John Wooden

Zachary was four years old, obsessed with the world of Thomas the Tank Engine trains and disconnected from our world. When I heard about a place in Lancaster, Pennsylvania, that offered a life-size Thomas train, I knew it was a way to connect with Zachary. On the ride there, I kept telling myself it would be a memory to treasure.

It was late when we arrived at the hotel. Zachary did not like new surroundings or a break in routine. A million doubts raced through my mind, but I held onto hope. I prayed Zachary wouldn't have a meltdown and get us kicked out. More than anything, I hoped this wasn't a mistake.

To our relief, Zachary's expressive brown eyes reflected wonder, the backpack chiming out its contents as he dragged it on the stairs. I inwardly cringed at the noise he was making, but decided his screams would be louder if I picked up the backpack.

Once we entered the room, Zachary pressed his palms against a wall, ran to the opposite side, and repeated the process several times.

I sat on the edge of the bed next to my husband, Joe.

"Jeannie..." He seemed deep in thought. "He's so..."

"What are you thinking?" I whispered.

"How beautiful he is."

On his next pass, Joe scooped him into his arms and carried him off to give him a bath. Zachary's effervescent laughter filled the room... and my heart.

When I slipped pajamas over his chubby legs, I realized how I treasured such a simple action. He'd overcome his sensory-over-loaded-clothing-hatred. I inhaled his still-baby scent and relished the moment. With Zachary snuggled between us, we soon fell asleep.

At dawn, Zachary woke me playing with his trains—my body his track. It actually felt good. Until he reached my face. Train wheels are detrimental to eyes, so I gave up on sleeping. Zach pounced on Joe's stomach, and woke him too. We were used to it. Zach never slept much. On a positive note, the sunrise was a sight to share. Then a toy train hit Joe in the back of the head.

"Do you still think our little guy is beautiful?" I asked through a fit of giggles.

Hope was our rope, and humor was the knot at the end of it. Still is.

We entered the Thomas the Tank amusement park, Zachary clutching our hands and lifting his feet to swing between us. Anyone looking at us would think we were a "normal" family. At that moment I felt that way. The other kids clamored around the costumed employ-ees, but Zachary ignored them and bolted to a line of people—a long one, twisting like a snake, and making my stomach knot with trepidation. Zachary did not grasp the concept of waiting.

Thomas the Train arrived, steaming and in full-size glory. Zachary hopped on the balls of his feet, flapped his hands, and droned. Everything would be fine as long as we kept moving. We were almost to the steps of the engine. Three more passengers and we would be on. Perfect. An announcement blared over a loudspeaker.

"The train is full. Please wait patiently for the next round."

I knelt in front of Zach. "The train will come back. Just like on the Thomas shows."

He smiled at me. I thought he understood. Then the train left without us.

Zachary's wail drowned out the train whistle, his agony misunderstood by anyone but Joe and I. I resorted to sign language, because at this point I knew words meant nothing. I assured him the train would come back for him. I promised everything would be okay, knowing in his world nothing was okay. When Zachary threw himself to the asphalt, Joe cradled him in his arms, protecting him. Our little boy thrashed, scratched, and keened like a wounded animal, but nothing compared to the utter sadness in his eyes.

My heart skittered into helplessness.

"I can help!"

Was I hearing voices? A red-haired woman bounded through the sea of frowning faces. "My son is autistic too." She thrust a laminated card in my hand. "Show him this."

Stunned, I did as she said.

His screams stopped so quickly, the murmurs from the crowd stilled. A breeze blew wisps of hair into his eyes, but he remained fixated on the four black letters on the yellow card. WAIT. Next to it, a stick figure sat in a chair… waiting.

I looked for the woman's wings.

"I'm Lisa."

I wanted to say, "You're an angel." I wanted to thank her for rescuing my son from his hell, yet I couldn't compose a complete thought.

Her red curls bounced as she spoke. "They're visual little guys, so this works great with our kids." Angel Lisa touched my arm.

Our kids. My throat closed with emotion. Mere words couldn't convey my gratitude and I felt adrift until I read the understanding in her eyes, bathing me in the light of hope.

All it took was an understanding angel to turn tragedy back into the adventure we sought for our son.

The train returned and I handed the card to Lisa as we boarded. "Keep it." She sat her son next to her and dug into her bag. "Here's a bunch more for you. It's called picture exchange communication." I felt she had given me a trainload of gold.

Our son's face filled with wonder at the sound of the train

whistle. The train chugged through the countryside, the moments of distress forgotten. It seemed a fitting place to be... on a train with my husband, our contented child, an angel, and a miracle.

On the ride home, Zachary clutched his backpack of trains in one hand and a WAIT card in the other. Over the years, he gradually gave up picture communication and spoke on his own. However, I will always treasure those yellow cards... and angels.

~Jean Marino

Reconnect

Three things in human life are important. The first is to be kind.
The second is to be kind. And the third is to be kind.
~Henry James

Joey paced back and forth at the top of the slide waiting for me to clear the puddle from the gravely dirt at the bottom, my last task on his take-off checklist. I'd spent the past ten minutes ridding the slide of its seventeen dew droplets, barely visible to the human eye, by using a dirty paper towel I had found in the trash receptacle. After twenty minutes, and the completion of five tasks, Joey tentatively sat down and slowly slid his way down to the bottom. He then proceeded back up the stairs to slide down again, exactly the way he had climbed up and slid down the time before... my much-needed break had come.

I sat down on the bench and took pride in my ability to resolve his issues once again. As my eyes took a brief recess from watching him, I noticed a flock of mothers looking at me. Disgust, irritation and disbelief were a few of the emotions I saw in their faces.

"I've heard of spoiled but come on—dry off the slide?"

No one understood and I didn't want to explain what Joey's issues were. I wanted to yell out, "I am not spoiling him! I am just making his environment one he can tolerate for twenty minutes to slide down a slide a few times... to do everyday things your children do and you don't have to think about!" At times, I secretly wished Joey had Down syndrome or some other "visible" disorder that people would recognize immediately, thus feeling instant empathy towards me. Rather, Joey, like many autistic children, was an adorable little boy with blond hair and big brown eyes.

I leaned back, brushed the gravel off my jeans and their comments off my mind and closed my eyes, taking comfort in my isolation. I didn't want to spend time with people who gave us dirty looks or didn't take the time to understand.

Then one day I was on the playground taking my break as Joey slid down the slide and one of the mommies approached me. She sat down next to me on the bench and handed me a paper bag. I opened it to find some dishtowels and a small bar of chocolate. Confused, I asked what it was for.

"I always kept a bag in my car when my oldest son was about your son's age," she said. "I got tired of going through the trash to find something to wipe down the slide. The chocolate bar was my reward after I helped my son get down the slide comfortably."

Through tears of disbelief I thanked her and she hugged me. I had been so alone for so long, I could barely contain myself. I began to sob. "We wanted to help; we just didn't understand," said the other mothers as they handed me tissues.

Many people make negative or derogatory comments about things they don't understand or can't explain. I've learned to look beyond those comments and take the time to "understand" them so they in turn can understand me. Since then, I have handed out a lot of paper bags, some filled with dishtowels, some filled with extra baby clothes for a new mother, or a spa candle and bath bubbles for someone appearing overwhelmed.

I have grown to realize that, though our children may lead us down different paths, we as parents all have the same wishes and instincts and that is what unites us. It's worth trying to reconnect with someone you feel has hurt you. Make a point to have coffee with your neighbor or a family member that you have disassociated yourself from. Maybe they just couldn't understand what you were going through. There's a paper bag with your name on it waiting for you.

~Anne Moore Burnett

My Trip to Home Depot

It's nice to be important, but it's more important to be nice.
~Author Unknown

My son Connor is autistic, and he loves to watch flowing water. Which means that in the warmer months, he likes to have the hose going in the back yard for hours at a time. While I have no issue with his love of water, it does elevate our water bill. Not to mention creating all that mud in our small yard.

One night I brainstormed a setup so that Connor could have flowing water, but we wouldn't need the hose to be constantly running. I pictured two small reservoirs—buckets, maybe—connected by a gutter. Then a recirculating pump could take the water from the lower reservoir and feed it back into the top one, so he would have a continuous stream of water flowing down the gutter.

I decided a trip to Home Depot was in order. I just wanted to look at the stuff in the gutter section and get some ideas as to how I'd make this work. I didn't quite have it all pulled together. Plus I wanted to price pumps, as I knew that would be the biggest part of the investment.

While standing in front of the gutters, thinking, I decided to take a couple down and contemplate the project ahead. A Home Depot employee approached me and asked if I needed help.

"Not really," I said. "I'm just trying to figure something out. It's a toy for my son, actually." I briefly explained, then I said, "Really, I'm fine. I'm just brainstorming."

A couple of minutes later, the man returned with another Home Depot employee named Glen. "I'm going to help you anyway," the first man said, smiling. So I explained to Glen about Connor and his fascination with flowing water. And the adverse affect on our water bill.

Glen and I started talking. He walked me back up the aisle to find another piece of the puzzle. An employee approached him with an issue, and I told him I was fine to go look at pumps if he could just point the way. I wasn't planning on buying the setup that day, so I didn't want to take up too much of his time.

He said he was going to walk me over, and he did. Along the way we ran across Jesse and Jeff, two more employees. Glen said they were the guys to help me out with the recirculating pump question. He described the project to them, and they came with us to the shelf holding all the pumps.

To my amazement, they then stayed there with me and helped me figure out the entire setup. Jeff went and got more pieces, and we laid out a mock relay of buckets, hoses, connectors, and a recirculating pump.

I started to worry whether I'd remember all the connections to tell my husband Roger about later on. So I said that maybe I'd buy the connections, hoses, etc. but leave the pump, which wasn't quite in the budget, for later.

We talked a moment about prices for a couple of the items, and then suddenly they said they'd see about getting me out of there with everything.

I looked at them. "What do you mean?" I asked.

"We'll give it to you. For free."

"Why?" I asked, incredulous.

"It's what we do," they told me.

Glen added, "Because you have an autistic son, and we want to help you out."

I was dumbfounded. Jesse and Jeff took the pieces we'd been

using, and headed up front to talk to the manager. Glen went with me to get one final piece. Along the way, he explained that Home Depot's mission was to become the number one service provider anywhere. That they wanted to make connections within their communities.

"Well, you succeeded," I said.

The manager agreed, they made a list of everything, and Glen put it all in my car. They told me to come back if we needed any help with the project. I don't know how many times I said "Thank you." I hope I said it enough.

I am someone who works with words for a living, and I couldn't express to them how amazing the whole experience was. I went in there intent on just looking, and wrestling with the details on my own. I left with a completed design, all of the parts I needed (worth over one hundred dollars) for no charge, and a sense of amazement at how genuinely interested, and how willing to help, these guys were.

I am still dumbfounded. Connor was over the moon with this setup. We saved a ton of money on our water bill. And I found out that there are people out there who are willing to help, often when you least expect it. One thing that I know is that this means a lot more to me than they realize.

Little miracles still do happen.

~Stephanie Carmel

Parting the Waters

May you live to see your life fulfilled.
~The Talmud

My little girl stood on the dais, facing a roomful of people. Her fine, brown hair was pulled off her face with a barrette. Huge hazel eyes, rimmed in dark, lush lashes, stared intently at the foreign words on the scroll in front of her. A colorful Israeli prayer shawl draped over her shoulders; her matching skullcap was bobby-pinned to her head. Her family—parents, grandparents, aunts, uncles and cousins, many of whom traveled far to be with her—sat in the front rows, looking up at her, waiting. My heart leapt into my mouth as Lauren began to chant.

We'd worked long and hard to prepare for this day—Lauren's Bat Mitzvah—none harder than Lauren. There were those who said it couldn't be done.

In fact, throughout Lauren's childhood, "experts" showered my daughter with all the ways she was different from her peers—all the things she couldn't do. She'd never learn much, never live independently, never ride a bike.

Lauren was our only child, and, like many first-time parents, my husband and I relied on experts for guidance. She had yet to be diagnosed with Asperger syndrome—that wouldn't happen until she was eighteen—but we knew she had developmental delays and learning deficits. She was diagnosed with nonverbal learning disabilities, which manifests in ways similar to Asperger's, and attention deficit hyperactivity disorder.

Fortunately, Lauren didn't rely on experts. When Lauren wanted to do something, she did what other kids do—she tried. She worked as hard as she could, for as long as it took to master what she wanted to learn.

One day, my husband and I looked out the window of our home to glimpse the back of a familiar-looking bicycle disappearing down the sidewalk. "Was that Lauren?" Avner asked me. We watched until the bike reappeared, heading our way. Sure enough, there was our daughter, peddling furiously. Not only could she ride a bike, she had taught herself.

What else could the experts be wrong about?

Lauren was mainstreamed in school, meaning she was a special education student who took mostly regular classes. A paraprofessional, a woman who sat in on Lauren's classes, helped her grasp the lessons and keep up with her studies. Lauren's assignments were modified to her ability.

How she tried. She sat at the kitchen table, reading, studying and asking questions until she understood the material. She earned A's through sheer diligence and brought honor on herself and her family.

When Lauren approached the age of thirteen, it was time to think about her Bat Mitzvah. Technically, all anyone has to do to reach that milestone is to read from the Torah. Just one line will do. Many parents of children with disabilities modify the experience according to what their children can realistically achieve. But Lauren ached to be like her peers. And so, we determined she would have her big day. There were no resources for children with special needs in our synagogue, so we created our own plan of action.

First, I became an adult Bat Mitzvah in a group ceremony when Lauren was twelve. The women in my class chose the portion of Exodus that includes Song of the Sea, in which the Israelites flee Egypt. When the Israelites get to the Red Sea, they're trapped. Discouraged, they're ready to turn back. But one brave soul steps into the water. Miracle of miracles, it parts, allowing the Israelites to cross on dry land. The sea then closes behind them, drowning the Egyptian soldiers chasing them. It's a story about not accepting limits, and having faith and courage in the face of fear.

Once I learned to decode the Hebrew, I was able to help Lauren learn it as well. We decided Lauren would have her Bat Mitzvah the next February, when she, too, could read from the portion of Exodus that contained Song of the Sea.

Then we went to work helping Lauren prepare. It took a village. I worked with her nightly. We got her a tutor, a learned man who refused to charge us for his weekly sessions. A dear friend, a cantor, taught Lauren the melody to which her Torah portion is chanted. Many Bar and Bat Mitzvah candidates speak their portions, but Lauren wanted to sing. What is Song of the Sea without a melody? Besides, Lauren's Hebrew name is Shira, which means song.

As she did with everything, Lauren tried. As hard as she could, for as long as it took to master what she wanted to learn.

The day of her Bat Mitzvah dawned bright and brutally cold. I was too excited and anxious to pay attention to the weather. I didn't sleep much the night before. I dosed myself with coffee. That and adrenaline gave me the energy to get through the day.

So here we were, an entire congregation watching my daughter as she began to chant. She recited flawlessly. She was a bit off key in places, but that made her effort all the more endearing. Most importantly, she radiated confidence and self-assurance.

When she finished her Torah portion and her interpretation of the portion, she read in Hebrew her haftarah, a passage from Prophets that follows a Torah reading. She then thanked her friends and family for being there and her teachers for helping her reach this day. Then Avner and I made our speeches to her—his recalling how she taught herself to ride a bike and travel the rings on the monkey bars; mine telling her how truly special she was and how she was my Shira, the song of my heart. At the end of my speech, I said, "And now Lauren, if the choir will stop crying, we'd like to sing you a blessing."

I thought I was kidding. The choir, to which Avner and I belonged, gathered and began to sing a beautiful rendition of Shehekeyanu, a blessing that gives thanks for unusual experiences and special occasions. We started off fine, but when it came time for the cantor to sing the solo, she choked. She was crying too hard to get the words out. It took only a beat for another choir member to jump in and recover the song. Then we all joined in. I was moved beyond words by what the rabbi later referred to as the spaces between the notes—the unplanned occurrences that amplify the meaning of an experience.

The rabbi, too, was moved. While we sang, he began to weep. Lauren, sitting next to the rabbi, comforted him with a hand on his arm and asked if he was okay. When the rabbi got up to speak, he told the congregation of Lauren's concern for him. "No one's ever done that," he said. "Ever."

The rest of the service went by in a blur. I felt so blessed that day, surrounded by loved ones, watching my daughter shine. Lauren once again faced a seemingly insurmountable challenge with grace and aplomb. Like her ancestors before her, she stepped into the Red Sea, trusting that it would part for her. And so it did.

~Robin J. Silverman

The Birth of
Camp Awesome

There is nothing—absolutely nothing—
half so much worth doing as simply messing about in boats.
~Kenneth Grahame

"I'm sorry, we simply don't have staff trained to deal with children of that sort." I slammed down the phone, the camp director's words ringing in my ears. Burying my face in my hands, I tried not to cry, or scream. This was our son Mark's twelfth summer and once again I could not find a camp to accept him. Not knowing, nor probably caring what autism is, the directors were deaf to my description of Asperger's as a milder form of autism.

My heart ached as I watched the neighbor's children playing happily in their yard on this sunshiny day while the thuds and squeaks of video games was the only indication my son was even awake. It was painful to see him always alone, spending most of his time playing those mindless games. Even the little boat a family friend had given him last spring didn't interest him for long. Mark didn't sail. No one in the family sailed, so what was the use? Sailing? Wait! Sailing! Hadn't I read about summer classes for kids in a sailing center brochure?

Mentally sticking my chin in the air, I dug through the stuff in my desk, found the brochure and dialed the number for the Clearwater Community Sailing Center on Sand Key in nearby Clearwater, Florida.

I fully expected they would also say they couldn't accommodate my child.

Richard White, Director of Programs at the sailing center, answered the phone.

I carefully explained Mark's challenges caused by his autism. They would soon discover his problems anyway.

"Will you take him in your camp?" I asked, trying not to sound anxious.

"I don't know," said Mr. White. "I'll be glad to see what we can do. Why don't you bring him to the center and we'll find out."

I couldn't drive us there fast enough!

Rich began by asking Mark to read the first two pages of the sailing manual. Returning a few minutes later, he was surprised to see Mark looking out across the water.

"Did you finish the pages I assigned?" asked Rich.

"I read the whole book," answered Mark. "When do we start?"

Sooner than I thought possible, Mark was belted into a life jacket and popped into a small boat. I don't know if I was excited or frightened as I watched my boy head out on that wide expanse of water in a boat that looked smaller by the minute. In that boat, however, he would go a lot farther than just across the water.

I was amazed at the changes in Mark as he interacted with the other youngsters in his class. He didn't settle for just sailing. He tried out the paddleboard, a sport where you stand on a long board with a long paddle to propel yourself across the water. To my delight my supposedly "challenged" son's strength and balance made him good at it. His social skills improved as he actually participated in playing with the other campers in a game of capture the flag. He even volunteered to assist the instructor.

These were not the only changes I noticed in Mark. He began waking up on time and had less trouble sleeping at night. For the first time, he was eager to go to a camp. In fact, every day he was excited about going to the Sailing Center, with no complaints about boredom or frustration. I couldn't believe how stress-free the summer became for both of us, in contrast to past vacations.

Eventually the time came for the campers to compete in one of the sailboat races held in a nearby city. I held my breath until Rich opted to be Mark's crew in the race.

"Mark was truly the captain," Rich told me. "I was the crew and, like a good crew, was careful to only make suggestions. The crew does not instruct the captain. So, as we approached the final mark, I only suggested that he tack before 'rounding the mark' to be in a better position for the finish line, but Captain Mark said, 'I think I can make it without tacking.'"

"And," Rich added, "he adjusted his sails and squeezed past the mark with inches to spare. His self-confidence won him the race."

Because Mark learned to sail so quickly and improved so rapidly, a national sailing organization called US Sailing named him "Sailor of the Week," complete with his story on their web page.

This recognition led to an interview on *Bay News 9*, a local television program. The reporter asked Mark, "How does sailing make you feel?"

His answer was, "Free and me."

The award gave Mark a whole new view of himself and did wonders for his self-esteem, which had suffered considerably from past bullying at school.

I still find the whole adventure so incredible, especially compared to Mark's experience in past summer programs. The Sailing Center crew showed great patience in working around his problems of impatience and self-esteem. It's the best therapy we have found for our son.

After camp was over Mark hung out at the Sailing Center. That's where he feels comfortable, welcome and, best of all, useful.

When I tried to thank Rich, he laughed.

"Don't thank me," he said. "Mark reminds me why I became a sailing instructor in the first place. He's a pleasure to work with."

In fact, Rich was so pleased with Mark's progress, he asked me what I thought of putting together a camp the next summer to teach sailing to other youngsters affected by autism. Remembering Mark's comment to the TV interviewer that sailing had made him feel "free and me," I happily encouraged Rich to pursue the idea.

When Rich said, "I doubt I can teach my instructors how to work with young people with autism, but I can sure make sailing instructors out of people who know how to work with kids with Asperger's," I went looking for instructors.

We found them in the county school system. Teachers experienced in working with autistic kids jumped at the chance to be their sailing instructors. We hired three of them. Rich easily taught them to sail.

We had eight kids with Asperger's participating in what Rich called Camp Awesome. I call it my own personal miracle.

Incredibly, this is only the beginning. Our guys and gals will continue to sail on a weekly basis. During the school year we plan weekend sails and family cookouts.

Better yet, US Sailing is introducing other sailing centers to have Camp Awesome for children with Asperger's. I'm so thankful for Rich and the Clearwater Community Sailing Center. They took me from frustration and discouragement to triumph and enthusiasm in one short summer. And the difference it makes for Mark is—awesome.

~Bonnie Monroe

The Market

One can pay back the loan of gold,
but one dies forever in debt to those who are kind.
~Malayan Proverb

write love letters to the man who bags my groceries. I have never sent them. I mostly write them in my mind. But I do love him. In fact, I love everyone at the grocery store by my house. I love the quiet, sharp-humored people who stock the produce displays, the handsome butchers, the high-spirited people who scan my groceries, the courtly gentleman who opens the door and greets me.

This grocery store is small. When I was new in town, and filled with complaints generally, I was irked by some prices and the lack of parking. But quickly I came to love everyone in the place, and everything they do, if only because they are so kind to me and my boy.

When we arrive at the store, every day, my son runs ahead of me and reaches the door even before I have had a chance to lock the car and find someplace to stash my key. I race to catch up, but he has already entered the store and gone deep inside. I can hear him whooping and laughing (making what his brothers call "Nicky noises"), but don't know in what aisle he is working.

Happily, it doesn't matter. I know he'll be fine. I get my cart and walk the usual path, past the produce (picking up bananas, apples, and green beans), past the dairy (milk for the other boys, lemonade for Nick, eggs for adults), on to the meat counter. While the lovely butcher is getting my chicken cutlets, I look around, since from this back corner I can see all the way to the south and the west corners of the store.

Usually, at this point I catch sight of Nicky, looking for me, his arms full of his groceries: ice cream sandwiches, crackers with peanut butter, dark chocolate sandwich cookies, brown paper sacks, and a toilet brush. Every now and again we miss this rendezvous point, but if I head down to the bakery counter and peer around, I see one of the young men stocking shelves who smiles and silently points in the direction he last saw my gorgeous, beach-blond wild man.

At some point, Nick started showing up with little containers of his favorite food: bowtie noodles with pesto, and I realized that he was somehow—with almost no expressive language—interacting with the people behind the prepared food counter. I wanted to thank them, for the gift of the effort on their parts that this transaction must have required, but was worried I would not be able to get through the sentence without bursting into tears. Recently, Nick danced past our cart and tossed in a newly wrapped butcher package of ground beef (a.k.a. "habooger"). Oh my god! The butchers, too?

Then we trundle together to the cashier, and Nicky dances up and down the space behind the young people bagging groceries, singing incomprehensibly and spinning wildly enough to worry the elderly shoppers and their companions. The cashiers offer Nick genuine and warm greetings, calling him "Hon," while requiring nothing of him in return. The baggers laugh good-naturedly when Nicky crashes into them. Nick is completely confident and at home here with his people.

I don't know why these people are so nice to and tolerant of the unusual shopper I bring every day. Cognitively disabled people have worked there over the years, so we know the management is comfortable with human diversity. But there is more going on in that store than management policy. There is powerful energy coming from the man laying out the zucchinis, the high school kid loading people's wine into boxes, the grandmother who might be excused for being sorry that she is still at work. They are sending me love letters daily with their rich and mellow kindness. Someday I am going to write back.

~Jean McAllister Brooks

Chapter 5

Raising Kids on the Spectrum

Finding the Funny

Oliver Wears the Pants

The only normal people are the ones you don't know very well.
~Alfred Adler

Sometimes I think I worry too much about my special needs son Oliver. It's not so much that I worry... but that I just always assume he's going to be the odd man out. Not without reason of course — my son is one weird little guy. I personally like this about him, but I'm also aware of the fact that "weird" isn't a sought after quality in elementary school.

The fact that he's in kindergarten makes everything a little bit easier. He's given some leeway for being a "little kid" and the other kindergartners are still kind of goofy in their own ways, regardless of how much more typical they are. So Oliver continues to fly under the radar, doing his own thing, his own way, and isn't largely concerned with how he may be perceived.

That's another thing I like about Oliver. He's his own man. So other kids are moving on from their old preschool interests and now run around playing *Star Wars*? Whatever — he's still happy with his Thomas trains. They think trains are for babies? Good — more trains for him. He's not abandoning his favorite toys just because of what someone says. He has staying power.

He is also so incredibly comfortable in his own skin. At five years old, he's a very big kid. Over sixty pounds, he's as tall as some of the second graders. And he is solid. I was also pretty tall for my age and a fairly sturdy little girl, but this always made me feel awkward.

Like I was just a little too much. I felt heavier and weighed down by my size. But Oliver is sure-footed and agile. He uses this sense of weightiness as an anchor. He stands firm and holds his ground. A physical quality that matches his personality.

And when I say Oliver is "comfortable in his own skin" I mean that quite literally. He likes to wear as little clothing as possible. Coats are constricting and only to be tolerated in the coldest of temperatures. He has little patience for layers. They are peeled off as quickly as they were applied. And once inside, clothes are hardly necessary. Really—what purpose do they serve when not protecting you from the elements?

Other children run in after school kicking off their shoes and flinging aside coats, seemingly deaf to their parents' reminders to please put them in the closet. My son does this as well, but he takes it a step further by adding his pants to the trail of outerwear.

Oliver doesn't wear pants at home. In fact, he doesn't wear pants in any home where he feels at home. It's not uncommon for me to walk into a neighborhood play date to find my pantless son building Lego towers or lounging in front of the television. It doesn't matter if all the other kids are fully dressed. To each his own, you know. It's not that he's rude—he's just comfortable. His state of undress is really just a testament to your superb hospitality. Kudos—you hostess with the mostess, you!

I've come to accept this little quirk in the same way that I surrender to my daughter's insistence on wearing nothing but pink. It's not my preference... but I respect their choices as long as they're not hurting anyone else.

At the end of the day, I'm just thrilled if Oliver is at least wearing underpants.

Aside from his current trajectory toward being "the naked guy" at college parties, Oliver is quite well behaved. He's a nice boy and very accepting of others. Feel free to take off your pants at his house too. He doesn't judge. He likes other kids as a general rule and will only be put off by unpleasant behavior. Even then, he doesn't take offense—he just moves on. It's like he has this innate sense of there being plenty of room for everyone. If you give him some space, he'll give you yours. And in such a "my team/your team" world, I find this both brave and wise. I hope he always has the strength of character and confidence required to maintain that approach to life.

So yes—he's a special needs kid. He's different. He's maybe even a little weird. But he's fine.

The other day at the YMCA, I glanced down at the Kids' Gym to see Oliver standing still while other children raced around him. I kept watching and realized that he wasn't just standing still, he was frozen to the spot. His arms were stiff at his sides and his knees were locked. He stared straight ahead and looked as if he was trying not to blink. He stayed this way for long enough that even I, the head cheerleader for Team Different, thought he looked totally bizarre.

Time stood still as Oliver stayed still. Blurred shapes of playing children swirled around him, but I only had eyes for my son, the statue. I thought, "What are you doing? Come on—just move already before the others notice. Walk. Play. Be normal. Please."

Then a small figure disengaged from the only vaguely perceived chaos around Oliver and tapped him on the shoulder. Just like that, he came back to life and ran out of view. And I suddenly understood. Oliver wasn't playing some strange game of his own, oblivious to everyone around him and their potential scorn. He was playing Freeze Tag. They all were. He was part of the game. One of them.

Talk about not seeing the forest for the trees.

Oliver isn't always alone. Sometimes he really is part of the group. And sometimes he's not, but it doesn't matter because he's always exactly where he wants to be. There is always a place for him.

I never need to worry about Oliver. He's not oblivious to the world around him. He just makes his own decisions about when and where he wants to engage with it.

He's come a long way in the past few years, and the truth is, he has a long way to go. But I have more faith in him than I do in almost anyone else in my life. He is my constant and he is true to himself. I have no doubt that he will always find his place in life. One where he is happiest, regardless of what anyone else thinks about it. He is now and will hopefully always be his own man. With the support of his family and friends, and without any fear of ever truly being alone. With or without pants.

~Kate Coveny Hood

The Little Man Inside

It is best to love wisely, no doubt:
but to love foolishly is better
than not to be able to love at all.
~William Makepeace Thackeray

Around age fourteen, our son Toby began to notice that there are two versions of the human race, and that the girl version comes in fascinating packages. Toby has mild/moderate autism, and although he is friendly and somewhat verbal, his communication and social skills are weak. This, combined with his newfound interest in girls, created some interesting situations.

Our daughter Kirsten and her bevy of sixteen- and seventeen-year-old friends were in and out of the house constantly. Where Toby had ignored Kirsten's friends before, he now started observing them with interest.

"Mu-therrrrr!" Kirsten screeched one day. "Toby is following Janice around staring at her legs!"

I walked into the room and saw Janice standing at the kitchen counter, drinking a soda, while Toby stood a scant six inches away, his eyes glued to her legs.

Janice has a lovely figure that would be striking even in a pair of overalls. That day she was wearing cut-off jeans. They weren't Daisy Dukes, but showcased in those shorts, Janice's legs would do credit to a Rockette.

"Well, girls… Janice does have very nice legs. I imagine most boys would take a second look. Toby, please come here a minute."

Once out of the room, I explained to Toby that one does not stare at portions of a young lady's body, no matter how attractive they are. I reminded him of personal space rules and as an afterthought said, "Absolutely no touching!"

Toby nodded virtuously. "No touching. Look only."

"Right. Now, you owe Janice an apology for making her feel uncomfortable."

Toby went back into the kitchen.

"Sorry staring pretty legs, Miss Janice," he said, staring at her derrière.

"Um, Toby…" I began.

"It's okay, Ms. D'Ann," Janice said with a giggle. "Kinda flattering, I guess. Mom thinks these shorts are too small, anyway."

"It's em-barr-ra-ssing!" Kirsten sputtered. "C'mon, let's go upstairs where he can't aggravate us."

Kirsten seemed to be the only one who was really bothered, but Janice nodded and followed her out of the room. As Toby watched Janice bounce up the stairs, I reflected that guys don't have it easy these days. Sighing, I told Toby again that staring at a girl's anatomy is unacceptable.

A few weeks later, I stood in the church vestibule, chatting with friends. Kirsten was with a group of her buddies, and Toby stood nearby, smiling. While Toby doesn't interact much, he enjoys being with people and often hovers near the edge of a crowd.

Kirsten's voice soared over the muted roar of after-church fellowship as if she'd been speaking into a bullhorn.

"Toby! Stop staring at Charlene's breasts!"

Everyone within shouting distance looked over at the group of kids. Toby leaned against a post, his eyes fixed on Charlene's generous bosom.

People started laughing. Kirsten and Charlene turned bright red. I wanted to hide behind the nearest potted plant and pretend I was childless. Instead, I apologized to Charlene, took one child by each arm and propelled them outside.

As we drove home, I scolded Toby for gaping and Kirsten for calling everyone's attention to her brother's behavior. My husband Paul smiled slightly and said nothing.

At lunch, Paul clarified the fine art of girl-watching versus girl-ogling.

"Son, it's fine that you're noticing girls."

Kirstin snorted. "Noticing? More like he's stalking them."

I glared at Kirsten. "He is not. Stop interrupting your father."

"It's normal to look at girls," Paul continued, "especially when they dress to be noticed."

"We do not!" Kirsten protested.

I crooked an eyebrow. "Really. Is that why you were talking about how sexy you look in your new jeans?"

Paul talked over us. "All us guys have this little man inside, saying, 'Look, look!' and jumping up and down at the sight of a pretty girl. Looking is fine, but you have to do it subtly."

"He doesn't understand words like 'subtle' Daddy," Kirsten said.

"You have to look quietly," Paul said. "Not obvious." Paul stood, came to within a foot of me. "Watch how I look at Momma. Not like this." He stared down at my chest.

"Ew, that's gross! Stop that!" Kirsten said.

"Not that way," Paul said. "Like this." His eyes swept me with a quick glance, and then he focused on my face˙ and smiled at me warmly. "See, Toby? Quiet appreciation."

Paul had me stand up. "Not like this," he said, giving my bottom an exaggerated leer. "Like this." His eyes encompassed me in a brief glance, and then he focused a charming smile on my face. "Hi, you're pretty," he said.

"Thanks, kind sir." I curtseyed. "Would you like to buy me an iced tea?"

"You guys are weird," Kirsten said, laughing as she left the room.

"Got it, Toby?" Paul asked.

"Okay." Toby rose to put his dishes in the sink.

I wondered how much of Paul's lesson he had understood.

A few weeks later, we had to take my car in for maintenance. Toby and I were waiting on Paul to complete the paperwork when Toby noticed a very pretty girl standing at the next counter. He started to stare, so I nudged him.

"Remember what Daddy said? You can appreciate and say hello, but don't stare," I murmured into his ear.

Toby bounded over to the girl's counter.

She looked up from her computer. "Hi. Can I help you?"

My son grinned from ear to ear and swung his arm back and forth like he was waving a semaphore. "Hello, Girl!" he proclaimed joyfully.

I was relieved to see Toby focus on her lovely face, rather than below her neck, but my relief was short-lived.

Toby began bouncing up and down on his toes, the little man inside fully celebrating the vision in front of him.

I said a silent prayer that the girl would "get" that he was special, and not call security. Toby is a handsome young man, but he's tall and muscular. The sight of 150 pounds of appreciation bouncing up and down could be intimidating. An explanation trembled on my lips.

A warm smile lit the young lady's face. "Hello! How are you today?"

"Good!" Toby said, giggling as he bobbed up and down.

Paul walked over. "All set, we can go now."

Paul and I smiled at the young woman. I mouthed "thank you" and we left. As we reached the door, Toby turned, beamed, and waved at her once more.

"Bye-bye, pretty girl! Appreciate!"

She grinned and waved.

We walked out into the warm afternoon sunshine.

"Toby," I began, but my husband shook his head and squeezed my arm.

"It's okay, Mama," he said with a reassuring smile. "Like I said before, all us guys have a little man inside who jumps up and down frequently. Toby's just more honest than the rest of us."

~D'Ann Renner

Return of the Prodigal Son

Laughter is an instant vacation.
~Milton Berle

My son Zach, now thirteen, spent the past three weeks at a sleep-away camp for kids with all kinds of special needs and disabilities. He has high-functioning autism, sometimes called Asperger syndrome. He is a very tall, cute, quirky guy with many challenges. He is also very bright and funny. Like most kids with autism spectrum disorders (ASD) he is very literal. For example, kids like Zach have difficulty understanding figures of speech unless they are explained and even then they have a tough time. If you say that someone is beating around the bush he looks around for shrubbery.

His arrival by bus on Sunday afternoon (in Toronto) was fabulous. When the three buses pulled up, I couldn't see him through the tinted windows but I guess he saw me amid the throng of waiting moms, dads, siblings and dogs. The counselors got all of the bags off the buses before letting any campers off. When the doors opened he was one of the first out and came running at me, full speed, with a look on his face that any parent recognizes as three seconds to teary-time. I thought that the impact would send me flying like the world's biggest bowling pin, but he slowed just a bit before grabbing me and treating me to the tightest and longest hug I have ever received from him. We went round and round for a few minutes before I could break out of his clutch, get a bit of distance and have a look at my five-foot ten-inch, golden-tanned cutie. (He grew at least half an inch in three weeks.)

He was ravenous, as usual, so we drove to our hotel and I got him a big burger and fries. He claimed to have eaten mostly bread for the duration of camp. (He has serious eating issues because of hypersensitivity.) He told me all about camp and how much fun he had. Trying new foods and new activities was a big goal we had set for him. Zach told me that he had tried sailing, archery, canoeing, kayaking and even high ropes. The one and only time he had cried at camp was when he was doing the high ropes. He was very scared but he had done it anyway. I told him that being very afraid and doing something anyway is the true definition of bravery. He'll be getting lots of rewards for these accomplishments.

Then I asked about the disposable camera we had sent to camp with him. He said he had had a great time with it. He had taken twenty-seven pictures, of his bunkmates, counselors, waterfront, trees, activities, etc. When I asked him where the camera was he rolled his eyes, gave me a look like I was a complete idiot and replied, "Mom, it was a DISPOSABLE camera, so I threw it away."

That's my boy.

~Lorri Benedik

Don't Call My Daughter "Normal"

Normal is overrated.
~Cristina Marrero

"Your daughter's autistic? Wow! She seems so normal!" This "compliment" is absurd to me. I realize it's intended to make me feel better. After all, people think I'll be thrilled to know that my daughter passes for "normal." But every time I hear this statement I can't help but think, "Normal? Oh God, I hope not!"

My ten-year-old daughter, Isabel, was diagnosed with Asperger syndrome when she was three. For years she had occupational therapy, speech therapy and social skills classes. I've done everything in my power to give her the tools she needs to be confident and succeed. And she's thriving! But let me make one thing perfectly clear—my goal has never been for her to be "normal."

I've seen "normal." And I'm not interested. "Normal" can't tell you the individual designs on every state quarter. "Normal" doesn't suddenly decide to go by the name "Bob." "Normal" doesn't answer the phone in the British accent she has been practicing all week.

"Normal" is overrated and I won't have it. Not in my house.

In fact, my twins are "normal" and I pay Izzy two dollars a week to teach them everything she knows. It's part of her allowance: Make your bed, take out the trash, teach your brother and sister to be abnormal. When they start organizing their plastic dinosaurs according to dietary restrictions, I'll know I've succeeded.

I'm "normal" and it took me forty years to get up the nerve to do what comes naturally to my daughter. To find a passion, speak my mind, and have the guts to go for what I want. Izzy knows she loves ducks. She loves everything about them (and can do a perfect imitation of a Scottish Wigeon). When she grows up she wants to work with ducks. Don't even think about telling her "that's silly" or that she should "perhaps consider dentistry." Izzy isn't paralyzed by what everyone thinks and I know enough "normal" people to know that that is definitely not normal. But because of it, the world is her oyster. Frankly, I'm jealous.

But you know what makes me the most jealous? You can't suck up to Isabel. She likes you or she doesn't. You're worthy of her attention or you're not. Sure, she knows how to be polite, but if you really want to be Isabel's friend, flattery won't get you far.

"You like my sneakers? They wouldn't fit you. They're for kids."

"You think I'm pretty? Thanks. Pass the pretzels."

I, however, am a pushover. I've befriended people simply because they say they liked my shirt. "Thank you so much! I got it at this boutique on Beverly. They have the cutest stuff. It came in green too, but I really liked the pink. Do you think it makes me look fat? I was worried my boobs looked too big in it. Can I have your number?" I'm paralyzed by my need to be liked.

Isabel isn't. I think she's got a future in Hollywood.

I wouldn't change a thing about Isabel. Of course, I want her to be happy. But being happy doesn't mean being normal. For Isabel, happiness will hopefully come from feeling loved for who she is, having skills to navigate the "normal" world, and being confident she can reach her full potential—which is limitless.

Isabel is an extraordinary girl. She is beautiful, loving and wholly unique. But call her normal to my face and you're asking for it.

~Sarah Maizes

Funeral Fun

Dying is a very dull, dreary affair…
~Somerset Maugham

We have a large extended family, and we were in a period of time when many of our elderly relatives were at the end of their lives. I prepared my nine-year-old son for the process that was about to unfold as we drove the forty-five-minute trip to visit the first of three elderly aunts in the hospital. We talked about how Aunt Bianca was old, how she lived a good and happy life, and how she was very ill from a heart attack. We discussed what the room would look like, what she would look like, and what he could and could not say.

"She's going to die?" asked Noah.

"Yes, maybe soon, but we don't discuss that when we visit her. It's too sad." I have to explain every detail to him, because he approaches many events with such a matter of factness that his comments or questions can be inappropriate. We also talked about how to behave in a hospital since this was a huge worry to me. His voice is very loud and he's not good at being calm. It was a boring visit for him and he tolerated it well. Noah was fascinated with how all the machines worked and what they did for Aunt Bianca.

He asked about the dysfunction of our aunt's heart, since the internal body was one of his topics of interest. Otherwise there wasn't much for him to do. He was uncomfortable and bored.

A week later, Aunt Bianca died. I prepared him for the process of viewings and the funeral itself. We talked about appropriate behaviors and conversations. Again, Noah was overly curious about what happened to her heart, why it stopped, how it became sick, how it got a clog in its own artery, what would happen if there was an artery explosion in her heart and on and on about every scenario he could think of concerning hearts. The viewings were long and boring for him. Driving forty-five minutes to and from the viewing and sitting for up to two hours in a room full of mourning adults required many vending-machine treat incentives from the funeral home lounge.

The next day at the funeral involved more than three hours of driving and hours of services and a somber family gathering with nearly nothing for him to do.

Just a few weeks later we had to repeat the same process when Aunt Bianca's sister had a heart attack. We visited her in the hospital, we discussed hearts and their dysfunction, we went to viewings, a full mass, the funeral, the gathering, and we drove. A lot. More promises had to be made for vending-machine treats. Privately he was more vocal and rude, and bordered on a meltdown, but publicly he kept it together.

It was barely a week later when the third aunt died. Aunt Myrtle was on my mother's side of the family and because it was so sudden there was no time for a hospital visit. "Looks like I escaped the hospital visit," he said with blunt honesty. Aunt Myrtle was one of those aunts who loved children. She really enjoyed her seven grandchildren, sixteen great grandchildren, five great-great grandchildren and all of her great-nieces and nephews. She was always crocheting sweaters for the next generation of great-grandchildren and great-great nieces and nephews.

The funeral home was another long drive away and Noah was banking on a vending machine in the lounge. So was I. He was reaching his limit and if there wasn't a vending machine, there could be a meltdown. He was already concerned with the next day's funeral and if we had to go to the "boring party" afterwards. Once we arrived and did a round of greetings and condolences, I was quickly given some groans and reminders about the lounge. As promised, I helped him find it while nearly holding my breath with fear that it would have no treats. What relief and surprise as we entered and found, not only vending machines, but a television playing cartoons. This was a double treat for my son, who rarely gets the privilege of watching TV.

He was not only placated, but happy!

The next day's funeral service was held at the funeral home and Noah had to be warned that he needed to stay with me, rather than in the lounge, out of respect for Aunt Myrtle and the family.

He was very loud about his disappointment and I was dreading the whole day. I was sure that he had been pushed too hard with all of this and that an already stressful time for us was about to turn ugly.

Once at the funeral home, he was quiet and handled the service well, but the day was far from over. We still had a visit to the cemetery and then the family gathering. The drive there was a breaking point. There was a lot of screaming, kicking of seats and refusals to get out of the van. I went into the house while my husband stayed with Noah and helped him calm down.

With all the children in the house, it was full and active. My parents greeted me with knowing apologetic looks after learning that Noah was still in the van with his father. When they finally came in, Noah looked tired, but brightened a bit after seeing the spread of sweets. It was a sugar fanatic's dream: cakes, pies, cookies!

After eating the required dinner in order to get the sweets, he was off investigating the piles of toys and the swing set. He kept busy following all the other children in their games. He needed a little help navigating the challenging social rules of the other kids and he was caught many times snatching more sweets from the buffet, but otherwise it was a smooth and pleasant visit for him, which meant it was good for us, too.

When it was time to leave, he was resistant. We gave him a ten-minute warning. After we said our goodbyes, we tried coaxing, bribing, and demanding that he leave with us. Finally we had to physically guide him away toward the van. Despite his loud protests, out of habit, we reminded him he needed to say goodbye.

We were surprised when he turned toward the crowd of mourning relatives to loudly scream, "Bye! BEST FUNERAL EVER!"

Our embarrassment left us pale and speechless as we piled into the van for the long trip home.

It was a few days before we thought it through enough to know this would have been a huge compliment for Aunt Myrtle. We're sure she would have loved that so many children were there joyously celebrating her life. I also think she would be pleased that her great-great-grand nephew, who struggles daily with social situations, regarded hers as the "best funeral ever."

~Angela Benam

Scared or Angry?

Some days even my lucky rocketship underpants won't help.
~Calvin & Hobbes

This morning my autistic son Benjamin was taking a shower by himself. I was enjoying his independence when I heard a loud thud. Then a scream.

The door of the shower had had the indecency to fall off its tracks.

I went into the bathroom. He was furious.

"The shampoo made it fall off! The shampoo is fired! Falling off is against the ten commandments!" His rant continued to include *Captain Underpants*, and *Family Guy*. He went so far in his exasperation that he declared Zack Johnson is no longer his friend. This was serious.

I tried to disguise my amusement. Benjamin was convinced that *Captain Underpants* and the bottle of shampoo were in cahoots in this flagrant example of espionage.

"It sounds like you are angry, or scared. It is upsetting when the door falls off. You were not expecting that." I helped him out of the tub.

"Want a hug?" The wrestling match between fear and anger continued. Fury was winning so he did not take me up on my offer.

"The shampoo is STUPID." His wet body was shaking. I wrapped my arms and a towel around him.

I was glad he was not hurt, and thankful that the shower door had not shattered. I wasted no energy on reprimanding him, or asking if he had any explanation for what happened. Gratitude and compassion had center stage, with a muffled grin behind the curtain.

While I feel fairly certain that the targets of his blame had no malevolent intentions, I could translate Benjameese into my native tongue.

"Someone or something made this happen! I do not know who, so I will pick a random target to catapult my feelings at. I can't tell the difference between fear and rage, but whatever it is it's exploding inside of me."

I can cut Benjamin some slack because he has this handy diagnosis of autism. But really everyone in my house suffers from the occasional implosion. They are savvier at choosing scapegoats, but I could offer them some leeway too.

One time my husband John got mad at me for asking if he wanted to go to the twins' school program. I was caught off guard. It seemed out of proportion for the question at hand. I became defensive, and we both lost.

I think next time I want to heave blame I will spare my family entirely and aim it at *Captain Underpants*. He can handle it. He is after all, a superhero.

~Lori Odhner

Dressing Up

I don't need easy. I just need possible.
~Bethany Hamilton

"I want to wear my Miranda Lambert costume," my son River informs me matter-of-factly. His autistic obsession with memorizing the Billboard Pop and Country charts has recently evolved into a passion for dressing up as the stars with top hits. In the world of autism this is a major development — imaginative play! I am thrilled, though unclear about how far to let it go when it leads me to looking for fishnet stockings for a ten-year-old boy who feels this is a must-have accessory for his Lady Gaga and Britney Spears costumes. And today, for the first time, he wants to wear one of his outfits in public.

Oh boy. My mind races ahead to figure out how to navigate this sticky wicket. *Don't push against, be creative, and especially, stay easy...* I tell myself.

"Okay," I say cheerily. "We can put on your Miranda Lambert costume for five minutes, and then we'll change into your clothes for the park." Yeah right. Like we can really pull that off. But both boys have a physical therapy appointment at the park, and we've already missed several because of tantrums and breakdowns, so I am resolute that we're not going to bail on this helpful professional at the last minute, again.

"No! I want to wear my Miranda Lambert costume to the park!" River protests.

Oh boy. I can't believe I have to do this. Me, of all people! Ms. Wear Whatever the Heck I Want and I Don't Care What You Think. Ms. Liberated Mother who's been encouraging the full and very colorful expression of my boys' outrageously unique selves for over ten years. My heart just breaks inside. But today I'm Ms. Discerning Mother of Autistic Twins Not Interested in Triggering a Child Protective Services Investigation. I don't think the soccer moms will find my boys dressed in tight, strapless dresses, four-inch platform heels, and cascading wigs of blond curls parading around the playground as fabulous as I do.

I take a deep breath, knowing we have ten minutes to get out the door, and that if I don't do this right, River will erupt into a violent tantrum that could last an hour.

Bodhi, his identical twin, best friend, and worst enemy, pops his head in the door. Lucky for me, he's feeling generous today.

"I recommend you let him do what he wants. He's gonna get mad if you don't."

"Thanks for your advice, Bodhi," I tell him sweetly, realizing that a strong odor is emanating from his Pull-Ups. There is no way I can pull off the UN-level negotiation needed to get him cleaned up, and also get River out the door in something G-rated—in the next ten minutes.

Triage time.

Okay, I think, no one's gonna call CPS on me for having an autistic boy in poopy Pull-Ups. His physical therapist won't be pleased, but tough. We'll be outside, and the odors will dissipate.

So I keep my attention on River.

"Let's wear your cowboy costume!" I suggest brightly.

"No! I want to wear my Miranda Lambert costume, and that's final!"

I can't figure out a way to do this without saying no, so I go for the direct approach. "No sweetheart, it's not appropriate to wear such a fancy costume out of the house."

Damn. Is this me talking? "Appropriate?"

River starts screaming. He shouts. "I'm really angryyyyyy!"

"I hear you, River! Thank you for telling me with your words!" Autism has a way of creating surreal Hallmark moments.

I re-open the cowboy conversation nonchalantly. "So what do you think—Brad Paisley or Jason Aldean?"

"Jason Aldean," he grumbles, but he's already starting to brighten. I gather the necessary country-rock-star elements—cowboy shirt, boots and hat, jeans and microphone—in record time and manage to corral both my sweet boys into the car, only ten minutes late. Whew. I breathe a sigh of relief. Only, it's not over.

"Why didn't you let River wear the costume he wanted?" Bodhi demands, as we drive away from the house. I can hear in his tone of voice, he wants real answers. I try to be vague but truthful. "Well you see Bodhi, it's a funny thing about the culture we live in. What is good manners to most people is not wearing really crazy costumes out in public, unless it's Halloween or you're going to a costume party."

"Are you telling me," Bodhi's voice is incredulous and suspicious, "that people wouldn't enjoy seeing River in a colorful costume?" He spits out his final words like a defense attorney delivering his final address to the jury.

I squirm, weighing how much I should say, finally judging that it's probably important to be a bit more transparent given that this is an issue that is not going away.

"Well, actually, I guess what it really is, now that I think about it more, is that some people would be uncomfortable seeing a boy dressed in a girl's costume." There. I said it, or at least more of it. No need to bring in child pornography, pedophiles, CPS, and homophobia at this point. But I'm not sure how my statement is going to land with my boys.

The response is immediate. Disgust. "That's RIDICULOUS!" Bodhi exclaims. "A boy should be able to dress up like Nicki Minaj if he wants to! That should be a RULE!"

"I agree!" I raise my voice to match his indignation, but Bodhi is not through.

"We've got to tell OBAMA about this! He's got to pass a LAW about this!" He breaks off his rant with an outraged huff.

It's enough to warm an activist mom's heart.

~Michele Bissonnette Robbins

Life Skills

Humor is the great thing, the saving thing.
~Mark Twain

I hear screams and breaking glass, then a click. I redial the number. More screams. More breaking glass. "Don't hang up! Tell me what is going on," I plead.

My daughter struggles through her tears, anger, and disbelief: "Carter couldn't find the orange juice so he called 911 and the cops are here!"

Oh, of course.

Finally, after so many years of continuous instruction, unable to take a day off, my husband and I felt we could take a vacation. So, there we were, in a hotel room far away from the current crisis.

"What about the house sitters? Where are they?"

"Mom, they are still asleep. I didn't want to bother them."

Oh, of course.

Take a deep breath.

We have come so far, I remind myself. After all, we had conquered banking....

"How can I help you?" the smiling bank teller asked my sixteen-year-old autistic son.

"I would like to order a pizza!" he replied with enthusiasm.

The teller smiled. "That sounds really good, I would like a pizza too."

I smiled too. Thank God for nice people.

"Carter, this is a bank, we can't order pizza here. We can get money here and go home to order pizza, remember?" I said with that slow, instructive voice of experience. We continued with the transaction, just as we had practiced at home, just as we had reviewed so many times.

The teller smiled. "How would you like your cash?"

"Well done, with lots of ketchup," my son replied with a look of pride.

"Not quite, Carter. That is what you say at the restaurant when the waiter asks you how you would like your hamburger. This is a bank. What he means is, what kind of bills do you want — fives, tens, or ones?"

Yes, we had conquered banking.

And phone calls... "Mom, is that enough butter?" he asked, like a racehorse out of the gate, no need to waste time on pleasantries.

"Oh hi, Carter. I'm not sure since I can't see what you are doing."

Or the time that I drove him to the library because it was raining and he couldn't ride his bike... and as I was pulling out of the parking lot, my phone rang. "I'm at the library."

"I know that, Carter. I just dropped you off. In fact if you turn around you can see me and wave to me."

Seriously? Is this what they mean by "mind-blindness?" And why did he decide then to follow the "call me when you get there" rule, when so many other times he hadn't bothered to call me?

Yes, we had conquered so many things. I remember that day when I asked him to stop on his way home and pick up a gallon of milk. When he walked in the door with the jug of milk and no bag, I was astonished. "Did you pay for it?" I asked, imagining that he just walked out with it and soon I would be visiting him in juvenile detention.

"Yes," he answered, handing me a receipt to prove it. I smiled. I thought I had died and gone to heaven.

I celebrated the moment. A little victory in life's never-ending battle for life skills. Oh, how he hates life skills!

"Is that another life skill? I'm done with life skills. How many life skills do we have to do?"

Banking. Phone calls. Groceries. We had battled them all, sometimes winning, sometimes trying again. And don't forget about ordering pizza online...

"Whoa! $200 of pepperoni pizzas? That's twenty pizzas. Do you really think you need that many?" I asked, grabbing the mouse out of his hand and clicking on "Clear Shopping Cart."

"I'm sorry. The computer was slow!"

Life skills. He needs them. I need them. All those years working in the emergency room have not prepared me for the daily crises of life with autism. Some days I think I'd gladly manage a cardiac arrest over the meltdown caused by a fly in the house. At least in the ER we have equipment, proven strategies, and teamwork. I have no equipment for the predictably unpredictable responses of autism. Proven strategies fail me in the downward spiral of anxiety produced by that nemesis of daily life: change. The better half of my team has to work for a living.

I need life skills: patience, perseverance, and perspective.

Patience, to live graciously in my son's challenging world, where love still wins more battles than strategies do.

Perseverance, to know with confidence that my efforts are not in vain.

Perspective, to celebrate the progress, thankful for all that he can do.

Life skills. How many do I have to learn?

Maybe just one more.

A good sense of humor.

~Carol Schmidt

Womb Pact

I know God will not give me anything I can't handle.
I just wish that he didn't trust me so much.
~Mother Teresa

t's a sunny April day as I sit in the overstuffed preschool conference room for Carter's case conference. I had finished Spencer's conference the week before and I had learned he was a bright boy ("scary smart"), had great teacher-pleasing skills and was making some progress in social skills and communication with other kids. He was a good listener; we just needed a way to help him find his voice so he could communicate with us.

So now I'm about to find out how his twin brother, Carter, is doing. Sitting around the table with me is his occupational therapist, the school nurse, the coordinator and his preschool teacher, Marje Snow.

I love Mrs. Snow. She's a wealth of knowledge and has this easy-going way about her that just makes you feel comfortable and safe discussing anything about your child.

The conference begins with a review of his goals for the year and the progress he has made. He, too, is a smart boy with a penchant for the alphabet and all things space and music. He flows fairly easily through the routine of the day. He is a loving child.

"He does tend to wander, though," adds Mrs. Snow.

My head pops up from the report. "What do you mean?"

"Oh, we've just had a couple of instances where he was gone from the room. That's why we have the child's gate at the door now."

I had seen the gate on the door for quite a while but had no idea it was due to my son's love of adventure.

"You mean, like, escape? Where did he go? How far did he get?" I ask.

"One time he got to the front office, another time he got to Spencer's room."

At the opposite end of the building. "Wow," is about all I can muster. I had no idea he was escaping and wish I had been told.

Mental Note: Talk to Carter about this.

"And we think he is capable of doing more than he is," continues Mrs. Snow.

"How so?" I ask.

"Well, for instance, he gets his coat and then hands it to Mr. Mike to put it on for him. I know he could do that himself but Carter likes others to do things for him."

I flash-forward to Carter living in my basement at the age of forty yelling upstairs, "Ma, can you bring me another grilled cheese and a glass of milk?" as *The Wiggles* play in the background.

I nod my head in agreement. "Of course. I'm sure I've been lax in teaching him or making him do these things at home. You know, sometimes it's just easier and faster to do them yourself... trying to get all the kids out the door on time. It's just us not making him do it. But I'll make him. I'll start teaching him to be more independent. Absolutely." (Because I am a good parent. And if I admit my faults enough perhaps I'll still be seen as a good parent. So let me just accept the responsibility for him and move on.)

She assures me she understands, but somehow I still feel like I failed Carter in his transition from toddler to preschooler.

"And probably the one thing we struggle with the most is his receptive language," says Mrs. Snow. "He doesn't process requests as quickly as others. He doesn't process two-step requests."

I look up again.

"The other night I asked him to take a bowl from the family room and put it in the kitchen sink. He took it to the table," I explain.

"I told him to take it to the sink and he took it to the island.

Again, I said the sink and he put it on the stove. Finally after the fourth time he took it to the sink. Is that what you mean?"

"Yes, exactly."

Mental Note: Tell his dad that it isn't a matter of Carter not listening to us. He truly doesn't understand what we are asking of him.

"So Carter communicates with us fairly well, he just doesn't always receive what we're saying," continues Mrs. Snow. "We need to…"

"Wait. He communicates okay but has a hard time understanding what we're saying, right?" I ask.

"Yes."

"And Spencer can understand everything we say but can't communicate with us," I continue.

"Well, from what I know of Spencer…" says Mrs. Snow.

"My boys… are the exact opposite… on the spectrum," I say with trepidation. "Carter can talk but doesn't understand what we're saying, while Spence can't say a word but understands everything. I have the entire spectrum! My boys are the spectrum."

The people at the table just look at me with raised eyebrows and Mrs. Snow nods at me with an "I-think-I-have-a-parent-about-to-lose-it" smile.

I continue with the meeting and making plans for next year, but in my head I keep repeating, "I have the entire spectrum. We don't get a break. We have the whole, entire spectrum."

Later that night as I watch the boys play together, I can't help but wonder how this happened. How could one boy communicate and the other not? How can one understand perfectly while the other struggles?

Knowing my boys and how mischievous they are, this is how I think it went down in the womb:

Baby A: "Hey, Baby B, wanna have some fun with the mother ship?"

Baby B: "Sure, what ya got in mind?"

Baby A: "How about if you talk, but don't listen to anything she has to say. And I'll listen but I won't talk. It'll be a riot!"

Baby B: "I LOVE it! Let's do it. Now, move your butt so I can get some sleep."

And so while I rested and nourished them with apple slices and peanut butter, they were eagerly plotting my motherly demise.

Mother: 0; Boys: 2.

~Sharon L. Martin

It Is, Because I Said So

Take rest; a field that has rested gives a bountiful crop.
~Ovid

n late June, we decamped. My husband, our typical ten-year-old, Aidan, and I left our comfortable, familiar home to spend a week in lovely Chestertown, Maryland. We had signed up our thirteen-year-old son, Conor, for his first, real sleep-away adventure at a five-day camp on the eastern shore of Maryland designed for individuals with special needs. (In addition to autism, Conor has Tourette syndrome.)

Actually Conor's first sleep-away adventure had been the summer before, a five-month stay at an inpatient behavioral unit designed to help my son control his out-of-control tantrums. It's sad and uncomfortable (and more than a little embarrassing) to admit, but it's important to know so you can understand how BIG a deal this camp adventure was... for all of us.

That year, Conor had been hospitalized twice, for brief periods, but the long-term inpatient unit was an intensive and necessary intervention. Thankfully, his behavior and medical team slowly got the tantrums under control, enough so that my husband and I were willing to try sleep-away camp eight months after he was discharged.

(My husband thought I was crazy to try. I blame the wine.)

We rented a beautiful waterfront home about ten miles away from the camp so that we could check in every day and make sure he had his sweet potato and his complex behavior protocol followed and take him on his earned community outings and blah-dy blah blah.

You know, all those things we helicopter parents do. My husband and I, we can hover like nobody's business.

I spent so much time preparing for camp, and then supporting him at camp, that I neglected some things on the home front. Little things like bills and taxes and birthday gifts. And my hair. My God, my hair was a complete and utter disaster. I looked like a street woman pushing her cart. (Except my cart-pushing was usually in Target and not downtown. But still.)

In any case, at the end of four days, we declared sleep-away camp a success. (If we say it, it must be so.)

My husband, Aidan and I got some time off, a much needed respite. It was enough of a break that I was able to read two really terrible books and get a migraine from too much sleep. Honestly, I think reading sentences like "Their bond was as strong as titanium, sheathed in diamonds" contributed to the migraine. (I know, really. I shudder to think of it, even now.)

At camp, Conor made a friend, a boy who loved shooting hoops in the searing 100-degree heat as much as he did. A boy who didn't mind that Conor tackled him during a short-lived game of catch with a football. A boy who talked Conor's ear off and hugged him in the swimming pool and held his hand as they wandered around.

We briefly adopted his one-on-one aide, as we often do with the good ones, an affable chap from Plymouth, England, just out of university. (He's British, so I can say "affable" and "chap" and "university." So awesome.) We were so smitten with Ted, we had him over to the rental house on Friday and taught him how to pick Maryland blue crabs steamed with Old Bay. Followed, of course, by a cold beer. (It should have been warm, though, shouldn't it have? His being British and all?)

It was Ted's first taste of blue crab. "Brilliant," he said. "Delicious." (See? He's a keeper.)

Conor rode a horse during a therapeutic session at a local farm. He looked right at home, tucked up in the saddle. Poor Ted stepped in a pile of horse poop and spent some of the session trying to regain his dignity.

Don't judge. It happens. Everybody poops. Let's move on, then, shall we?

While Conor was busy sitting atop a pooping horse, my typical ten-year-old son (in typical ten-year-old boy fashion) wanted to do nothing but fish. He fished from the dock and he fished from the rocks and he fished some more. (He took a break one morning to play golf with his dad and his grandparents. Then he came back and fished.)

So… Conor made a friend. He had a great one-on-one aide. He rode a pooping horse and shot hoops. He did arts and crafts, navigated a ropes course complete with zip line, and swam in the pool. He slept through the night and the rest of the family got some R&R. We fished, I read, they golfed, I shopped. We ate too much, didn't drink nearly enough, and we all survived.

Oh, he did have one tantrum at camp. But not until the second to last day. Since he came home only one night early, I deem sleep-away camp a success.

It is, because I said so.

~Alisa Rock

**Chapter
6**

Raising
Kids on the
Spectrum

School

The Most Popular Girl

Friendship isn't a big thing—it's a million little things.
~Author Unknown

W e were late for school again. It happens more than I care to admit. I tell myself that most parents, even single ones like me, don't have to wake an autistic child who is exhausted from a grueling forty-hour-per-week therapy schedule and doesn't want to be touched. They don't have to explain in sign language and pictures why her favorite sundress is inappropriate in winter, wrestle her into velour leggings that won't assault her overtaxed sensory system (again, without touching), pack a nut-, dairy-, preservative-, and gluten-free lunch, and calm her after a meltdown (or two). They don't administer a witch's brew of supplements that make the cod liver oil chaser seem downright delicious. And they definitely don't drive to another school district in hellish rush-hour traffic in a minivan that disgorges cereal, broken toys, and mangled bits of crayon whenever the sliding doors open. But I know this is an excuse.

I should have gotten up earlier, guzzled espresso, and omitted my shower (again).

I'm fairly certain sending Katie to school in her blue cupcake pajamas would be frowned upon, even in a special-needs classroom.

Plus it was raining, which meant more traffic and a guaranteed bad-hair day.

I hustled Katie through the half-empty parking lot, mentally running through the day's schedule: work meetings, deadlines, another lengthy round trip to the school, paperwork, grocery shopping, afternoon therapy. A group of kids straggled to the front of the school just as the sun broke through brooding clouds. They were probably first graders and clearly going on a field trip. Their excited voices mingled with the rainbow-hued drizzle.

Like most parents, I'd taken it for granted that friends and conversation would fill my daughter's life. But friends and conversation don't come easily to an autistic eight-year-old. For Katie, they hadn't come yet, but on that morning, listening to the children's laughter, I had (almost) stopped fearing they would never come at all.

Katie splashed through puddles and commented on her pink leopard-spotted rain boots as if I wasn't there. We approached the covered entry and a child shouted, "Hey, look. That's Katie." Out of the corner of my eye, I saw a cluster of children turn. "Hi, Katie," they yelled across the parking lot, waving frantically.

I looked down and met my daughter's stormy blue-grey eyes. "Are you making friends?" A note of surprise colored my voice. She smiled shyly as the kids continued to wave. "What do you say?"

"Hi," she said and waved at them with loose-limbed grace.

Turning away, she fiddled with her raincoat as if it were no big deal—except it was. If those children had continued to talk and ignored Katie as we walked past, no one would have thought twice, least of all me. The school and its teachers promoted tolerance, but still, those children made the effort. It would take that, plus hard work and a miracle, for Katie to make a true friend.

A few weeks later, I picked Katie up from school. The campus swirled with chaos and chatter. Crowds used to push Katie past her limits, but she had learned to tolerate and even enjoy them on days when the mood bubbled over with excitement.

A girl with long silky hair and a brilliant smile ran up.

"Hi, Katie," she said.

Katie grinned and studied the clouds, her caramel curls glinting in the sun.

"Katie," I said. "What do you say?"

She glanced at the girl, flapping her hands like a quail struggling for flight. "Hi, Katie." When she can't recall names—a common occurrence—her name serves as placeholder.

"Try again." I looked at the girl, who beamed up at me, clearly unfazed by Katie's response. "What's your name?"

"I'm London," she said, looking at Katie. "Lon... don."

The name suited her. She oozed big-city sophistication.

I said hi, and Katie echoed my response. Her gaze darted from me to London, then away.

London smiled. "I'm friends with Katie. I sit with her every day at recess." She paused but I was too stunned to speak. "Well, I sit with her in the lunch room. I would sit with her at recess but Katie doesn't sit much."

"No," I managed to laugh. "She doesn't."

How was it possible that this gorgeous, chatty girl was friends with my quirky, quiet daughter? London had "most popular" written all over her. She could play with anyone she wanted at recess. Why Katie? It pained me to think it, but why Katie?

"Katie runs really fast and she climbs the monkey bars with the boys." London's face filled with awe.

"You could climb them too."

"No," she said. "Not with the boys. I just watch Katie. She's really good."

It saddened me that a first grader considered certain activities limited to boys. Did it make me happy or sad that Katie would never understand these subtle, unwritten rules? I wasn't sure.

"I can climb," Katie said. She did a little dance and burst into song: "The itty bitty pider climbed up the water pout...."

London laughed. "She's funny too."

I nodded. It was true. Katie could crack you up if you took the time to listen. The problem is most people view Katie's autism as a deficit rather than a difference. But this extraordinary seven-year-old saw my child for who she was and embraced her.

"Hey London, if Katie talked more, I know she'd say she likes sitting with you at lunch."

She flipped her blond hair and shrugged.

London had never been shunned by her cousins or kids at the park. Her mother had never watched her stand by the swings, silent and ignored. Tears pooled behind my eyes. "It means a lot to me, and I'm sure it does to Katie too. So thank you."

I fought the urge to hug her. I adored this girl, so beautiful for reasons that had nothing to do with appearance.

"I like her," she said, as if that was the only reason that mattered.

My lip trembled. I worried she'd think I was strange—a parent, crying at school. I took a deep breath and told her we needed to go. I didn't tell her I had just enough time to make Katie's afternoon therapy session, assuming I encountered no traffic.

London smiled. "Okay. Bye, Katie."

Katie assembled her response. "Bye, Li... bye, London." She grinned, pleased with herself, and the three of us shared a round of high fives.

I cried on the drive home.

My daughter had a friend.

I never thought I'd view that statement as something close to miraculous, but autism changed me. I no longer take friends—mine or my daughter's—for granted.

I eased off the highway—on time for once—and silently thanked London, as well as her parents, her family, her teacher, her school. Yes, the years of hard work were finally paying off, but the miracle was London.

Thank you, thank you, thank you.

My smart, stubborn, beautiful, barely verbal, autistic daughter had a friend.

~Cynthia J. Patton

Yes or No?

I can remember the frustration of not being able to talk. I knew what I wanted to say, but I could not get the words out, so I would just scream.
~Temple Grandin

held the most beautiful list in my hands. Blinking in disbelief, I stared down at what I had just been given. I couldn't take my eyes off that glorious list.

That morning had brought me bright and early to the office of our older son's new speech therapist at school. It was his first year working with her, although at ten years old and with very little spoken language, he was no stranger to speech therapy.

We had seen countless therapists since our journey with autism began eight years earlier. In the early days, they were like part of our family, entering our home each morning, sometimes before the frost had even cleared from the windshields of our cars. They worked in shifts throughout the day, saying goodbye late in the afternoon, knowing that the next morning we would start the routine once more.

Over those years, we shared in one another's celebrations and setbacks, happiness and heartbreak—all spread out among the countless hours of therapy, therapy which I thought was going to cure our son of autism within a few short years.

When our son aged out of the early intervention system at five and started school away from my constant watch, I hoped that some kind soul would find him on her roster, someone who believed in his future the way I did. Certainly, tens of thousands of autism parents out there had the same wish.

No longer in the driver's seat of his daily education, I sat more on the sidelines, watching therapists come and go. I had no idea who they really were, for that matter, or if they would bother to go the extra mile for our son.

Early that morning, I sat down across from this year's new therapist knowing very little but hoping for everything.

"You know," she said, "your son really has a great sense of humor. He's very sarcastic."

Her insight caught me off guard.

And then, she placed before me a list of questions she had asked him during their morning session the day before, all phrased so that they could be answered with a simple "yes" or "no" by pointing at a picture.

"Do fish fly?"

"Are you patient?"

"Did you go to the mall last night?"

"Did you just get a haircut?"

These questions seemed so simple and yet they weren't simple at all. They were nothing short of a breakthrough!

For the first time, a method of communication had reached him. She had actually succeeded in establishing two-way communication with him on a level that nobody else had. During her time spent with him, she had somehow managed to tap into our son's thoughts!

Could this really be true?

It had been a decade — ten long years spent nurturing this special child. We had always wondered when we might be able to catch a glimpse of his thoughts.

I stared down at the answers to these questions listed on the page before me. They were answers that came from our son. He did know things — lots and lots of things! He was in there... yet trapped.

Our meeting came to an end, and I walked out of the building in a daze. I fumbled my way to my car, got in... and I cried.

I cried for our son who had learned to live life alone with his thoughts.

In the days that followed, I would wait with anticipation for the notes to come home from the therapist in his backpack after school. Our child—the one I gave a book of nursery rhymes to the last holiday—was answering reading comprehension questions on checking accounts, tsunamis and yellow fever. He knew the definitions of words such as "scowl," "illegal," "bashful" and "frail."

How did this happen without my knowing? Thank goodness that it happened in spite of me.

One afternoon, fresh from greeting him at his bus, I pulled the latest update from his backpack while he ran upstairs to decompress, and I decided that I just couldn't resist the urge any longer. I simply had to try this for myself! Quickly fashioning my own crude "yes" and "no" cards, I made my way to his room.

My heart was racing. It seemed as though we had traveled this road for a lifetime. Sleepless nights, GI problems, ABA, DIR, GFCF, Tomatis, DAN! doctors, homeopaths, colonoscopies, endoscopies, therapy, therapy and more therapy. It had all driven me to the point of insanity and back.

How did my son feel about it?

I reached for the doorknob to his bedroom with a lifetime of questions to ask him. Inside his room, I found him sitting on the floor with his favorite toy, a retired Dirt Devil upright vacuum. He looked at me, immediately seeing the "yes" and "no" cards in my hand.

"All done," he said.

He was in no mood. Those cards were just like schoolwork, and he was home. Home was not school.

"I won't take long," I told him.

He didn't want me there. He had been with people all day, and he needed a break. I had to respect that. A lifetime of questions would have to wait.

"I promise, I'll only ask one question," I said.

He looked at me, awaiting his fate, and for a brief moment, I paused. Looking into the eyes of our son, our partner in the war of our lives, I became aware of the little boy. He was a magnificent boy, one who deserved a childhood free from the emotional burden that his autism sometimes brought.

Holding the "yes" and "no" cards in front of him, I looked him in the eyes and simply asked, "Are you happy?"

Without hesitation, he lifted his right hand and pointed to the card that read, "Yes."

I choked back my tears of joy as I told him that I loved him, certain that I would always remember the method of communication that allowed me to first talk to my child. There are simply no words to express the feeling a mom has when, for the first time, her child is actually able to tell her that he is happy.

On that day, I caught a glimpse into the mind of our ten-year-old son, whose thoughts have been all but silenced by autism his entire life. And, on that day, I saw hope.

~Amy McMunn Schindler

He's Not Even Wrong

The problem with pounding a square peg into a round hole is not that the hammering is hard work. It's that you're destroying the peg.
~Paul Collins

I am always apprehensive about parent-teacher conferences. My eight-year-old son, Jack, is autistic but he goes to school in a mainstream inclusion third-grade classroom and even though I always hear at these conferences that he is very smart, that he is "making sufficient progress to meet goals," I am always waiting for the other shoe to drop. I never really hear anything that surprises me, but I am still anxious walking into those meetings.

Last fall's conference was different. I had noticed Jack struggling more and more. I had started to wonder if an inclusion classroom was the best setting for him. I started to see his autism-specific deficits bumping up against the curriculum, and I started to see the social divide between Jack and his peers widening.

Third grade is where it starts getting harder for Jack to slide by just because he's bright, his teacher told me. Then she blew my mind. She showed me some examples of his work and went through his answers. She showed me one worksheet and said, "I didn't know how to grade this. It's not even wrong, but it's not right."

I gasped when she said those words, when she said, "not even wrong." That is the name of one of my favorite books on autism, by Paul Collins.

That phrase—Not Even Wrong—refers to what was originally

a derogatory way of dismissing someone's answer to a problem. It's not right, it's not wrong, but the solver's frame of reference is so far off base that it is not even wrong. It perfectly describes autism and it perfectly describes Jack.

It also perfectly describes what I want for my kid—a place, an existence, where it is okay for him to be not even wrong. Because I love the way Jack's brain works. I love the way autism has given him a unique perspective that lets him come up with some of the most amazing things. I adore his not even wrongness. I want him to find a way of life where starting from a fundamentally different point of view is an asset to him and where he can be valued for that.

In his book, Collins wrote, "Autists are the ultimate square pegs, and the problem with pounding a square peg into a round hole is not that the hammering is hard work. It's that you're destroying the peg."

I want to help find more square holes and I am trying to get to the round holes and make them at least trapezoidal before my kids and your kids get hammered into them. I want to spread awareness of both autistic kids and autistic adults. I want this to be a world where it is okay to be a square peg without having to pretend to be round.

I don't want to change Jack. I want to change the world.

A few weeks before my conference, I started trying to change the world by changing Jack's class. I went in, armed with nine pages of notes, and I told Jack's classmates about autism.

I told them how each one of them is different and how they can be a friend to Jack and other kids with autism. I told them to go forth and be different themselves, and to show other kids that it is okay to be different. I listened to them at the end of my talk when they told me, "There is a kid on my soccer team with autism," and "I have an uncle who doesn't talk," and I knew that some of them were getting it.

Not all of those kids are going to make it. They will not all stand up for the different kids and adults that they run across in their lives. But some of them will. And some of them, even if they don't act on it now, just might remember learning about Jack and autism later in life when they come across someone who acts different. And they might help that square peg find a hole that isn't round.

At Jack's conference, his teacher told me the story of a short passage that Jack had to write, which would get a grade of zero to three points. His original sentence earned him a zero. After a long process of reading his passage to the class, being prompted for more, and adding information, Jack finally earned his three.

The teacher has a Hall of Fame wall where passages that are really, really good and earn threes get hung up. Jack's passage was undoubtedly not up to the standards of what was already posted there. But Jack got some tape and he took his paper, on which he'd crossed out "0" and written "3," and he put it up there all by himself. He knew that he had worked hard and that, for him, his work was Hall of Fame worthy. And the teacher made a square hole for him and let it stay.

The world is slow to change. We have been hammering square pegs into round holes for so long that it takes a huge leap to put down the hammers. I'm hopeful that I got to some of those kids before they even pick up the hammers. And I hope that some of those kids told their parents. And I hope that some of you read this and tell your kids. And I hope that we, all of us together, CAN change the world.

~Jean Winegardner

59

Seeing Eye to I

Little stones that are pelted into the lake of consciousness
should not throw the whole lake into commotion.
~Paramahansa Yogananda

Casey is reliably emphatic. Arm swung out, shirt turned around backwards, he gushes with frustration about Hat Day. "Why is your Polo shirt backwards?" I ask. Casey throws his arm forward with each syllable, "They didn't tell me it was Hat Day at school! I had to do SOMETHING!" He's not quite angry. A subtle hint of pride trails behind him as he weaves into the kitchen, Polo shirt still backwards, buttons open. I smile.

The following autumn, Casey is emphatic when returning home from his first day of school. In the front entryway he leans his small body forward, letting his mass of untrimmed sandy blond hair fall into his eyes. "My teacher doesn't even look at me when she's talking." Casey is rigid, angry, engrossed in rule recitation. The importance of maintaining eye contact has been drilled into him since he received the diagnosis of Asperger's six years ago. Back then, he sat fixated on airplane models for hours, noting rudders and flaps and parts called ailerons (he taught me this word). Now, he spends hours planning his future airline: the equipment, the amenities, the brilliant name Everywhere Airlines.

"She doesn't look at you at all?"

"No!" Now both of Casey's arms are thrown out, illustrating the size of the problem. "She looks away! She doesn't even look at me!"

When he was younger, Casey conversed with walls, floors, geometric forms—anything but the person standing in front of him. His body twisted and turned mid-sentence, and words smashed together in an avalanche of information. Eye contact was only one social hurdle. Those days were square one, early intervention, an introduction to life in the mainstream.

It's difficult to believe that Casey's teacher has poor eye contact. She's an eye contact instigator, a specializer in the spectrum, and a maven in the mainstream. She knows the value of eye contact.

Yet Casey comes home again, exasperated, dramatic, wanting to throw his backpack down but knowing full well that it would break a rule of decorum. He's good with rules. He thrives on them. But he's at an age when he realizes some rules are actually about personal boundaries, not laws. Therefore he takes the frustration out on himself; he curls up in a fetal ball on the corner of the couch and moans. Practice tells me to wait until he's down to a simmer. When he turns and uncoils, I can ask him questions subtly, carefully.

The moans cease. He uncoils.

"How was your second day of fourth grade?"

"She did it again!" The words spring out, and Casey recoils into his ball. His shaggy hair is slick with sweat, glued to his temple. Every other year Casey's hair is buzz-cut-short and easy to manage. This year he actually notices how the other boys are growing their hair out. The social worker calls this a huge step for Casey. "He's trying to fit in," she tells me. What I value about Casey is that he doesn't. Yet he's growing up, and I need to give him a little space. But not right now.

"What happened?" My hand presses firmly against Casey's back. The deep pressure might calm him. In the early days, I administered soothing deep pressure with a plastic therapy brush and joint compressions. He wiggles to reject the pressure. The hand doesn't work.

"She did it again!" A pillow on the couch muffles his voice.

"She-won't-look-at-me-when-she's-talk-ing!" Casey's words are a string of angry syllables. I'm not sure that I hear him correctly. This is precisely the reason Casey is still receiving speech therapy. His mouth can't match the pace of his ideas. The words come out in a soup of vowels and accents and consonants. If you break it apart, you hear the intelligence—the professor-like words such as "improbable" and "continuity" and "indeterminate." As a jumble, he simply sounds his age or younger.

"She won't look at you when you talk?" I ask. Casey groans in response and pulls his knees tighter to his chest. "Are you absolutely sure about this?" Casey doesn't respond. It's the beginning of the year with a new teacher—a teacher with whom I will undoubtedly have numerous interactions. Contacting her so soon seems, well, too soon. But Casey isn't giving me much to go on.

The school calls me a day later. It's about administration, not behavior. There are forms to be signed, congenial smiles to be exchanged, and other new-school-year rites of passage. At the school, I'm thinking about forms—not eye contact—when a hand is extended. The knobby, arthritic hand belongs to a pear-shaped woman in her early 60s. Her hair is sprayed up and out like a yellow spun sugar.

"I'm your son's teacher," the woman smiles. Her eyes are too big for a human head—triple magnified by her double thick glasses. And there's something else about those eyes. The alignment? The focus? Her spun sugar head is directed right towards me, but those eyes are not.

"Did he enjoy his first day?" Her magnificent smile begs for affirmation.

"Historically his first week or so of school is a little rough, but I'm feeling good about this year!"

"So nice to hear!" She nods but one iris can't keep up with the gesture and slides towards the bridge of her nose.

Casey says his third day is fine aside from his juice flooding his lunchbox and rendering his sandwich strategically damp and unfit for his finicky consumption. The details are both banal and magnificent. He describes the crust of his sandwich bread as a melting fortress's wall. Individual fissures in the bread are explained in painstaking detail. "A circle in the crust expanded to a large oval—like a swimming pool—and the juice drained through it making a tsunami over the peanut butter…" Casey makes an exquisite explanation of something otherwise trifling. But he does this many times a day. I interrupt.

"Casey, I met your teacher today."

"Did she look at you?" Casey's body goes rigid.

"Hon, she has a condition. One of her eyes doesn't work like it's supposed to, so sometimes it seems like she's looking elsewhere. But really, she's trying very hard to make good eye contact." Casey mulls it over.

"Oh," he's still thinking, but not quite as hard as before, "…that's too bad. It's kind of like a disease, right?"

"Right."

At that the topic is over—buried. Casey grabs one of his model airplanes—a McDonnell Douglas MD-80 to be precise. Casey talks to himself but knows I'm within earshot. "I think my airline will have special goggles for pilots with crooked eyes." His emphatic arm springs out in jubilation. "That way anyone can be a pilot!"

"That's a great idea!" I tell him. And it is.

~Julie Casper Roth

60

The Storm Before the Calm

There is no greater loan than a sympathetic ear.
~Frank Tyger

A h, summer. The brief hiatus when I can finally exhale, temporarily released from the rigorous demands of the school year, and allow myself a mental respite before tackling the strategies for the coming year.

Grade four was bittersweet for my son. The first term was deceptively uneventful. I was ecstatic, believing we had this autism thing licked. Surely he was learning to integrate, molding his quirks to fit unobtrusively within acceptable social parameters. Maybe he was maturing, grasping the fundamentals of self-regulation and outgrowing the tantrums just as he was outgrowing his clothing. It could happen, right?

Apparently not, as it turned out. By the second term, it was clear that we needed help. There had been some social skills classes and specialists sitting in on the classroom in years past. The result: general coping skills and strategies designed to help him fit in and follow the routines. But this despair, this volatile anger, was completely out of my league. Belatedly I realized that the only way to help him was to really understand what it was like to live in his skin. I began educating myself, amassing reference books, reading first-person accounts, attending autism caregiver workshops, listening to other parents' stories. A whole new world opened up for me: Simon's world.

Imagine an existence where everything you see, hear and feel is magnified to an almost painful intensity. I've seen Simon clap his hands over his ears often enough to figure out that he finds sudden noises and loud crowds intolerable. I've noticed that securing his attention when his focus is elsewhere is a constant challenge. But where I had thought that he was incapable of hearing me amidst background noise, I was surprised to learn instead that he, in fact, heard everything. Every word uttered, every creak in the floorboards, every car speeding by outside, every drip of water in the sink. He wasn't shutting out my voice so much as absorbing everything, sorting through it and trying to integrate it in a way that his brain could make sense of it all. From a very young age, he had to learn how to process multiple simultaneous auditory, visual and physical stimuli, while other children were learning to walk and talk.

Imagine a world where you must live by arbitrary rules that make no sense to you or risk being ridiculed or ostracized. Imagine feeling like you are constantly walking on eggshells, afraid of offending someone or embarrassing yourself without really knowing why. Each unfamiliar situation would be akin to negotiating a minefield. His anxious tears when confronting changes to routine or unanticipated events make so much sense to me now.

Imagine not being able to escape the smell of vegetables being chopped in the next room. Gagging because the neckline of your shirt grazed against your throat. Struggling to adequately communicate how you feel or what you're thinking. Having every sense heightened and your limits of tolerance tested relentlessly, and in the minutest of ways. Now imagine not being on edge or frustrated from dealing with all of these encumbrances for most of your waking hours. Personally, I can't. All things considered, I am amazed at Simon's usual calm demeanor. His momentary blips of panic or anger now seem completely justified to me, and I'm in awe of the inner strength he must possess in order to function day-to-day with the kind of challenges the rest of us will never truly understand.

The best part about my self-education is that Simon and I started reading about autism together and discussing his own perspective. I learned that he recorded visual memories the way we store images on film, and could rewind and scan this cerebral footage for precise and efficient retrieval. This explained his photographic memory and the way, when recalling something in the distant past, he would momentarily stop and stare intently into space. (I swear I can hear the wheels whirring as he scans his mental recordings.) He also described how he can devise and manipulate objects in his mind in three dimensions, much like a sophisticated imaging software program. This is how he has been able, since preschool, to create intricate 3D models crafted out of a single, uncut sheet of paper, formed meticulously into the vehicle he had envisioned long before making the first fold.

As it turned out, Simon's stormy end to the school year resulted in many steps forward. In finally addressing his autism openly, he discovered that there were others who understood how it felt to be like him. And it was a relief for me to know that I could rely on other, more experienced voices to provide him with answers and guidance. More importantly, I've been reminded of autism's dual nature. We are quick to label it an affliction, and equally quick to forget that it might also play a part in some of the characteristics we admire most. When I think of Simon, I think of his quick wit, his kind heart, his honesty, and his steadfast sense of honor. Whether these traits are due to autism or in spite of it, separate from it or enhanced by it, doesn't matter to me. What I do know is that autism is nothing more than one of the many shining facets of his personality. My son is a marvel to me, and I wouldn't change a single thing about him.

Right now, I am savoring the small triumphs of the past few months. This is the short-lived peace between the end of a school year and the start of another. This is the calm, his safe haven. I'd like to think that the worst of the storms are behind us. But the truth is that finding the balance between having to curb his natural impulses to meet social expectations, and living a life that is true to who he is, will be an ongoing, perhaps even lifelong, undertaking. For now, armed with a better understanding of the roots of his troubles, I feel hopeful that we will find better coping strategies and ultimately, a place in this world where he can confidently, unapologetically, be his true self. Storms and all.

~Jennifer Doelle Young

Letter to My Child's First Teacher

The best teachers teach from the heart, not from the book.
~Author Unknown

Two years ago, my husband and I took our daughter school-supply shopping for the first time. Armed with our list, we searched for the requisite items, allowing her to pick out the colors and designs. We were nervous about her first day. I was emotional, wavering between excitement and pride, and fear of putting my precious little girl into someone else's hands. We talked it up to her and made a big deal out of it, allowing her to choose a special first-day outfit and hair clips. Then we walked her into her classroom, helped her find her cubby and seat, kissed her goodbye, and left. I teared up as I left, like many mothers—but knew in my heart all would be well. And at the end of her day, we delighted in hearing from her about each and every new experience.

Last night, we made preparations again, this time for her little brother's first day of school. We went to the store to buy school supplies. Only, this time, we picked them out ourselves. My son, mostly nonverbal and autistic, doesn't have an opinion about his lunchbox. He doesn't know his colors yet, nor does he express a preference. He doesn't even understand that he is going to school today. This experience of the first day of school is altogether different for us. And at the end of his first day, he will not tell us what he thought or how he felt.

In a couple of hours, we will—supplies in hand—walk him into a very big building. In it will be hundreds of children who can follow directions, feed themselves with a spoon, use the toilet, and can—if frightened or in pain—express their needs. My son cannot. Yet I will be placing his tiny, almost three-year-old hand into someone else's—someone who does not yet know and love him. Someone who will not be able to understand the few words he has and the peculiar ways he attempts to communicate. Someone who will not know how to soothe him when he inevitably gets lost in confusion and frustration. I cannot begin to convey the terror I am feeling right now. He is so little and helpless. And it is such a very big bad world out there.

I met you last week at his IEP. I tried to use every instinct I had as a teacher to get a feel for you. My instincts tell me I made the right choice. You weren't assigned to him by chance. Teachers know all about homework, and I did mine. Yes, I shamelessly queried every connection I have made in my years in the school system to find just the right classroom for him. You are rumored to be the best. I can tell you that some mighty fine people whom I like and respect think very highly of you.

Having done that, I now have to step back and let you do your job. I have to trust in your experience and love for special little ones like mine. Let me assure you that, though I feel confident in my choice of you as a teacher, this is the hardest thing I've ever had to do. For, somewhere in your classroom, there is a cubby with the name of the little boy who encompasses my entire world.

And though I am trying, there really are no words.

As a teacher, I know what you need from me. I have been where you are. And I want you to know I plan to support you. I will take into consideration that you are a person—not a saint. I know all too well how bone-tired you can be at the end of the day. How hard it is for you to see child neglect and parent apathy. How critical the powers that be in education really are. I know how all of your planning time is stolen for stupid meetings and unhelpful consultants.

So, here is my pledge to you. I am not going to make your life a living hell over the little things. You are allowed to be sick, sometimes you will have to come up with things on the fly, have your head turned during a minor bump on the head, and even forget a note home or phone call. You aren't superhuman. I pledge to not expect perfection from you.

In return for this, I would like something from you. I would like you to remember that this little boy is mine. I would like you to remember—when he is being difficult—that he cannot speak for himself, cannot share his fears, his desire for mommy and daddy, and his confusion over the new expectations placed upon him. I would like you to remember how fragile and defenseless he is while learning how to navigate this world. I would like for you to grow to love him for the sweet, loving little boy who cuddles with me and holds my hand each night. I know that, having chosen to do what you do, you already know these things and have already made that commitment. But, please—on the most difficult days that all teachers have—remember you are holding my world in your hands.

Thank you for your sacrifice. For though we both know the rewards of teaching are many, I know the time, dedication, and expense you put into it—for little pay and a great deal of hassle. May you be blessed with patience, love, determination, optimism, realism, and the stamina that I know is required to do what you do well. If you need anything at all, please pick up the phone and call. For I know for certain that, in this sacred trust, I am calling on you already.

~Leigh Merryday

Let Me Tell You About Jake

What a teacher writes on the blackboard of life can never be erased.
~Author Unknown

Jake walked into my kindergarten classroom with a *Wall Street Journal* and a *Chicago Tribune* sports section tucked into his backpack. His parents led him to his seat. He sat down and pulled out the newspapers and began to read, oblivious to the other children playing with a variety of toys at the table. I'm not sure who was more nervous, Jake or me, his teacher.

Jake was not only able to read and understand the newspaper, but he had a terrific grasp of statistics. Although I don't remember him participating in physical sports during his school years, he would often come to class after a weekend with the statistics of the players of the teams he supported. As he relayed play-by-play descriptions of a game, I wondered if he would have a future career as a sportscaster.

It was an interesting and challenging year for Jake, my assistant, his family and me. As a teacher, I have always felt that the classroom should be a community that functioned like a family and every member was important.

Jake was not the first child I had in my classroom with Asperger syndrome. There were two things that I felt I could safely assume. First, each child had a very special gift of in-depth knowledge in a subject area well beyond grade level. The second was that the child with Asperger's that I had the year before was completely different from the present year's child, who came in with a different knowledge base and a different set of behaviors.

With Jake, I noticed that he would rarely interact or communicate with the other children. Much of the curriculum was set up so that students would move to different tables throughout the day, where they would be taught various subject areas in small groups. Jake found it very difficult to transition from place to place, to stop one activity and begin another. My assistant was integral to guiding him throughout the daily routine.

Even when the class sat in rows on the floor during story and calendar activities, Jake seemed isolated. During free play and on the playground, Jake enjoyed his own company.

Working with Jake required special strategies. Fortunately, communication between his parents and me was constant and we worked as a united team. We tried to encourage behaviors that would be consistent at home and school.

Jake was not always aware of what was happening around him. His safety was always my main concern, especially when he was outside of the classroom. Fortunately, his parents always volunteered to go on field trips, an older sister came to the classroom to take him to the bus at the end of the day, and the playground supervisors were on alert to notice where he was when he was outside.

When I think about that year, I believe the greatest breakthrough came one day when the children came to sit on the carpet. Jake dove into a row between two boys who usually sat together. Everyone was shocked as an eruption of movement and tussling occurred. The boys didn't want to separate and Jake couldn't understand why he couldn't just jump in where he wanted to be. It was, however, a joyous moment for me. Jake wanted to sit between these boys. He wanted to interact, but he didn't know how to communicate it.

Once Jake moved on to older grade levels I was not able to track his year-to-year progress. I was fortunate though, to have moments in time where our paths would cross.

I remember that when he was in fifth grade, many of the students were part of a parent-run basketball program. Although Jake did not have the coordination skills to play basketball, he had the ability to announce the "play-by-play" of the games. He announced students' names and followed their movement as well as their scores. Every time a player made a basket, Jake whooped with delight and his face radiated pure joy. Although he tried to stay within a script provided, he improvised a bit and made each game sound like a professional sports event. He also provided a "public service" announcement about the Parent-Teacher Organization's snack bar and safety tips upon leaving the school. How wonderful it was to see his awareness of what was taking place around him and his emotional response to the activity.

About two years later, I was invited to Jake's Bar Mitzvah. As I sat in my seat, tears rolled down my face as I listened to Jake share what it meant to him to reach this milestone. He very clearly articulated what it was like to know that he learned and communicated differently from others. It was among the most moving speeches I had ever heard and I learned that he had written it completely on his own.

A few weeks ago, I ran into Jake and his family at a community dinner. He is now seventeen and towers over me in height. It's always nice to run into former students, but I was particularly happy to see him and to know that he remembered me. His mother told me that they would not be staying for the planned program after dinner because they had to get ready for a special day. She asked Jake to tell me what was going to happen.

Jake said, "Tomorrow I am going to college! I'm going to major in Communications-Sports Broadcasting."

~Jean Ferratier

Field Day

Tears are the safety valve of the heart when too much pressure is laid on it.
~Albert Smith

T he parking lot is packed. As I drive around in circles trying to find a spot, I begin to wonder what my son's first Field Day will be like. It seems like all the other "special days" that typical parents look forward to with their typical children always turn out to be a nightmare for us.

Would it be like the Tea with Teacher Day when my son grabbed and ate his new classmates' cookies? Or like Picture Day when he ran uncontrollably and almost took out the photographer's entire backdrop display and equipment?

Miraculously, I find a parking space and as I get him out of the car, I try to get him excited about the field day festivities to come. "This is going to be so much fun! You'll get to watch a lot of running and I bet you'll even get a ribbon at the end!"

Since my six-year-old son is on the moderate to severe side of the spectrum and is currently nonverbal, I do this not knowing if he understands what in the world I am talking about.

On top of the ASD, he also has a rare genetic anomaly which affects all of his motor movement, so I have a tight grip on his little hand so that he doesn't fall flat when he trips. As we are walking and stumbling along in the crisp spring air, I can see the flags waving against the blue sky, the PA being set up, and a bunch of overly excited kids with their parents on the field.

"Oh, look at the flags blowing in the wind! Aren't they pretty? This is so exciting!"

I blather on with a smile plastered on my face, while my mind races with negative scenarios, imagining the sting as I watch kids skillfully run relays while my son is stimming on the sidelines. I keep the smile on my face and say, "Wow! We couldn't have asked for better weather!"

I leave him with his class, and move around the field to find an opening so I can see what is happening. I smile and nod at the other parents while they talk to me—"Kaitlin couldn't sleep last night she was so excited and she took forever deciding what to wear today!" and "Ryan started playing soccer and he is the fastest one on the team, so he should do well today!" Since I can't really relate to anything they are saying, I just smile and nod, smile and nod.

Another mom I don't recognize comes up and asks me which one is my child. I point out my sweet boy and she points out hers, who is another kindergartener but is in another class. As they start getting into their groups for competition, I notice her staring at my boy. She then turns to me and asks, "What's wrong with your son?"

My smile slips a little, and I want to reply, "What's wrong with you?" but I decide to take the high road and educate her on autism. She says, "Oh! Well he is such a cutie!" and walks away. At this point, the only thing I can see when I look over the grassy field at my son is what is "wrong" with him. He walks haphazardly, can't talk, and probably doesn't even know why he is here. I realize I must leave.

I rush past my neighbor, who has an older son in a wheelchair, and she takes one knowing look at me and says, "I'll take pictures for you." I race to my car, slam the door and start sobbing. People are taking quick, uncomfortable glances in my direction, but I don't care. Tears are running down my neck, but the pain is so heavy in my chest that I cannot breathe. Why me? Why my beautiful son?

Even though I cannot see through the tears, I put my key in the ignition, but something stops me from turning it. I stop and think about my son, my angel.

Yes, he walks haphazardly, but at one time we weren't sure he would walk at all. And yes, he cannot talk, but he tries with all his might to speak and is starting to say approximations of some words. I just know he is going to speak someday! And sure, he might not know why he is there, but how do I know that for certain? In fact, he probably does know and is wondering where his mother is so he can show off his new moves! This makes me giggle a little between the post-blubbering heaves. I dry off my face with my sleeves and blow my nose, thinking that there is nothing "wrong" with my son. He is his perfect little self and no one does it better. He deserves a ribbon every day.

I get out of my car and put one foot in front of the other to go back up to the field. I hear cheering and whistles and something else—a chant.

"Aidan! Aidan! Aidan!" Why are children chanting my son's name?

I walk up to see my son holding hands with his aide as he clumsily puts his feet in the tires on the obstacle course, with his entire class on the sidelines cheering him on. My son, with a ridiculously huge grin on his face, knows exactly what he is doing. The weight lifts, and this time I start sobbing tears of joy.

Whenever I start thinking about all that is "wrong" with my son, I just say "Field Day" out loud. I know that he may never come in first in a competition, but I know in the end that he will have touched the spirit of everyone he meets. And that is worth more than all of the ribbons in the world.

~Adrienne B. Paradis

Student Teacher

Attitude is a little thing that makes a big difference.
~Winston Churchill

When you hear the diagnosis Asperger syndrome, a million things go through your mind: Will my child be independent? How will he do in school? Will he be able to socialize with his peers?

David had been diagnosed not long before he started kindergarten and we had explained to him that just like every child, he had strengths and he had challenges. We let him know that he wasn't disabled, he was differently-abled, as was everyone in some way or another. He accepted that information, like all other information, and saved it for later use. The first day of school, David asked his teacher, "You mean the rest of these kids can't read?" He decided that this must be their challenge and he decided to help them work on it.

He became the teacher's youngest assistant, reading to small groups of children so that she and the adult teaching assistant could work with others. He could be a great help in class and the children didn't seem to mind that this very serious, very kind, very adult- acting child sometimes stimmed. For them, that was just David.

Of course, that's not to say that all his instruction was helpful. One day, I got a call from Barbara, his teacher, who was trying to keep from cracking up. David had apparently decided to teach a class in biology in the back of the school bus and explain to his classmates where babies came from. When the kids got off the bus they strolled into class suddenly knowing all the medically correct words for all the body parts and the procedures. (We had bought an older children's book with the correct terminology because he was asking questions. David had taken it upon himself to read ahead and share with the class.)

Not knowing whether to be proud or mortified, I asked, "Well, did he get all the terms right?"

"He did a better job explaining the science of birth than my freshman college professor did, although he did get one term wrong."

"Which one?"

"Can you let him know when he gets home, it's not the Filipino tubes?"

That night, we gave David a talk on what subjects students should teach, what subjects teachers should teach, and what is reserved for parents to teach.

Thankfully, that small stumbling block didn't deter him from helping his fellow students with their challenges. Before they called his name to get his eighth grade diploma, he was recognized for starting a student tutoring program in middle school. When they called his name, my son, who I had worried would not be independent and would not be accepted for having Asperger's, received a standing ovation from his fellow students.

By helping others deal with their challenges, David had shown them how to accept his.

And when they asked him what he wanted to be when he grew up, his answer was clear and proud—"I'm going to be a teacher!"

~René Thompson

Never Giving Up Hope

Optimism is the faith that leads to achievement.
~Helen Keller

Twelve years ago when my son was diagnosed, he did not speak. He could be aggressive and had many severe behaviors. His loss of eye contact and focus made it difficult for him to learn picture communication, so we moved to sign language. I remember clearly his first sign was for "more." So basic... the need to be able to ask for "more water" or "more food." But it was communication. By the time he was four years old, he was able to speak in four-word sentences. It gave us something to hold on to... it gave us hope.

Five years ago my son continued to regularly melt down and escape from the typical classroom. After an adverse reaction to medication in third grade, I feared we would never get him back to where he was. The doctors offered us no option but to wait and see. Pray. Hope he would get better while we watched him suffer.

Four years ago his behavior started to decrease in school. Yet we still had many hard days and calls from the teacher. Things seemed to slowly get better by the end of fourth grade. He learned how to play the drums. He was getting good grades, and we could see that he could function well in an inclusive setting for the long term. We started to really hope.

Last month he stood strong at his first IEP meeting. I was nervous for him but he did it. We discussed his challenges but we also discussed his strengths. The reading teacher complimented him on his independence and hard work. His pre-algebra teacher told me she wished all students were like him. For the first time in his life, he is able to do his science and math homework by himself. In fact, many days, he has his homework completed on his own before he comes home from school. He is doing well academically. He has his autism friends and loves school.

Tonight I watched my son play his drums in the seventh grade band concert. He independently went to the band room when we arrived and later took to the stage with the rest of the children. Even though his regular band director was absent due to illness, and there was a substitute, Tyler handled the change as if it were not an issue. In my eyes, he was nothing short of amazing.

And once again, I am reminded of the miracle of his progress. It has been happening often this year but I am surprised every time it happens. I know how fortunate we are. My son works so hard to keep it together in school, but we can never assume the progress will just come to him. Hope, yes. Assume, never.

And I am so grateful. He was not always high functioning. Believe me… I had many hopeless days. I kept a journal and read it today. From 2003, I wrote, "Please God… heal my son." But the healing did not come quickly. I could not see it. Things were sometimes unbearable in those dark days. Having to quit work to care for my son. Meltdowns. Calls from teachers. Fighting for services. Facing the unknown on a daily basis was daunting.

When I went to the concert tonight I thought of other parents. Parents of children with autism and other disabilities, just like me, who also face the unknown. Maybe they too felt the hopelessness that can rear its ugly head on any given day. I want you to know to never give up hope. I have been there. Things can get better. Even though it can take a really long time to see the progress, it can happen.

When you face the unknown, the joy of witnessing a huge accomplishment can bring you to your knees. You can finally let yourself feel happiness and allow yourself to dream about your child's future.

Tonight, a band concert brought tears to my eyes and strengthened my hope. I am grateful for the experience of hearing my son play an instrument. I am grateful that he can work with a group of children and create beautiful music. He can experience the wonderful feeling of belonging. So simple, but incredibly important. It may be a small event in the grand scheme of things. But to me, it is as big as the universe. And I am filled with hope as we continue this journey, at least for this moment.

Sure, I am still worried about what will happen when my son becomes an adult or even what might happen next week. Truth be told, I am really scared. But I don't give up hope for where he will be in another five years. He deserves my hope, and he will get it. I will never give up. The beat goes on.

~Kym Grosso

Thank You, Diane

*I would maintain that thanks are the highest form of thought,
and that gratitude is happiness doubled by wonder.*

~G. K. Chesterton

Sometimes people save you. You know the ones I am talking about; they swoop in and pull you off the tracks. That happened for my family in 1990. The change came in a bright, loving, energetic package. My brother Jeff was five, embarking on his educational path, and an angel came to guide him. That angel was Diane.

To say Jeff was a handful is an understatement. Programs and services didn't exist the way they do now. Jeff was attending a Boards of Cooperative Educational Services (BOCES) school where the population was diverse. It would be unfair to say that his learning was stunted, but options were limited. There were people who loved and cared about him there and he was safe, but the weekly phone call that "Jeff drank the water in the swimming pool" was growing old. Quite frankly that was the least of our worries—at home we were dealing with no sleep, smashing VCRs and other electronics out of frustration, bathroom issues, etc. We were just working to get through each day.

Enter Diane.

It was love at first sight when we met Diane. She was bursting with positive energy. Diane saw Jeff and her students as people—people with potential. She didn't look at their disabilities. Diane respected them for their courage and fortitude in facing the world each and every day with their varied challenges. They were all celebrated for their accomplishments, but were held accountable when they broke the rules. You couldn't put anything past her.

Diane helped to spearhead the move into the public schools. I was lucky enough to be part of the incredibly unique and loving family that was Franklin Avenue School. The initial class had six students and they became known as "the boys." To this day, people still ask about "the boys," who are now grown men.

Because the school was so small at the time, with roughly 200 students, everyone knew the boys. Diane created a "Buddy Program" where kids would come early before school to play on the back playground. It was the place to be. Often she would have to turn children away because it was too packed! I never had to deal with peers calling my brother "different." Instead, he was the "cool" kid. The buddy program paved the way for Jeff's school career. When he was a senior in high school, fellow seniors, who were former buddies, would be warm and friendly to him.

Diane assembled an incredible team, who approached each day with such spirit. Nothing fazed them and they were able to find humor in even the stickiest of situations. They were innovative and developed different techniques for each student, providing love and support along the way. It didn't take much, but Diane got the entire school on board. The boys were welcomed with open arms into any classroom or project. Franklin Avenue was, and still is, a wonderful place.

When the time came for the boys to graduate Franklin, they participated in the graduation ceremony, singing along with the songs and accepting their diplomas just like everyone else. Diane would have it no other way, and there was not a dry eye in the house.

Change and transition are hard, but I think this move was more difficult for the families than it was for the boys. Diane prepared them for the middle school, but selfishly, we didn't want to let her go.

Then came the summer program....

Jeff had access to a summer program through the school district, and guess who took the reins to be the teacher? Yes. Diane. For years and years Diane created the most amazing summers, not just for Jeff, but for me as well.

Diane believed that the most important education these boys could get was being out in the "real world." The classroom, which they spent next to no time in, was in the same building as a summer playground camp. The boys played kickball and board games with other campers. Diane also created a store to sell goodies—they would go out to shop and then sell them, cash register and all. They would swim every day and go on all of the trips the camp would go on. Diane welcomed me with open arms into these magical summers.

She would cheer for me, with her fist pump and kick, when I would beat every single boy in camp at "Knock Out," the same way she would when Jeff ducked his head under water for the first time, or when Adam would hit a home run in kickball, or when Joey would use his PECS to spell out exactly what he needed. Diane was genuinely thrilled for our accomplishments, no matter how small.

As summers passed, Diane decided she was going to get her bus driver's license so that she could up and go whenever she and co-teacher Karen decided to. We would head to the beach, amusement parks, sports games, and so much more. A bus ride was not complete without 101.1 WCBS FM blaring from her boom box. Those days were fun.

As summers passed Diane's boys became men.

I grew up as well. Diane saw me go from a toddler to a young adult. I remember so vividly talking to her about Jeff and being upset—she let me. She always validated my feelings. I also remember the days when I was "up to no good," making some adolescent mistake. She listened and laughed and I am sure was thankful that her beautiful daughters had grown out of that stage.

I could never say enough about Diane or do her justice in the written word. She was there for me in ways that no one else was. I know that I could walk into her classroom and be greeted with the same beautiful smile and warmth that only she could provide. Diane helped me to see my brother in ways I wouldn't have known how.

She also helped me see myself. I know that I am different for having a brother like Jeff—different for the better. There are moments in life when it is difficult to see the light at the end of the tunnel. But because of all that Diane has taught me, through her example, I am always able to see the light.

So Diane should know how thankful I am to her for pulling my family off the tracks all of those years ago. But most of all she should know how thankful I am for, well, everything.

~Alison Dyer

Raising Kids on the Spectrum

All in the Family

The Salutation of
Slapping Palms

*A high-five is done when two people congratulate each other
after they achieve success.*
~Online Encyclopedia

No one taught Hope the art of the ABA discrete trial or the use of repetition to facilitate learning. Nor has she yet learned to quote that old proverb: "If at first you don't succeed, try, try, try again." She does not know the Biblical parable of the persistent widow who continually petitioned an unjust judge until she wearied him into granting her request.

However, she, in all her nineteen months of wisdom, has been employing these principles for one important ambition, that is, what the playwright Daniel Kamenetz referred to as "the salutation of slapping palms."

Her sister Rhema never stops moving.

But Hope, with her chubby, toddler legs, chases Rhema day after day, week after week, month after month. With her arm raised in the air, Hope calls out imploringly, "High five? High five?"

According to Wikipedia, "If one initiates a high five by raising a hand into the air and no one consummates the celebration by slapping the raised hand, the initiator is said to be 'left hanging.'"

Until today, Hope had always been left hanging.

Rhema has been a tad bit peeved with Hope since the day Hope was born. It was understandable in the beginning: all siblings go through adjustment periods when the new baby arrives. For Rhema, I had always been her means for communicating and getting what she needed or wanted. She was queen of the "autistic leading" technique. Without words, she would simply grab my hand, drag me to the desired object and thrust my hand at it. I believe my preoccupation with Hope as a baby caused Rhema to view her as an intruder and interference, and she has tenaciously held onto that view.

Rhema's game plan has been to basically ignore Hope's existence until Hope has a Popsicle. Then Rhema steals the Popsicle.

The response to the plaintive request for a high five has been no response... or a fast run in another direction. In the past I have felt bad for Hope—getting dissed and all—so I have offered her a high five. But she shakes her head... she doesn't want it from me; she wants it only from Rhema. I have attempted to tackle Rhema and force her hand to slap Hope's, but it always reeks of phoniness.

Nevertheless, Hope possesses that defiant boldness and strong devotion that embodies hope. She insists on sharing *something* with Rhema—not her Popsicle, not her toys—no way!—but a *connection*, a greeting, an acknowledgement.

Today, finally today, Hope got her breakthrough. She was in hot pursuit when Rhema stopped abruptly, causing Hope to crash into her. Hope stepped back and raised her hand in the air.

"High five?"

Rhema awkwardly, all the while grinning and avoiding eye contact, slapped the palm of her sister.

What word suffices here? Momentous? Stupendous? I cheered like the Red Sox had won another World Series.

Hope, of course, couldn't get enough and requested high fives all afternoon. And Rhema obliged her every time.

Sistas at last.

~Jeneil Palmer Russell

Do Dogs Have Autism?

You don't choose your family.
They are God's gift to you as you are to them.
~Desmond Tutu

"**M**ama? Do dogs have autism?"

"I really don't know... but that's a very good question, Lil."

It really was a good question from my seven-year-old. Lily is an interesting girl. Headstrong, independent, so full of joy and energy that at times it can turn on her, making her restless and obstinate. She knows what she wants and isn't afraid to tell you. Of all my kids, she is the most like me in temperament, which sometimes makes her my most difficult. Have you ever tried to butt heads with yourself?

We were new to all things autism when Lily was an infant. I used to worry that I wouldn't ever be able to give her enough time, energy, attention. That somehow, because her brothers' needs seemed so enormous, hers were going to be put on the back burner. It took me about five minutes to get over that. Lily never saw autism. Instead, she saw her brothers — her competition. To her they were all on equal ground. If she wanted attention she learned how to get it. I don't mean that in a negative way. It's more like she sees herself as any sibling does. The parents are fair game and if you want something from them you jockey for position to get it. She does a very good job.

So although I wasn't surprised by her question, it was the

reasoning behind it that made me think. "Autism" is a word that we use at home. Our boys are of an age where they notice that they are different. So we have been very open with our kids—how could we not? Lily, however, sees this as her brothers and little sister having something she doesn't. "Sam has autism?"

"Yup."

"Oscar has autism?"

"Yup."

"Zoe has autism?"

"Yup."

"So they all have autism and I don't."

"Yup."

"Well that's not fair! What do I get?"

"A big hug and kiss from me?"

"Maaama!"

We have always talked to the kids about how people are different, and that some people by their behavior or words or lack of words might appear more different than others. But no matter what the differences, everyone was deserving of dignity and respect. Everyone. We didn't use the word "autism" until we saw it on the television show *Arthur*. You know, the show where the lead character, Arthur, is an aardvark? It wasn't as if I was ashamed of the word. It just needed to be put in a way they could all understand. Sigh... sometimes, I guess it doesn't take a village... sometimes it takes an aardvark.

All of my kids require some sort of accommodations. All of them, and yes, some more than others. (We are a great example of what a spectrum is.) That's just the way it is. I don't weigh one against the other, assessing the degree of need. They are my children and they are equal.

So, do dogs have autism? I couldn't tell you. What I said to Lily was, "Would it matter if they did?" She thought about it for half a second.

"I guess not." The conversation was left at that. She was already off and running on to the next thing that caught her interest. Because autism doesn't really matter to her. She looks at our family and sees just that—her family. Where she knows she is loved and cherished for being who she is. A sister and a daughter who sometimes thinks she is queen. She gets that last part from me.

~Kathleen Leopold

Back and Forth

Any man can be a father, but it takes someone special to be a dad.
~Anne Geddes

For William's third birthday we got him a swing set. Not just swings, but swings, monkey bars, a climbing wall, a slide, a ladder, a rope ladder, and bars to hang from — it was amazing!

We got it for him because I got tired of hauling him to the park. We had a few neighborhood parks near our house, and had a good time on Saturday mornings taking a ride in the red wagon down the block to the park. That part I didn't mind; in fact, I enjoyed pulling William in the wagon. He wouldn't talk or make much noise, but I would still talk to him. I would tell him about the homes we were passing and I would describe the materials or the architectural style of the homes, or I would comment on how pretty or ugly I thought the houses were. That part I enjoyed, maybe because I held out the hope that he would just "snap out of it" and say, "Gee, Dad, you're right, that soffit is painted the wrong color for a porch," or something like that.

What I got tired of was getting to the park and then him not wanting to play there. We'd get there and he would just sit in the wagon or want to run away and I'd have to beg him to play.

But when he did fixate on the park, it was always the swings. I swear, he would swing for hours if you would push him... and that's where I really got aggravated. I would start pushing him and he would say, "Go fast," or "Higher," and that's all he'd say for about ten minutes or more. Yes, I was grateful that my child was speaking, but I didn't want to hear "Go fast" or "Higher, higher, higher" over and over—this from a child who wouldn't respond to any of the other things I'd said to him.

Of course, my brilliant stroke of genius to get him a play yard for his birthday didn't change anything except the fact that I didn't get to comment on the neighborhood homes as we walked to the park. He still said "Go fast" or "Higher" constantly, and when I say "constantly," I do mean constantly!

I will teach him to swing for himself if it's the last thing I do. One day he will understand the concept of "Bend your knees, straighten your legs" that I have recited to him about a billion times to no avail. I can't wait for that day!

Or can I? Amidst all my angst and frustration about pulling him to the park, only for him not to want to go to the park, or pushing him for twenty minutes or more while he shrilled out one-word orders to me over and over and over… amidst all that, I have realized that we found a common ground.

I don't know if William will ever go to a game with me, or if I'll ever be able to take him for his first haircut, or if I'll ever build a model with him. But we found something to do together. We have our thing. It might not be fun all the time; in fact, sometimes it gets really tiresome, but you know, it's our thing. When the day comes that he learns to move his legs back and forth and doesn't need his daddy to make him go fast or go higher, it'll be a bittersweet moment for sure.

~Seth Fowler

Don't Sweat the Stimmies

What we see depends mainly on what we look for.
~John Lubbock

would venture to guess that every spectrum parent has, at one point or another, looked for the autism in themselves—perhaps even questioned their own neurotypical-ness. For myself, I didn't have to look very far.

From the time I was an infant, I hand flapped. Not with a gentle motion, but with a powerful intensity that engages my entire person. My body tenses, I take a deep breath, my mouth opens, my head cocks to the side and my hands flap wildly at the wrists. Anyone who saw me in full flap mode, without knowing me in any other context, would probably think I was mentally handicapped, certainly not capable of doing all of the things that I do on a daily basis.

As a young child, I didn't realize that there was anything strange about it. My family found it endearing, and no one made me feel weird until I started first grade. I clearly remember a little girl asking me, "Why do you do this?" while simultaneously mimicking the behavior. She wasn't teasing me. It was a genuine question, but it was the first time that I understood that it wasn't considered "normal."

After that day I started trying to suppress it. It wasn't easy in the beginning. You see, hand flapping wasn't something I decided to do. It was the natural outflow of what I was feeling in the moment. Often

I wasn't even aware I was doing it for several seconds. With practice, I learned to catch myself sooner and sooner, until eventually, I could stop before it started without consciously thinking about it.

However, the feelings attached to it never went away. I still felt the rush of excitement and my body tensing. I needed some type of release for that. So subconsciously, a new, more socially acceptable option emerged. I started tightly squeezing my thumbs inside my fists. I was able to keep my arms at my sides and do this very subtly without drawing attention. Still, though I never consciously thought about it, the hand flapping would always resurface whenever I was alone—even to this day. The thumb squeezing is never quite as satisfying as the flapping. It helps to suppress the urge, but it doesn't truly replace it. It's kind of like when you have to sneeze. You can hold it in, but it doesn't produce the same relief as actually sneezing.

My husband Nick was the first person who ever mentioned the thumb squeezing to me, but it was clear to me that he found it as precious as my family had found the hand flapping when I was a child. One night when we were out on a date he said, "You're happy." I asked how he knew. He gestured toward my hands, clenched into white-knuckled fists with my thumbs tucked under the pointer fingers. "You do that when you're happy." Yes, this guy was a keeper. He paid attention, and he loved me for every last morsel of who I was—quirks and all.

Fast forward to motherhood. I was teaching Luke to play with a racecar toy he had just gotten as a present. He was seven months old. He finally got it and I started yelling with glee: "Yay! You did it!" Immediately I saw Luke's eyes widen and light up, and his whole body tensed until it shook with excitement. I knew that face and smiled. He got that from me.

Stimming is a very positive experience. It's the ability to feel joy and excitement and satisfaction beyond what most people do. The word in the English language that best describes it is euphoric. It's enjoyment on a whole new level. For me, the urge to flap is most closely linked to feelings of pride and accomplishment. I can't manufacture the sensation. I can't tell myself, "Okay, I'm going to hand flap now." If I did, it would be no more satisfying to me than it is to anyone else. It has to be spontaneous, based on the circumstances of the moment. As a teenager, I most often flapped while doing homework. Type a sentence. Flap, flap, flap. Type again. Flap. Reread it to see how it sounds. Flap, flap. In case you're wondering, I'm flapping as I write this story. Flap, flap.

Today, it most frequently happens while watching my children. For some reason, I have never suppressed it in front of them. I suppose because I don't feel the need to keep up appearances. I'm sure we are quite the sight to behold. Luke is tensing with excitement while playing with his iPad. I'm flapping away while watching him. Faith is doing it too, although it is clear that she is only copying us. She doesn't have the hand-flapping gene, and I'm sure that as Luke gets older and becomes more socially aware, he'll learn ways to mitigate his stimming just like I did.

I was uniquely designed to be Luke's mom, and I'm thankful to have an extra special glimpse into his psyche—to feel what he feels, and to be able to tell others about stimming from first-hand experience.

~Joyce Rohe

Rocky Road

Sometimes being a brother is even better than being a superhero.
~Marc Brown

magine you are an ice cream fanatic. You love vanilla ice cream. There is nothing you ever want more then just plain vanilla ice cream, and so you go to the ice cream parlor to get one bowl of vanilla ice cream. Then they give you Rocky Road. You never asked for it, and you probably don't even like nuts. But they've closed the ice cream parlor, and there's no going back.

That is how my family tried to explain my brother to me.

When you're eight years old and your brother has just been diagnosed with a condition you can't possibly understand, everything you do gets seen through a different lens. I was an only child for six years. I got more care and attention in a day than most children would get in a month. When I thought about getting a little brother, I didn't see him as competition. I saw him as a sidekick, as an accomplice. I had my place at the top of the mountain. No one could move me.

My descent started when Charlie turned two. My parents sat me down, told me that he had been labeled as autistic. It meant nothing to me at the time. But time passed, and things began to get clearer. Charlie had aides, a special school, an entourage that followed him and tried to console him and cater to him. He got everything he wanted. I did not. I wanted him to give me something. All he did was take: he took my attention, he took my toys, he took my place at the top of the mountain.

Time has passed. Eight years later, Charlie is still my brother. And he still has that label. He has moments where he'll lose control and just rant at my parents or at the walls. He'll ignore the world and slip away, closing off his mind, no matter how hard we try to pull him away. People who meet him for the first time sometimes come away asking questions and shaking their heads. He's not like other kids, and he never will be. But he goes to public school and plays on the soccer team. He eats all kinds of food. He can have conversations for hours now, not seconds. Most people see him as how he is. I see him as how he's changed.

Charlie has his challenges, but he has his strengths. He has the most amazing memory I've ever seen. He memorizes plays, musicals, songs, numbers, words, systems, games, anything he can wrap his mind around. Then he can recite it all back to you, without prompting. He just works like that. Others don't. The difference is that simple.

It's not like I asked for vanilla ice cream and they gave me a shoe. They still gave me ice cream. It's just not the flavor I asked for. I think of what we as a family have tried to teach Charlie, but then I can't help but think about what he's taught us: empathy, compassion, reserving judgment, the true meaning of a challenge. Challenge is having to see someone or something in a way no one else will. He is the most caring ten-year-old child I have ever met. We give him love, and he takes it and gives it all back to us twofold. He's generous and faithful. And he's my brother. And he's autistic.

I wouldn't want him any other way.

~Eric Tor

Finding
My Inner Spectrum

*If I could snap my fingers and be nonautistic,
I would not. Autism is part of what I am.*
~Temple Grandin

My autism was discovered when I went to the doctor for a concern about depression that really wasn't depression. One hour into our session, the doctor said, "Have you ever considered the possibility that you have autism?"

I had not considered this possibility. For the last eight years, I had been raising a child with autism. The autism with communication and social impairment. The poop in your pants and spread it all over the walls autism. The I'm never going to grow up and go to college autism. I always ignored the possibility of my own spectrum-y behavior, because I had been dealt the hand of being the mother of a child on the spectrum, and didn't really have time to worry about what was causing my issues.

There are three things that make one autistic. They are a social impairment, restrictive and repetitive behavior, and a communication impairment. You look at me, interact with me, and say, how could that be? I will be the first to admit that I'm socially inept. I cannot read people. I cannot tell if you like me or dislike me. I always assume that you don't like me, unless you straight out tell me that you like me. I also have a significant lack of empathy. I can pretend to be empathetic, but I really am not, and most times I'm a horrible actor. I actually make checklists to remember to ask my friends how their grandmothers are faring, how their children are doing, and whether everything went okay at that last IEP meeting. These checklists are on my smartphone, sometimes hanging on my fridge, and many times simply memorized. I lack empathy, but at least I have a photographic memory. I also have to constantly remind myself that people are not interested in my obsessions, whether it's weather, *Star Wars*, or running.

Don't even get me started on restrictive, repetitive behavior. I run marathons, and weeks prior to my races, I will write out my running schedules, my menus, my shopping lists, what I'm wearing if the weather is a, b, or c. If something goes wrong with my schedule, I can't cope. If anything goes wrong with any number of things in my schedule, I end up doing nothing, but pace back and forth through my home. It's a miracle that I get anything done. Besides my running schedule, I'm very restrictive about my menu. I can't eat vegetables that have the same colors two days in a row. I can't have meat from the same animal two days in a row. Leftovers are eaten with a day between when they are served, as to not break the rule of eating the same foods two days back to back. When I get pulled over, I cry, not to get out of the ticket, but because I feel so guilty about breaking a rule.

The last autistic trait was the one I had most difficulty coming to terms with, and one that I still struggle with. I don't comprehend spoken words well, specifically instructions. When I was in the military, this made my life, and the life of the people who worked with me, absolute hell. I did not understand verbal instructions. I would repeatedly ask for clarification. Not only did I have issues with spoken communication, I also had issues expressively communicating. Needless to say, I have a lot of regrets about serving in the military. I loved my job, I loved the people I worked for, but I feel like I let everyone down, because I was not smart enough, or good enough to realize that my weaknesses would have ultimately not qualified me for military service.

So there you have it. I am a mother with a child who is moderately autistic, dealing with autism myself. A lot of my family and my friends would prefer that I keep this to myself. They fear that I open myself up to scrutiny about how good of a mother I am, about whether or not I am capable of handling this condition and my son's condition, and they fear that I will ultimately be unfairly judged because I am open about my condition. Some family members discount my diagnosis as being just quirky. I am quirky. I have decided that if people want to judge me at face value, they will. Mothers are judged incredibly harshly on a daily basis by other mothers. I'm no different.

The main reason I have been open about my condition is to provide hope. Although it certainly isn't always rainbows and butterflies, autism is not a death sentence. Having a diagnosis does not mean that your life is over, or that you cannot find happiness, peace, and love. I have found all these things, despite having an Asperger's diagnosis. I have been happily married for fifteen years, I am college educated, and I have two wonderful children. Only one child has autism; my daughter is typical.

I also want to share the importance of diagnosing even the cases of Asperger's and autism that are high functioning. Even though I lived my life for thirty-five years without knowing I had a form of autism, knowing now gives me a sense of accomplishment. I have persevered despite having something considered a disability.

For a long time, I thought of myself as less of a person, because I just wasn't good enough or smart enough; now I know there is a reason why some things came harder to me than most people. I feel that I am intelligent, vital, and can contribute to society. I don't face the challenges my son faces, but Asperger's does present some challenges in and of itself.

If I had known about my condition as a teenager or young adult, I think that I would have benefited from a few of the services that my son currently receives. I think I would have been a better person, a better employee, and a better leader if I had some of the coping mechanisms, knowledge, and support children are getting now.

My diagnosis does not reflect on my child's diagnosis. We are all individuals—people with autism are not a "we." Each and every person with autism is an individual with hopes, dreams, loves, hates, frustrations, and aspirations. My son will benefit from the therapies that were not available to me as he pursues his individual path.

~J. Vetter

Our Passover Story

Other things may change but we start and end with family.
~Anthony Brandt

"Why doesn't Josh talk?" my niece Abby asked. I knew that this question would eventually come up. I'd tried to prepare for it.

We had all arrived in Florida the day before, a Passover vacation courtesy of my mother. Apparently the yearly spring ritual of switching dishes over and removing every speck of leavened bread had worn her out the prior year. She had called me post-holiday and declared, "I'm never doing this again. You and your two sisters are invited to join us wherever we decide to go."

After researching options with her travel agent, Orlando was the chosen destination, and I was presented with a decision: stay home for eight days, or take my spouse and son with autism on a three-hour plane ride to a new environment.

"What do you think, Aaron?" I had asked my husband.

"I think it's a crap shoot," he had replied honestly.

"Crap being the operative word?" I cynically retorted. If our then four-year-old didn't comfortably handle all the changes and transitions involved in accepting my mother's generous gift, crap is exactly what everyone joining this excursion would be dealing with. My parents, sisters, one of their husbands, and their twin ten-year-old boys, eight-year-old daughter and a four-year-old son, all of them "neurotypicals," would be coming along. We'd all be sharing a five-bedroom rental house with a pool. It wasn't only our comfort that we had to take into consideration; it was theirs too.

We thought about it and decided that it was worth the risk. Not only would the April weather in Florida be more predictable and enjoyable than that of New York, there would be so much more to do. I'd researched activity options online and found that both Disney World and Sea World have accommodations for children with autism. All you needed was a copy of a medical evaluation confirming your child's diagnosis; then you were granted immediate access to those rides that have VIP lines. If a given ride only had one line, there were designated areas that were less noisy and more shaded for those on the spectrum. If nothing else, we knew we were headed into theme parks that were sensitive and tolerant of our situation.

Like any parent with a child going on an unpredictable flight, I loaded up on Josh's staples and reinforcers. I had a magnetic drawing tablet, a DVD player loaded with his favorite *Sesame Street* DVDs, cookies and potato chips. Surprisingly enough, once we finally got to the airport and settled on the plane, it all went relatively smoothly. Josh drew and munched from the time we took off until the time we landed. It wasn't until we landed in Florida that behavioral issues arose.

I couldn't blame Josh for the meltdown. We had asked a lot of him over the past several hours, herding him from car to airplane to shuttle van. When we arrived at the car rental place, we were all hot, tired and worn out. The fact that the three cars we had ordered weren't ready and the building that we had been brought to was miniscule didn't help. My practically nonverbal child threw himself down in the parking lot and flew into full meltdown mode.

After what seemed like hours, we finally obtained our vehicles and headed to what would be our home for the next eight days. We all unpacked, got settled in our rooms and did what we had to do to prepare for the holiday, which started the next day at sundown. It wasn't until we were all swimming together the following afternoon that Abby asked her question about Josh's condition. And since all of my sister's children were present, as were both their parents and mine from a distance, this was as good a time as any to discuss it.

"Josh has something called autism," I explained. "One of the symptoms is that it makes it hard for Josh to speak. That's why he goes to a special school that tries to teach him how to talk."

"Will he ever talk?" asked Evan.

"We don't know," I answered honestly.

Sam looked sad and said, "I feel sorry for him."

"Don't feel sorry for him," I replied, and immediately regretted saying it. I had no business telling any of them how to feel about this and resolved to not do it again.

"If Josh can't talk, how do you understand him?" Abby wanted to know.

I smiled and said, "I'm his mommy. That's why I stay at home with him; so I can better understand what he needs and try to find people to help him get it."

"Will you work when he talks?" she asked.

"Probably," I answered, wanting to give them at least one concrete answer. The truth was that I hadn't a clue. It was all so hypothetical. I hadn't lived in definites since the day of the diagnosis. But my nephews and niece weren't asking anything that I didn't ask myself daily. And I wanted answers even more than they did.

Over the remaining course of the holiday Josh was himself. He slept through the Seders, which meant that Aaron and I could partake in them relatively easily. During the day, he ran back and forth in order to fulfill his sensory needs. He bounced off the couches and had nights that were difficult. My family all dealt with this graciously and sympathetically.

As our stay neared its end, Aaron and I discussed what we would do on our last day in Florida. "Let's do Disney again," I suggested. Josh had loved it and Aaron agreed.

Sam had been listening and asked, "Can I come with you?"

I looked at him and said, "You know it's difficult with Josh, right?" Sam had really made an effort to bond with Josh over the course of the holiday; in fact, he had such a positive impact that Josh was saying Sam's name on command by the time we left Florida.

Sam nodded solemnly and said, "I'll always love Josh, Aunt Jennifer, even if he's crazy."

I smiled and said, "The word is 'hyperactive,' Sam," but I was deeply moved. For the first time over the course of the holiday, someone bedsides Aaron or myself had expressed unconditional love towards my son, and that in and of itself was far too good a feeling to pass over.

~Jennifer Berger

Joseph's Wish

A brother is a friend given by nature.
~Jean Baptiste Legouve

It was almost Christmas. Most of our shopping was done, and we planned to spend the next few evenings wrapping presents, baking cookies, and watching Christmas classics.

"Mommy, there's a new Christmas movie on tonight called *Annabelle's Wish*. Can I watch it?"

"Sure, Joseph," I replied.

Joseph, my enthusiastic four-and-a-half-year-old, could barely wait until Christmas. Even during the brutal year following his younger brother's diagnosis, Joseph was full of joy.

"Why can't Stuey talk?" he asked one day.

"Because he has a boo-boo in his brain." In another year or so, Joseph would be ready for us to share with him the words we heard that black April morning. Stuey has autism.

Joseph cuddled up with my husband, Stu, to watch the adorable animated movie, while I spent the hour guarding our Christmas tree. Stuey loved to grab the ornaments and smash them on the floor. He would celebrate any successful attempt by clapping and jumping on his tippy-toes.

Annabelle's Wish is the story of Billy, a young boy living on a farm, who has been mute since surviving a fire in which his parents died. Early in the movie, a calf named Annabelle, born on Christmas Eve, becomes Billy's Christmas present. Billy and Annabelle's friendship grows stronger with each passing day.

Every Christmas Eve, when Santa arrives, he sprinkles magic dust over the animals and says, "Let the talking begin." The animals receive the gift of speech for one day.

On Annabelle's first birthday, she learns that Billy can't speak.

"Oh, that's so sad," Annabelle replies. And she decides that next year she will have a special wish for Santa.

A year passes, and Santa arrives to share his magic dust. Annabelle whispers in Santa's ear and he nods. On Christmas morning, Billy finds a golden box under the tree. It appears to be empty, but as he lifts it over his head and turns it upside down, some of Santa's magic dust falls gently upon him.

"There's nothing in here," Billy announces.

His grandpa jumps up and runs toward him.

"Grandpa, I talked!" Billy exclaims as his grandfather cries and embraces him.

Billy runs out to the barn, shouting, "Annabelle, I can talk!"

"Moo," is all Annabelle can reply.

"She gave her voice to you," Annabelle's mother tells Billy. "To hear you talk, that was Annabelle's wish."

After the movie, Stu tucked Joseph into bed.

"I've got my Christmas wish for Santa. I'm gonna wish that Stuey could talk," Joseph said and then closed his eyes.

Stu walked downstairs and told me what Joseph said. My husband's eyes were red and glassy as he tried but failed to fight his tears.

"I want him to have his dream. How can I tell him his wish won't come true?"

The next morning, Joseph described the movie as he slurped cereal.

"Will you watch it with me after school?" he asked.

I managed to have two kids fed, washed, and dressed for school, clothes ironed and lunch boxes packed, but I wasn't ready to talk about this movie. "Okay, go get your coat," was all I could say.

I could think of little else while Joseph was gone. All of us wanted Stuey to talk and to be a part of our family in every way. Stu and I were hopeful it would happen someday, if we worked very hard, and if Stuey got the best treatment possible. How could we tell our dear Joseph, who saw a solution amid the promise and magic of Santa Claus, that this would be a lifelong journey.

Joseph popped in the video as soon as he arrived home from school. As he snuggled against me, I could see his thoughts as clearly as the veins of an autumn leaf revealed by a ray of sunlight. When the movie ended, I called Stu at work. "We have a problem."

"I agree. I'll talk to him tonight," Stu promised.

The warm glow of our Christmas tree flowed from the living room into our kitchen. Joseph was coloring at the table while I stood at the counter, chopping carrots, deep in thought. In the year leading to Stuey's diagnosis, I learned how to function on three hours sleep, how to keep Stuey from running away or flipping the furniture in our home, how to work with and advocate for my disabled son while serving as Joseph's class mother and play-date-broker. I learned to bear up under pressure, exhaustion, and despair. But, I didn't have the strength to break Joseph's heart.

Joseph and I began to chat, and he dropped hints about his Christmas wish. I knew it was impossible to avoid the issue any longer. "What do you want Santa to bring you?" I asked, feeling a growing sense of strength from within, and beyond.

"It's a secret," Joseph said.

I never loved him more than I did at that moment. No matter what else I had to deal with, I had a son who cared more for his little brother than he did for himself. He gave me the strength to face the truth, and now I had to share that truth with him, no matter how much it hurt. As his hopes climbed with each passing moment, I knew they would have that much farther to fall.

"Joseph," I said, waiting for him to turn toward me.

"Santa can't make Stuey talk," I said softly, when his eyes met mine.

"Why not?" His shoulders slumped, and he began to cry, my

words shattering his dream of talking and playing with his brother on Christmas morning. I knelt down and embraced him. The sum of our pain was immeasurable. My attempt to be strong failed, and I sobbed with him. We held each other and cried for what seemed like hours. Finally, I explained.

"Joseph, *Annabelle's Wish* is make-believe. Santa doesn't have that kind of magic. But Stuey can still get better. If we work hard with him every day, slowly he'll begin to talk. You'll see."

Christmas has come and gone fourteen times. With the grace of God, and the dedication of his family and many professionals, Stuey has slowly improved.

"JoJo!" Stuey exclaimed when he heard the car door slam. He ran to the driveway and embraced his big brother, home from his first semester of college, where he studies Special Education.

The warm glow of our Christmas tree flowed from the living room into our kitchen. I stood at the counter, chopping carrots, as Joseph and Stuey decorated our Christmas tree, reciting the names of the ceramic Disney ornaments as they gently hung them on the evergreen branches.

There was no magic dust for Stuey. But he has been given a greater gift. A brother who has a magical love for him, like Annabelle loved Billy.

~Terri Manzione

Thank You, Las Vegas

You can learn many things from children.
How much patience you have, for instance.
~Franklin P. Jones

We are late yet again and the pressure is building. The therapist has been here for two hours. I have no excuses. There has been enough time to clear breakfast, get myself dressed and prepare for another day. I have had a break from my shadow and her constant, repetitive questions. "What's gonna happen? Can we play Batman? Who's the bad guy? What's gonna happen?" It's not so bad for a few days or weeks or even months, but this has been years. Four years, going on five, with no end in sight. It is time for our next appointment and it's time to hurry, but rushing only seems to make things worse.

"No, Daddy! No!" my daughter pleads. "No brush. Bad brush!" Her dark, Asian hair is so fine and so unlike my hair or my wife's. It is easily tangled and difficult to brush, especially when we are in a hurry. I am doing my best but I can feel my anger rising. No one has to comb my hair—especially the hair I have left. I'm a man—damn it! What do I know about brushing hair? I'd be happy to stop if she could only do this for herself. I don't like this any more than she does. In fact, I don't like this any more than most aspects of my current life, like the cold or the snow or the chaos of a messy house. I want out—out of the God-forsaken winter in Wisconsin. I need a break—to a place that is warm and green, a place where I can shed my coat, bask in the sun, and feel the weight of a golf club in my hands.

That break will come soon, when I find a deal for a quick weekend getaway. As the plane makes its final approach and the lights of the Vegas Strip come into view, my wife checks Sophia to see that she is safely buckled into her seat. With exasperation in her voice, my wife says, "Now tell me, once again, why exactly are we in Las Vegas?" When I made the reservations, the trip had seemed like a good idea, but already I am having second thoughts.

When we wake up the next morning, the reality of our situation is starting to dawn on me. The February air is cool, much too cold to use the outdoor pool. With Sophia, going to shows is not an option. And we don't like to gamble. There really isn't much for us to do. By default we spend our time sightseeing, walking the many miles between and through the various hotels and casinos.

Moving about in a culture far removed from the rural Midwest, I am annoyed by the swarm of self-critical thoughts that keep buzzing around in my head. On the billboards and in the shops I see a glamorous life that is nothing like my small-town existence back home. I keep thinking, "I need some new clothes. I look like a slob. I look fat. I need to go on a diet." The sights make me feel poor, boring, cautious, and slow. Insult is added to injury when I finally visit a golf driving range.

Even though I am an average golfer at best, golf remains my joy and my passion, a priority that ranks just behind my wife and my child. Taking some tentative swings for the first time in several months, I am asked by an older man in the neighboring stall if I have played much golf. He says, "You'll never hit it straight if you keep sliding your front hip." He then demonstrates how to fix this serious flaw. Once he has finished sharing, another golfer steps forward to ask if I am interested in learning how to hit with power. In just a few moments, I am reminded that I am neither long, nor straight, as a golfer. In a word: pathetic.

This is the final straw. The damage to my self-esteem is complete. It is time to go home. I find myself questioning the priorities and direction of my life.

Between hotel checkout and our flight home we have some time to kill. We find a cab and tell our driver to take us to the library, which is also near the driving range. Driving by the amazing sights of the Vegas Strip my daughter is bursting with a manic energy. Question follows question after question about the casinos, our schedule, the people she sees along the street, our flight, where we are going, why we have to leave, and so on. We eventually arrive at the library, where my wife and daughter will spend some time among the books. The taxi driver then takes me back to the driving range. On the short trip she asks me about my daughter.

"Is she adopted?"

"Yes," I answer. "We adopted her from China."

"Is she always so full of questions?"

"Yes," I respond. "She has some learning delays related to autism. Her anxieties really take off in new surroundings."

"I was adopted," the taxi driver says as she makes eye contact through the rearview mirror. "You guys are so patient and so good with her. Trust me. No one was ever that patient with me. Sometimes I babysit for my nephew. One hour with him and I need a break. You guys are really good with her. She is very lucky."

And with that we have arrived at the driving range. As the cabbie drives away I feel like I have arrived at a new destination. Of all the places in the world, Sin City has delivered a clear message of affirmation about my life and my priorities:

I am a stay-at-home father.

I provide care for an autistic child.

This is important work.

I do a good job.

Thank you, Las Vegas.

~Steve Spilde

76

Beacons of Hope

Anything I've ever done that ultimately was worthwhile...
initially scared me to death.
~Betty Bender

t all began so unexpectedly with a trip to Barnegat, New Jersey, where we were visiting friends who suggested a trip to the local lighthouse. Why our son, Ben, was so attracted to "Old Barney" is still a mystery. He made a beeline for the door and flew up the stairs with my husband on his heels. Our older son, Alex—who was extremely afraid of heights—refused to make the climb. I was more than happy to sit this adventure out.

I should have known my persistent little boy was not going to let me off so easily. Having flown down the stairs as quickly as he had raced up, Ben announced he was ready to go again. My stomach churned with each vibration of the metal staircase under my feet as I raced to keep pace. What propelled me up those stairs was fear. My adrenaline-addled brain manufactured images of Ben flying over the railing at the top. Autism is not for the weak-hearted.

I caught my breath as we passed through the door together. The wind was whipping ferociously as I paused to deal with my jelly legs, still shaky from the exertion of the climb. With my back pressed to the wall, I eased my way to the far side of the observation deck. When both the air and the shaking stilled, I took in the view and shared what he saw.

Magic.

His beaming smile was pure joy as his eyes met mine briefly before focusing again on the horizon. For a moment, we were connected by the intensity of his experience, his elation. It was hard to remain afraid of something that captivated him so totally. These are the moments I live for. As elusive as they can be, these connections are possible in the most unexpected of moments.

The following summer, we visited the old Cape Henry Lighthouse in Virginia Beach. We decided to take an early morning climb before the day's heat became too oppressive. When we arrived, we were the only visitors there and I recognized an opportunity to try the climb with Alex too. If he got angry and had a tantrum over the suggestion that he try the climb, we had the privacy to work through it with him. So many of Alex's fears at that time in his life were not based on real factors as much as they were about sticking to routines and not taking risks. After many years of tag-team parenting, Joe and I were beginning to realize that we needed to do more things together as a family. I suggested to Alex that maybe he could try.

"I AM NOT GOING UP!" The screaming was blood-curdling and he dropped to the ground and kicked for several minutes.

I waited for the storm to pass. He became quiet and stood back up, so I continued: "There are times we do things for Alex, and there are times we do things for Ben. Ben always goes to the aquariums with you and tries the things you like. Now is a time when we do something for Ben. This is what families do; they take turns."

Alex dropped back to the ground and yelled some more. "It sure is hot," I continued, as I sat down on the floor near him, deciding that I had reached a point of no return. We had long ago decided that tantrums like this would not deter a request; this would only reinforce his tantrums as a means to avoid an unpleasant task, so I decided to sweeten the deal for trying. "As soon as we're done climbing up, we'll go back to Grandma's and go in the pool."

I had his attention now. "Do you want the pool?" I asked.

"YES!" he said.

"Well, let's climb up and get it over with, okay? First we climb, then we swim."

"YOU ARE THE WORST MOTHER EVER!" he screamed.

"Alex, if you really, really hate this you will never have to climb up another lighthouse again. I promise. You'll never know if you don't try."

"Alright, alright! But then we are swimming!" He stood up, approached the stairs and took a step.

"Good job, Alex, I'm right behind you!"

The 191 steps to the top were in some respects the hardest I have ever taken. I second-guessed myself, wondering if I had pushed too hard. The verbal assault continued the entire way up, and I couldn't help but notice that my boy had a knack for constructing beautiful sentences when he was mad, a stark contrast to years earlier when he was losing words at an alarming rate.

As Alex stepped onto the deck of the lens chamber from the opening in the floor at the top, I heard him draw a breath in sharply. I prepared myself for the worst.

"Wow," Alex admitted. "It's great up here!"

Magic.

When we reached the bottom and made our way outside, I posed the boys in front of the lighthouse and snapped a picture of them, both smiling, arms wrapped around each other in a moment of tactile tolerance.

"Alex, I am going to put this where you can see it at home, because I always want you to remember how awesome you are for overcoming your fear! There is nothing you can't do as long as you try!"

His eyes darted to mine before slipping away; his voice caught as he tried to hold back his tears. Before I knew it, I was receiving a very rare hug.

"Thank you for making me do that, Mom. Thanks for making me go to the top."

•••

Six years later, we have climbed more than twenty structures across seven states, including a weeklong trek to the Outer Banks to climb the Cape Hatteras Lighthouse, which is the tallest in America. Alex and Ben handled the changes in routine and unfamiliar surroundings on that trip better than we had ever hoped, no doubt because of the role the lighthouses played.

Many of our successes are wholly dependent upon how we choose to view the challenges autism presents. What if, along the way, we had decided that Ben's lighthouses were truly a negative "perseveration" that we somehow needed to quell or otherwise control because the intensity was out of whack with what might be considered "normal"?

Instead, by joining Ben in his interest, we grew together as a family. By pulling Alex out of his comfort zone and into his brother's, we have given him a powerful memory to sustain him in the frightening moments when he has to try something new. In these beautiful, enduring structures, climbing with other enthusiasts, people who meet Alex and Ben don't see two boys with autism. They just see two boys who share their love of lighthouses. They are a helpful, hopeful symbol to me, linked to both of my sons' continuing triumphs over autism in so many ways.

~Christine Bakter

77

The Boy from My Dreams

Whatever we do lays a seed in our deepest consciousness,
and one day that seed will grow.
~Sakyong Mipham

Like many little girls, I dreamed of the day when I would get married and have children of my own. The dreams would change slightly over time, but one thing remained constant. Images of a towheaded, smiling little boy named "Arthur" haunted my dreams, and I just knew that one day this child would be my son. Nothing ever deterred me from the conviction of that dream, not even the day I learned that bearing a blond-haired child would be genetically impossible for a Filipino girl like me. I just knew.

So you can imagine how my heart skipped a beat when, on our very first date, my now husband informed me that he had a young teenage son named Arthur. My head instantly filled with images of the child he described, matching them to the boy from my dreams. Arthur was blond with blue eyes. He loved animals, kids, and he had an affectionate nature, quirky sense of humor, and Asperger syndrome.

Asperger syndrome?

"It's a high-functioning form of autism."

Oh. Then I told myself, "I think I can handle that. After all, this is potentially the man of my dreams. And he has a son named Arthur!"

As the relationship with my husband progressed, I researched the topic of Asperger syndrome. I asked my husband many questions and volunteered at a local charity for developmentally disabled people. I did everything I could to learn about Arthur's condition, and what I learned concerned me.

Because Arthur lived with his mother a thousand miles away, everything I knew about Arthur's personality was through other people. The geographical distance and Arthur's dislike of disruptions to his routine meant physically getting to know him would be challenging. While he was basically a caring, sweet-natured boy, his difficulty expressing his feelings became exasperating to him when he entered his teenage years.

It turns out I didn't need to worry. I met Arthur a week before his father and I got married. This giant of a boy draped his arm around my shoulders, peered down at me with a big smile on his face, and asked, "How's the weather down there?"

I fell in love with him on the spot. Three months later he moved into our house. I had instantly become a full-time stepmother to a child with autism.

They say you can never prepare for parenthood, no matter how much you try. The same is true for step-parenthood, where you are suddenly responsible for a child you did not bring into this world and had no part in raising for the first sixteen years of his life. Add to that a diagnosis of Asperger's and you could say I was in over my head. But in some ways, I guess being the stepparent gave me an unexpected advantage. Unlike other parents with an autistic child, I didn't experience the crushing realization that my dreams would have to change with my child's diagnosis. I never went into a mourning period for "what could have been." Instead, I gained a child knowing full well that his Asperger syndrome meant that I still had a lot to learn. And I found that I really did love the boy.

Arthur is intelligent, sensitive, funny, and unbelievably patient with kids and animals. I never know what Arthur is going to say, or when and where he is going to say it:

"Gwen, you mean to tell me you've never been bitten by a horse?" (Loudly asked in the middle of a crowded Costco store.)

"Do you think vampires live longer because of the iron they consume in people's blood?" (On the drive home from school.)

"I should be elected supreme ruler of the universe because I have been certified in both animal and homosapien CPR." (Written for a school paper.)

On the outside, our child looks and speaks typically. Because he looks normal, people expect him to behave normally too. And nothing ever prepared me for the fierce protective streak that surges within me whenever someone accuses Arthur of being "weird."

"But he doesn't look autistic," people tell me with disbelief when I try to explain Arthur's behavior. They think he's just being rude. At the very least they think he's awkward. There was the doctor who left the room after he started to take stitches out of Arthur's leg (he broke it and needed surgery). Arthur looked down at the doctor's handiwork and commented, "I fail to see the logic in how you are attempting to do this." I could only giggle when the nurse came in to finish the job and Arthur took the tweezers out of her hand so he could finish taking the stitches out himself.

Situations like this make disciplining Arthur even more difficult. He doesn't understand that sometimes being who he is will offend people, and that he should apologize even if he didn't mean it. And accepting his condition does not mean we can excuse unacceptable behavior. Arthur wants to convey the truth so badly that it physically causes him pain when he realizes a misunderstanding has occurred. So he resists acknowledgement of wrongdoing with every fiber of his being. Sometimes it takes herculean efforts to help Arthur see when he is acting inappropriately or hurtful. But it's rewarding to see him learn from his mistakes and it really makes me proud to see the fine young man he is growing up to be.

And what of the boy from my dreams? I look at this incredible, smiling, and loving young man, and my heart speaks the truth. Arthur is much better than my dreams ever were.

~Gwen Navarrete

The Biggest Losers Win Big

It is never too late to be who you might have been.
~George Eliot

"So your son's autism drove you to overeat?" The woman asking the question was a casting director for NBC's reality-TV show *The Biggest Loser*.

A week earlier my wife Amy had "tricked" me into attending a casting call in Atlanta on Valentine's Day for the popular prime-time weight loss show.

Amy's proposition to me went something like this: "Honey, we need a romantic weekend away, and, by the way, while we're there, I want us to stand in a line with 600 other fat people."

We went, and were chosen for a second audition. And that's how we ended up in a hotel room talking about our struggles with an NBC casting director.

Our son's autism had, indeed, driven us to food. Together, we weighed 560 pounds.

I'd always struggled with weight, but Amy's battles with emotional eating began in earnest when autism turned our world upside down.

Sometimes I'm struck by how dramatically life can change in an instant. Life can be going one way and, in a heartbeat, everything can change and you find yourself heading in entirely new direction.

That's exactly what happened to us in the spring of 2002.

Our third son, Rhett, was two and a half, and everything about how our little guy was developing was right on track.

Then one day everything changed. Rhett regressed in skills and vocabulary. He stopped making eye contact and began to withdraw into himself.

In the hardest two years of our lives, we pleaded with doctors for answers. When Rhett was finally diagnosed with autism at age five, we were devastated, but relieved to finally have an explanation.

By then, Rhett was sleeping very little and we couldn't reason with him at all. When he did talk, he "parroted" what he heard. If Amy asked, "What color is this apple?" he repeated, "What color is this apple?" He couldn't answer simple questions, like what his name was or where he lived.

He was unpredictable and had no concept of danger. We lived in constant fear that he would climb out a window or wander away, unable to tell anyone his name or where he lived. We nailed shut the windows in his upstairs bedroom to keep him safe. And when Rhett wasn't awake in the middle of the night drawing on walls, he would lie in bed peeling the sheetrock paper off the walls.

Teachers told us Rhett would probably never read phonetically, nor could he follow simple instructions like "get your backpack from on top of the dryer" because he couldn't understand abstract concepts like "on top." Every night we worked with him for hours on homework, eventually giving up and telling him all the answers.

Depressed and exhausted, Amy started eating for comfort. I called her every day on my way home from work to gauge her level of sadness. Should I pick up Rocky Road ice cream? Or should I pick up ice cream and Reese's Peanut Butter Cups?

Amy was obsessed with "fixing" Rhett, and increasingly burdened knowing there were therapies out there we couldn't afford. Plus, we'd been told there's a window of time when an autistic child is very young when you can make a difference. After that, it's too late.

Soon Amy was spending every Tuesday night in bed with a big bowl of ice cream, watching *The Biggest Loser* on TV and crying.

I'd never felt so helpless as a husband or father.

We told our story to the casting director. Two months later, we got a call saying we were perfect for the show.

Earlier I said that life can change in a heartbeat, that in an instant you can find yourself on a brand new path. It happened, tragically, when Rhett began showing signs of autism. It happened again, this time for good, when we were selected to participate on *The Biggest Loser*.

Amy and I were different: I had no idea what a calorie was, and Amy was an experienced dieter. But we were both stuck, and desperately needed someone skilled who could coach us through the changes that would make our lives better.

Out of sixteen contestants, Amy came in second and I third in weight loss percentage, dropping a combined total of 256 pounds. Suddenly we had more energy. We had more hope. We even parented differently, for the first time emphasizing healthy living.

We were also getting e-mails from parents of other autistic kids, saying they'd seen us on TV and been encouraged by our story. Daily challenges still overwhelmed us, but we didn't feel as alone in our struggles.

One day we got an e-mail from a local tutoring and brain training organization that wanted to help Rhett. At this point Rhett had officially been in kindergarten for three years, with little hope of being promoted to first grade. After the tutoring, the changes were so dramatic that Rhett was admitted into first grade and has advanced every year since.

Today Rhett is in fifth grade, and is in regular classes most of the time. He loves to read. He does his homework by himself in about half an hour. And when he's looking for his backpack and we tell him it's in the living room on top of the bookshelf next to the couch, he knows immediately where to look.

We recently had a birthday party for Rhett. Surrounded by friends and family, he read every card aloud, then thanked each guest one by one. Watching him shine, I thought, "He still has autism, but he has friends. He has skills and dreams. He has a future, and it's brighter than we imagined it could be."

We're so thankful for the coaches who so dramatically changed our lives—Bob Harper and Jillian Michaels who helped us change our bodies, and our local tutors who helped Rhett catch up to his classmates.

Life really can change in a heartbeat. Things can be really hard, then something happens and you find yourself heading in a whole new direction.

~Phil Parham

Chapter 8

Raising Kids on the Spectrum

Snapshots

79

Sound of a Sunset

A sunrise or sunset can be ablaze with brilliance and arouse all the passion,
all the yearning, in the soul of the beholder.
~Mary Balough

riffin, my fourteen-year-old autistic son, makes a lot of noise. A LOT of noise. If he is not sleeping there are always loud sounds emanating from him. We have the maniacal laugh and other verbal stims. There is the sound of him slapping his torso for hours on end. Most of all there are the questions. If he weren't so cute I would swear the relentless questioning is some sort of KGB plot to drive me insane.

Sometimes, I want a tattoo that says "Yes, I like elevators and Wilford is awesome" on my forehead to at least cut out fifteen percent of the questions I get every hour. "No. We are not moving," and "To the bathroom. I am going to the bathroom," would eliminate about another nine percent.

Considering the relentless noise, when Griffin is quiet we get nervous. It sneaks up on you. Like the other evening when Mrs. Big Daddy and Lil Sis were out and the boys were left at home. I was doing a crossword and heard Griffin go to the kitchen with the stated purpose of getting a drink of water. I heard him fill his cup and then… nothing. For about forty-five seconds I heard nothing. He had not left the kitchen. He wasn't giggling. I got no questions. Silence.

I went to the kitchen to investigate and there stood Griffin, staring out the window at a magnificent sunset. He turned to me, as lucid and "in our world" as I've ever seen him, and said, "Daddy. That is a beautiful sunset."

It was, without a doubt, the most beautiful sunset I had ever seen. Before I could answer him, Griffin was off to his room to start giggling and, I'm sure, to think of new ways to ask me the same questions I've already answered thousands of times. In the meantime, I stood in the kitchen, crying, for what seemed to be an hour.

~F. Lewis "Big Daddy" Stark

80

The Blister

If you don't like something change it;
if you can't change it, change the way you think about it.
~Mary Engelbreit

Click. Clack. It was the soundtrack of my day, the sound of my five-year-old son Judah tapping his wooden toy trains together. A pot of soup simmered on the stove.

I sat at my kitchen table and picked up the dog-eared notebook Judah carried back and forth to school. That notebook. Every day like clockwork it came, its black and white marbled cover an intruder in my daily routine. My husband would be home soon. Judah and his brother Seth, two and a half, were watching *Mr. Rogers' Neighborhood* in the next room. Time to read the notebook.

Next to today's date was a sticker. "This is what I did today!" exclaimed the bright yellow happy face. "Language therapy today: He/I; I/you. Judah still confuses these words. Echolalia noted. Comments: We are trying to redirect Judah's behavior regarding unstructured free play. He has a tendency to go off on his own and become engrossed in one object, e.g. trains. He is in his own little world. He isolates himself and will not tolerate other children. Self-stimulatory behavior observed. Poor eye contact."

The clear message was this: Your son is imperfect, damaged, broken. God's mistake. Sometimes it felt as if we were locked in a night-marish tug-of-war with my husband and me on one side desperately pulling our son's body from the jaws of a monster. The monster was autism.

Click. Clack. Judah wandered by, a toy train in each fist. He had chewed his turtleneck collar to shreds.

"Hi, honey." I leaned toward him, cupping his chin in my hand and twisting his face to mine. My eyes captured his and grasped them forcefully. "Judah, it's almost time for dinner." I paused, watching the blank face for signs of recognition.

It was like waiting for a gumball machine. The quarter went in, chugged its way down. Then, the gumball climbed a conveyor belt to the top of the transparent dome, and descended, sliding its way through roller-coaster turns, riding up and around and down until it finally plopped into the cup.

"You are having macaroni?" Judah finally said.

"You mean you would like macaroni."

"Okay."

"Okay, Judah. We can have macaroni. Will you help me?"

Again, the wait.

"Judah can help me?" he suggested.

"Judah can help me."

"Okay."

I propped him up on his tiptoes on top of the stepstool, and turned on the faucet. Together, we filled the saucepan and set it on the stove, moving the stool as we went along. While Judah perched near the stove, gawking at the water, I turned to stir the soup. Judah must have reached over, because suddenly I heard, "W-a-a-a-h!" Face red, mouth contorted, Judah wrung his hands, his shriek exploding over the house.

I dropped the spoon and swept him up in my arms.

"Oh, honey, are you hurt? What is it?"

He raised one trembling hand.

"Did you burn yourself?" Amidst his screams I pushed his hand under the faucet and let the cool water run over the burn. Then I used a clean dishtowel to swaddle his hand.

Judah glared at the bundle.

"It's a burn, honey. I know it hurts, but Momma will make it better."

I unwrapped the finger like a present. There it was, a new blister. My breath stuck in my throat.

"A tissue!" he screamed.

"A tissue? What for?"

"Wipe it off! Wipe it off!"

"Judah, no, it's a blister. Part of your own skin. It doesn't come off."

"Take off the Band-Aid!"

"It's not a Band-Aid. It doesn't come off. It's a kind of boo-boo and it will get better soon." I touched the blister to my lips.

He sniffed.

I gathered him up in my arms, wrapped myself around my son's bony body. Judah needed my reservoir of calm; I dipped into it with both hands.

He said nothing and did not return my embrace.

And then I realized. I'd said it myself. The blister was part of his own skin—like autism. His chewed-up shirt, his gnawed fingernails, his confused pronouns, his tantrums, were all part of him. They wouldn't come off. They were woven into his gentle nature, inseparable from the presence I saw in those unfathomable hazel eyes.

He studied me as if I were a hieroglyphic, and I found myself deciphering him the same way. I dwelled on his flushed cheeks, his tearless eyes, the small sucking motion of his lips, almost picturing the gears, lifts and pulleys running the colorful mechanism of his mind.

I could see his question landing with its familiar plunk. "You are playing with trains?"

"No, honey. You, Judah, you want to play with trains." I pointed to him.

He looked down at my finger touching his chest. The quiet eyes inched over my hand like a caterpillar, climbing the skin of my arm to my shoulder, neck, face. Eyes.

Eye contact. Something in me let go. I felt my heart fall backwards and land, surprised to look around and find that the tug-of-war was over, and Judah was safe, looking at me with his hopeful wordless eyes.

In that moment Judah gave me a great gift. I knew then something it takes most parents years to learn—that my child doesn't belong to me, he is himself, not a reflection of my ego. That he is not broken but whole—created in the image of God, a God who understands disability, because there are things even God can't control, things for which God needs our help.

Supper could wait. I took my son's hand. "Yes, Judah. I'll play trains with you," I said, and I turned off the stove.

~Faith Paulsen

Just for This Day

Give your stress wings and let it fly away.
~Terri Guillemets

Just for this morning, I am going to smile whenever I see your face and laugh when I feel like crying.

Just for this morning, I will let you wake up softly, all rumpled in your flannel and I will hold you until you are ready.

Just for this morning, I will let you choose what you want to wear, and smile and say you're beautiful.

Just for this morning, I am going to step over the laundry, and pick you up and take you to the park to play.

Just for this morning, I am going to eat a huge breakfast, with bacon, eggs, toast and waffles, and you don't have to eat any.

Just for this morning, I will leave the dishes in the sink, and let you teach me how to put that 100-piece puzzle together.

Just for this afternoon, I will unplug the telephone and keep the computer off, and sit with you in the garden blowing bubbles.

Just for this afternoon, I will not yell once, not even a tiny grumble when you scream and whine for the ice cream truck, and I will buy you one if he comes by.

Just for this afternoon, I won't worry about what you are going to be when you grow up or who you might have been before your diagnosis.

Just for this afternoon, I will let you help me bake cookies, and I won't stand over you trying to "fix" things.

Just for this afternoon, I will let you put all kinds of barrettes in my hair, and put lipstick on my face, and I will tell you how pretty you have made me look.

Just for this afternoon I will take you to McDonald's and buy us both a Happy Meal so you can have both toys.

Just for this evening, I will hold you in my arms and tell you a story about how you were born, and how much we love you.

Just for this evening, I will let you splash in the bathtub and not get angry when you throw water over your sister's head.

Just for this evening, I will let you stay up late while we sit on the porch swing and count all the stars.

Just for this evening, I will bring you glasses of water, and snuggle beside you for three hours and miss my favorite show on TV.

Just for this evening, when I kneel down to pray, I will simply be grateful for all that I have and not ask for anything, except just one more day.

~Sally Meyer

82

Chicken Soup for the Soul

Tuesday Morning

No man can possibly know what life means, what the world means,
until he has a child and loves it.
~Lafcadio Hearn

It's nearly three o'clock on a Tuesday morning when my autistic eight-year-old son walks into our bedroom, backlit by the bathroom nightlight. He needs help going to the bathroom. I get up and walk him in, talk him through it, help him. When he leaves the bathroom he turns toward our room. I try to steer him toward his, but he twists away and through our door, climbs into our bed. I scooch him over and climb in, pulling up the covers, drifting back to sleep.

A few minutes of stillness, then he rolls around a bit and sits up. He slides out of bed. "What are you doing?"

"I'm leaving."

"Where are you going?"

"Away." He walks down the hall, to the kitchen.

"Everyone is trying to sleep. Let's go back to bed, your bed or our bed."

"No. I wanna get up."

"C'mon, let's go. Our bed or your bed, but you have to go to bed."

"No."

In a perfect world a perfect father would negotiate, but I'm tired and I don't want to risk more late night rambles. "Let's go to bed," I say in my firmest tone, trying to keep my voice level, knowing that any agitation on my part will feed his own. "Either bed, you choose, but we have to go, now."

"No. No. No. No. No."

I try to shepherd him toward his bedroom, saying, "We need to go to bed." He goes limp and sits on the floor. I try to pick him up, but he stays limp and squirms. He's not very big, but he can be awkward to handle when he chooses. I try again to force him to go. Big mistake. His agitation level rises.

"No. I wanna go watch a movie."

Now I negotiate. "How about if we read a book?"

"No." I offer a snack, to be followed by bed. He's quietly considering my offer.

He says something about not wanting a snack but heads toward the kitchen; sometimes, when he is agitated, he gets confused with his language. He goes past the kitchen, into the family room, and rummages through the library box. He grabs one of his favorite comic book collections and sets it on the kitchen table, standing beside it. I turn toward the cupboard to get him a snack. He grabs the book and heads down the hall, into his bedroom, and turns on the bedroom light. "You don't want to read," he says, clutching the book to his chest like a talisman. "Read to me. Don't read."

Things have moved beyond the immediate issue, into deeper fears and feelings. Tears rise in his eyes and drip down his cheeks. I gently take the book from his hands and begin to read. He really likes this book and I hope he will get engrossed in it. "No!" he shouts, grabs the book back and tosses it on the floor.

"You want to read!"

"Then let me read."

"No." I sit on the bed beside him. I reach over and gently rub his shoulder, feeling the tension in those muscles. We leave the book on the floor.

He looks at me, his always-big, jet-black eyes magnified by the tears welling in them, then he looks away, into space. Eye contact is difficult for him, he feels safer staring at nothing. "I'm, not, happy," he sobs, each word coming between gasps of air. "I'm not happy." I slip my hand under his nightshirt, actually one of my T-shirts, really too big on his slight body. I rub his back.

"You're not happy," I echo.

"No." I'm a little surprised that he lets me keep rubbing his back, even more when he leans against my hand. I look around the room, at the dark blue walls, the white blinds against the window, which is still black with night, at the large wall calendar, worn from his pressing against it when he counts out days, at the few stuffed animals that have fallen from the bed to the floor, at the colorful rug, the comic book lying on it, open, the cover splayed.

His words are true for this moment, and I feel bad for his feelings, for him. But I am secretly thrilled that he says them, that his statement matches the situation. Appropriate and timely communication is something we have long prayed for. He says again he is not happy. I ask why. He's quiet for a moment, then slips back into his usual communication style, naming concrete things in his life, listing them, in no real order and without real meaning. I'm not surprised; he has difficulty conceptualizing emotions and feelings and finds it hard to articulate anything that can't be counted out or physically measured.

He feels more than he can say; I can tell he knows it, and that knowledge frustrates him. I know, from experience, that the tone of my own voice is more important to him than its content, that he and I need to work through this tension; he needs to relax and return to his comfort zone. As much to fill my words as anything else, I remind him that I love him, his mother loves him, his sister loves him. I know those things are true, and I know he hears me, but I don't know how much he really comprehends what I am saying. He sighs, though, and leans back a little harder against my rubbing hand.

I find myself thinking about just how alone this little boy can be. I picture him walking in the faint light, from his room toward ours, through a long and sometimes eerie hallway, seeking something he cannot quite name. For most of us, the darkness leads to somewhere, the night fades into morning, we see, we name, we seek, we find, we share. But for him, I think, the hallway sometimes goes on and on. He lives mostly alone, sees shadows on the edges, hears strange sounds from around corners, sometimes finds a place to rest. But, most often it is just him, in his world, at three a.m., not knowing what lies beyond, uncertain of the dawn, not knowing exactly what he wants, not knowing how to ask.

He leans back against me. I lie down and he lies against me, his head on my stomach. I see by the window that it is still night; I think about getting up to turn off the light, but I know he would object; he has had enough of darkness. So I close my eyes. He lies against me. I drift off. When I awaken, he is lying beside me, breathing heavily. I get up carefully, gently move him so his head is on the pillow, and cover him. I turn off the light, but it doesn't get dark. Dawn has come, at least for me.

I glance back at him, watch him sleep, and gently close his door, leaving him alone in his room, and to his long gray journey. He is unhappy, but I am happy that he told me, that he could find the words to make the connection, to express himself, to bring him closer to the dawn.

~Douglas E. Baker

83

Chicken Soup for the Soul

They Think He's Dancing

Dance is the hidden language of the soul.
~Martha Graham

"Oh, look!" says the well-meaning cashier, laughing heartily. "He's got a little song in his head, don't you, honey?" She tilts her head, looking for William's gaze. "I see you dancing, buddy. Are you thinking of a song?"

He doesn't answer her. Just keeps waving his arms in that tried-and-true, rhythmic motion.

"I'm sorry, he won't answer you," I say. "He has autism. He has a hard time with the commotion of a public place, and waving his arms like this makes him feel better."

She smiles, not comprehending. "It's so busy in here today. I have a two-year-old little girl, and she just cries at the grocery store. I have to keep after her with Cheerios, and then we're all ready for a nap when we get home. You're probably ready for a nap, aren't you, buddy?"

"Yes, I am," I reply, deadpan. She laughs, and I get the heck out of there.

It usually goes like that. I'm not trying to make them feel bad. I have about three self-deprecating jokes I rotate in a feeble attempt to educate the general public about autism, without the humiliation.

Even so, I often go blank and say, "It's probably a jazz song in his head. He loves jazz." And then we talk about how unusual it is for a preschool-age kid to enjoy jazz so much. Or, you know, sometimes I just whip out a "No, he's not dancing. He has autism. What was the total again?" Those are the days I'm kind of a jerk.

The latest one was different, though. My grandpa plays sax in a big jazz band. We live two states away, so we don't have much opportunity to attend concerts. But there's one venue they play every year that nobody in the family misses. The acoustics are just right. They play all the old standards — "In the Mood," "I've Got You Under My Skin," "Hey, Mr. Zoot Suit," and the crowd is always huge and has been known to randomly get up and dance. And when they introduce my grandpa, everyone in the first four rows screams and whistles, because all of us are Wagners by blood.

This year was the first year we knew how to handle the concert with William. Previously, we sat down in the front like we always had, and when the music started, it startled both William and our neurotypical daughter so badly there was no recovery. But this time, we started out in the back and worked our way forward once the kids had the chance to acclimate to the volume and recognize some of the music. And at that point, there was no holding him down.

I sat down in the second row next to my parents, and stuck William on my lap. He didn't like that. He squiggled and slithered until he'd found the aisle, and started in on the arm waving. Up, in, out, in, down. Up, in, out, in, down. Then he brought his legs into it. Up, in, out, in, down, kick. Step, kick, kick. Up, in, out. Step, kick, kick. And then he looked up at me, once, eyes brilliant and twenty teeth shining, as if to say, "Don't you see this, Mom? Don't you hear how awesome this is?" and turned back to the band, waving and kicking and beaming.

I took my eyes off him and realized that I was getting those looks again. Those "knowing" smiles exchanged between the elderly husband and wife sitting across the aisle. The inevitable eye contact and smiling-shaking-the-head-in-wonder thing I got from both of the singers. The joyful giggles of children across the room, who took a cue from William and stood up to dance with one another. It seemed the whole front section of the room was watching him and loving him.

I knew I would be approached at intermission by at least three people who wanted to comment on William's sweet dance, and I contemplated how to politely correct them. At first, I felt some strange combination between irritation and a sad knowledge that these people would likely never know what they were seeing. I felt sad that my husband and I and some of my relatives did know what we were seeing, and we were all alone in that. And I felt the blank-out coming. What were my funny, self-deprecating educational comments again?

That's when I realized I had no idea what to correct. Was I supposed to correct their ignorant belief that he was... happy? Enjoying the music? Recognizing some of the songs? Dying, in some way, to express his joy?

They thought he was dancing. And... well, he was.

So, this time, when perfect strangers expressed their enjoyment of my son, I smiled. I said, yep, he loves to dance. I said he loves jazz. I said we've got a future pianist or drummer on our hands. And when one of the singers asked to introduce him to the crowd, I said sure.

They got it right enough.

~Maura Klopfenstein-Oprisko

84

Twirl with Me, Mommy!

When you dance, your purpose is not to get to a certain place on the floor.
It's to enjoy each step along the way.
~Wayne Dyer

My daughter Kylie's favorite place to play is at the Pottery Barn Kids store in one of our local malls. Kylie goes immediately to the Madeline Play Vanity, sits on the little pink tuffet and admires herself in the mirror. She then finds the jewelry box display and spends the good part of an hour investigating the interior of the boxes. She opens each one slowly as though they contain a great secret. The treasure within is a beautiful, tiny ballerina that twirls in perfect time to the music.

On this particular day, my daughter is mesmerized by these simple wooden boxes, and I silently observe as she studies the ballerina, takes a step back, places her sweet little baby arms in the same position as that of the ballerina and slowly begins to turn. I try not to make a sound, as I don't want to break the beautiful spell of the moment. My precious daughter is in a world of her own, pretending she is that sweet little ballerina. I feel tears pool in my eyes and I choke on the stifled sobs that gather in my throat.

I realize then that we are not alone. A small group of ladies, employees and customers, have gathered. A hush falls over us and, as I glance at their faces, I realize they are feeling the same tug at their heartstrings. They, too, are taking a little walk down memory lane.

When they rouse from their reverie and realize that I have noticed them, they comment on how beautiful Kylie is and how adorable she looks as she dances to the music—so innocent and oblivious to the audience that has been watching her.

What they don't know is that my Kylie experiences autism. They don't know all the work, steps and conditioning it has taken to be able to even approach a mall, let alone ride an escalator or elevator. What they don't know (at least not yet) is that when I tell Kylie that it is time to go, this sweet ballerina will morph into someone entirely different—a very loud and unhappy someone. A someone who most likely will lie on the floor and scream because she cannot process why we can't stay. She doesn't understand what it means that the store is closing. Her communication difficulties are a barrier to expressing appropriately how she feels.

I have a decision to make. Do I take the time to explain to these ladies, who are admiring my daughter, that she experiences autism so that they will understand when they see the transformation take place? Or do I protect my daughter's privacy and let them think that she is a spoiled, horribly misbehaved child and that I am a terrible mother. I know I'm not supposed to care about what others think, but I do—I always do.

Just then, Kylie catches my eye and reaches for my hand. "Twirl with me, Mommy?" she asks and how can I deny her? I gather her little fingers in mine and we twirl faster and faster. The struggle of what I know is to come falls away from me. I feel less overwhelmed. I feel like I can breathe. Kylie begins to giggle and I feel a smile tug at my lips. Now we are laughing together and this mommy is getting dizzy. We twirl and twirl and twirl! Kylie could keep spinning for much longer but mercifully, she gives me a break. What FUN we have together! Can we freeze this moment? Do we HAVE to endure a transition?

Oh, what I would give to stop the clock. Right here, right now with my baby's hand in mine. The autism seems so far away. I inwardly plead for more time. I capture the memory in my heart. I savor the moment. I indulge. I enjoy!

"Again! Again? Twirl again?" she asks, with a sparkle in her eye and a giggle in her voice.

"Yes!" I reply. "Yes! Sweet Kylie, let's twirl again... and again... and again...."

~Amy L. Stout

85

The Island

If the sight of the blue skies fills you with joy, if a blade of grass springing up in the fields has power to move you, if the simple things in nature have a message you understand, Rejoice, for your soul is alive.
~Eleanora Duse

Today something happened to Alexa and me, and as it was happening, I had the clear but strange thought, "This is a metaphor for your life." So I began to pay attention to the details.

It was April and we were on vacation from school. The warm weather was just beginning. Sensing the pull and tease of the sun, I said to Alexa, "Let's take a ride to the beach!" She climbed into the car, as eager and restless as I.

We drove to Plum Island. It's a small barrier island just off Massachusetts's northern coast. Named after the beach plum bushes that are scattered across the landscape, it is home to the Parker River Wildlife Refuge, a gorgeous, protected piece of earth. Driving past the entrance of the Refuge I passed the first parking lot where we could stop and walk onto the beach. I realized I had never seen the south edge of the island, had never driven all the way to the end of the road. I didn't even know how far away the end of the island was. I decided to keep on driving, passing more beach access parking lots along the way.

After about three and a half miles of state park driving at twenty miles per hour, the smooth pavement of the road became dirt. I slowed down to five or ten miles per hour. Dust swirled around our car. I wondered out loud to Alexa, "Is this road ever going to end?" Glancing in the rearview mirror I saw my question reflected on her face. Eyes filled with concern stared straight ahead. The road came to a T. On the left was another beach area. A sign, "Sandy Point State Reservation," stood on the right, where the road continued. I turned left and parked the car.

We got out and walked along the footpath to the beach. It was crowded and rocky. For a few minutes we watched people off in the distance carefully choosing their steps. "You know what? This isn't the end. Let's go to the end," I said. With renewed determination, we took the road heading farther south.

Within seconds, we hit a huge pothole and felt the whole car bounce. Trying to avoid more large potholes ahead, I slowed to a crawl, weaving the car from one side of the road to the other.

"This is ridiculous," I told Alexa.

"Diculous," she agreed.

Then abruptly, it was over. We were at the end. I pulled into a parking space and turned the engine off. With huge grins on our faces we got out and stepped onto a boardwalk that brought us up to a small sheltered landing before turning and spilling us out again on soft sand.

We were on an aisle of sorts. Ropes swept loosely from stakes, protecting sea grass and plovers on either side. The pathway was wide and generous. Seashells were scattered at our feet. I noticed green growth springing up from the same roots as brown withered leaves. The deep blue expanse of the ocean lay before us, covered with rippling white foam. The wind was wild with celebration. Long flowing grass was bowing down. There we were, my daughter and I, at the very tip of the island, at the very end of the road, smack dab in the middle of reverence.

Alexa started uttering words I had never heard her say before.

Her silence, like many other times, had seemed heavy when we were in the car. There's stillness in her silence sometimes that is hard to describe. I am used to not being able to have a conversation with her but I like how her cheerful repeating of phrases fills up the air. When she is silent even those words are gone and it reminds me of all that is missing.

Now her voice, high with excitement, was breaking free. She grabbed and held on to my arm, pulling me forward. That in itself is rare. I am usually the one who has to coax her into moving along.

"This is beauty! This is beauty!" she burst out. And then as if her own voice could not be contained, "Hallelujah!" Over and over again she sang out the words. "This is beauty! This is beauty! Hallelujah!"

My eyes filled with tears. I understood the metaphor. I understood what she said.

This is beauty. Just to have gotten the chance to taste this kind of love in my life. The kind of love that goes beyond limitations. The kind of love that gives everything it has, and if everything else is stripped away, unyielding and unbroken, it still stands. The kind of love that makes the price of a difficult road seem like pennies to pay, after all.

It's not that I think I am so noble or anything. I struggle with loving plenty of people. But in this one person, I know that I have experienced the purest and most powerful side of love. So powerful, I never felt or thought it was a choice.

This is beauty. For just a moment, the dust clouds of my life cleared and I could see the gift shimmering there. It was love, beautiful love. My voice joined with Alexa's as the breeze gathered up the sound, lifted it higher, and carried it off toward the sea.

This is beauty. This is beauty. Hallelujah.

~D. Alison Watt

Flying the Friendly Skies

Trapped by reality, freed by imagination.
~Nicolas Manetta

Clarkie was amping up, his agitated whine growing louder, his head swaddled in his yellow blanket and his hands clamped over his ears. A broken vent hissed out a powerful jet of air above Seat 7F, where my six-year-old struggled to stay in control after a long day of travel, airports and delays.

The malfunctioning air vent—a simple annoyance for most people—threatened to push Clarkie into a full-fledged meltdown even before the plane left the gate in Detroit.

Travel tests the patience of any parent, but when your child has an autism spectrum disorder, as the younger of my two sons does, it helps to be resourceful, daring and lucky. Delayed nearly three hours by a mechanical problem, the darkened plane was full of irritable passengers trying to fall asleep. And yet Clark's high-pitched whine began to amplify.

"I can't stand it!" he cried, as the vent hissed unrelentingly.

I called over the flight attendant and explained. "My child has autism, and the noise from this broken vent is unbearable to him. Can it be fixed or can we change seats?"

"I'm sorry, the flight is full," the attendant said, before hustling off to her duties.

As Clarkie's whining continued, tears of frustration filled my older son's eyes, his patience frayed by his brother's all-too-frequent agitation. Desperate, I jammed the yellow blanket against the vent—silence!—then considered whether I could hold my arm in that position for sixty-three minutes until we touched down in Baltimore. Then... a glimmer of inspiration.

Fumbling in my purse with my free hand, I found tissues and stuffed them into the vent crevice. A woman across the aisle offered me two Band-Aids to tape the tissues in place. I gratefully accepted, and the mood around us seemed to lighten. Seeing the makeshift repair, a man joked that I should've been called in to fix the plane in the first place. What could have been an emotionally turbulent flight turned into something positive. The rest of the flight was smooth. And later, as Clarkie darted about at baggage claim, passengers recognized him and smiled at his antics.

The two bandage strips covering crumpled tissues made a comical but effective fix for the broken vent—one that required a measure of ingenuity, desperation and goodwill, much like the life that we manage to pull together every day. For all things about autism that chafe against our family, we travel on, coping with what we can and delighting when we find empathetic people who lend a hand, even when they may not totally understand our difficulties.

I cannot always make the world a quiet, easy place for my "Quirky Clarkie"—nor can any parent do so for a child—but on this one day, in this one way, I was his hero.

Once the offending vent was silenced, Clark calmly removed his hands from his ears, looked up at the wadded tissues and grinned. "Mommy, you saved the day!"

~Michelle Landrum

Because Night Turns into Day

Some see a hopeless end, while others see an endless hope.
~Author Unknown

Every now and then, my fourteen-year-old son Marshawn, who has autism, goes through phases where he wakes up very early. I'm talking 4 or 5 a.m. early, when the alarm is set for 7:30. It's frustrating to say the least, particularly because he doesn't fall asleep until pretty late, and I'm usually exhausted. By the time I get him to fall back to sleep, it's time for us to wake up.

One morning after an "early awakening," I asked him why he had gotten up so early. He said, "Because night turns into day. The sun rises."

That was the last thing I expected him to say. Honestly, I didn't expect him to give me a real reason at all, as he often repeats my questions rather than answers them. As a person who loves watching the sky, all I could do was appreciate his response, although I'm grateful he doesn't wake up at the crack of dawn every single day. For days after that brief conversation, I couldn't stop thinking about his words, and it had nothing to do with the sky. It resonated with me, because I felt a sense of encouragement that he didn't even know he had blessed me with.

Life can definitely be hard, and I sometimes find myself in a dark place trying to find balance and make the right choices from one day to the next. I often feel lost, and think that there has to be more to life than feeling like this. Parenting, in my opinion, is one of the toughest jobs there is. Being a single mom of a child with autism presents a whole other dimension of challenges which affects every single decision that I make—important choices like work and child care, and more subtle things like whether a public place we choose to visit has family bathrooms, because I can't send my teenaged child into a men's room alone. Transitions, puberty, social and behavioral difficulties are just a few of the things that cloud my mind on a daily basis.

However, life is not always a sad song. Despite the tough times that we've encountered, his words ring true. "Night turns into day. The sun rises." During my son's evaluations and around the time of the initial diagnosis, I was beyond overwhelmed. It's hard to see the bright side of a difficult situation when it blindsides you.

As time goes on, and with each milestone, with each goal accomplished, with each amazing thing that my son does, I have seen night turn into day. I have become more optimistic, gained a lot more clarity of mind, and things have become brighter. Marshawn helps me to see life differently and to look beyond the obvious. Days are sometimes stormy, but his presence always reminds me to see the beauty in each one... to see the beauty in life with a son who is unique, loving, brilliant and the greatest gift I could have.

~Janoah M. White

Transformation on the Trail

In every walk with nature one receives far more than he seeks.
~John Muir

We hike single file. For a change, I lead the way. I am exhausted, moody, and yet eager to soak in what could be the last nice day of autumn. Joel, our youngest son, is in the middle as always, walking slowly, tentatively through the leaves, afraid of tripping on a root. My husband Wally brings up the rear. Joel's constant chatter has subsided and we are quiet, our feet doing the talking as we scuff across the yellow-carpeted forest floor.

I hear Joel's footsteps quicken and turn to see him approaching at a near-run. Surprised, I stop. He grabs my hand, looks me in the eye, grins, and pulls me forward. I wait for him to drop my hand, as he always does, but instead he squeezes it and swings my arm, his grin widening at my delight. For a moment, it feels so right, his hand a perfect fit in mine. A jolt of joy shocks my body, answered almost immediately by my mind, which says, "No, don't go there." There are no happy endings with twenty-six-year-old sons with autism. There are no happily-ever-afters when they move away from home and you are left, not with "this is the way it's supposed to be," but with guilt, and sleepless nights, and often, regret.

Joel holds my hand tight, matches my gait stride for stride, steals sideway gazes, his eyes playful, a smile flitting, now-you-see-it-now-you-don't, across his handsome face.

For a month he has been constant motion, constant chatter. Lashing out at staff with hands. Running around the sixty-acre farm for adults with autism that he moved to last year. Manic swings, which we thought he'd left behind with adolescence, erupting again, keeping him awake at night, and keeping everyone in his house on edge.

Dreams die hard. It will never be what we expected, our third son's adulthood. You think you've moved into a place called acceptance, when yet another transition takes place and you grieve all over again. Letting go of this son is nothing like letting his brothers go. That was the natural, normal progression of life, something to celebrate. Knowing you did your job as a parent, giving them roots and wings. This feels like an amputation, so deep is this son's need, so intensive our caregiving, a quarter century's worth.

Joel's hand, still clutching mine, is warm and sweaty. I leave my doubting behind for a moment.

Friends tell me I must cut the cord, not hold so tight to this broken boy-man. But this connection — this hand in mine — tells me what my gut already knows. This cord is a living cord, a cord of flesh and blood. Unlike an umbilical cord, this cord can never be severed. Yes, like the towering maples and beech along this trail, we will go through fallow seasons. Like this past year, with his move away from home, a seeming death for him, for me, for his father.

Every October I mourn the passing of summer. Dread the dank days of winter to come. I want to hold onto this moment forever. But my head reminds me that spring always follows winter. Spring, when the sap flows upward, bringing with it new life, new possibilities, new ways of being.

This is what is true: I am his mother. He is my son. And we are walking up a hill, hand in hand, through sunlight streaming golden through a canopy of maple and beech.

~Kathleen Deyer Bolduc

Raising Kids on the Spectrum

Hope and Expectations

Ma Tovu

God gives us dreams a size too big so that we can grow in them.
~Author Unknown

The first four times we went to Sharing Shabbat, the weekly children's service at our synagogue, we didn't make it through the opening prayer of Ma Tovu. I cried after the first two weeks, and by week four I was ready to give up. Perhaps it was a mistake to think Jodie could become a Bat Mitzvah.

Jodie was diagnosed with autism when she was two and a half. Many parents of children with autism say the day their child was diagnosed was the worst day, and that after that initial shock, things improved. That hasn't been our experience. Every family celebration and milestone is bittersweet, because it is a reminder of Jodie's constant struggles. Looking at the empty seat at the Thanksgiving table after Jodie has gotten up after two minutes because she can't sit still is just as hard for me as it was to hear the initial diagnosis. I felt a huge emptiness at my brother-in-law's graduation; the whole family was there, except Jodie, who, despite being the oldest cousin, had to stay home with a babysitter. But I knew the hardest of all would be to let her Bat Mitzvah date pass by as if it were just any other day, without any sort of recognition or celebration.

Jodie has gone to special needs Hebrew school through a wonderful program called Matan since kindergarten. In our home, she says the hamotzi (the blessing over the bread), as well as the blessing over the candles, because she learned them in Matan. She has always loved music, so I thought maybe, just maybe, she could learn a few more songs and prayers and become a Bat Mitzvah in more or less the traditional way.

And so despite our initial failed attempts, and thanks to a well-timed, very encouraging phone call from the Sharing Shabbat coordinator, we labored on at Sharing Shabbat. Yes, we labored on Shabbat; it was not easy for either of us to get through those first few weeks. I brought her favorite Sesame Street books, and then from time to time slipped the prayer book inside and used hand over hand to point to the words. Usually she'd respond by screaming "No Book! No Book!" so loudly that everyone turned and stared. But eventually Jodie seemed to get used to the rhythm of the service. By week six, we had made it through two minutes and had sung Ma Tovu. Halleluyah! And sure enough, the next week we made it to the song Halleluyah, a full four minutes in. A few weeks later we were joining in the blessing for the Torah. And after three long months, we actual ate bagels at the oneg after services.

It was certainly not easy for Jodie, as I'm sure it was not easy for the families at Sharing Shabbat. Jodie struggles to sit still, to pay attention, to be quiet. Her behavior is unpredictable and at times loud, disruptive, and aggressive. It takes many attempts at something new before she will accept it. But somehow she came to find comfort in the music of the service and in the repetition of the prayers week after week. Her favorite part seemed to be the end of each prayer, when she would smile broadly and sing a super loud and quite off-key "Amen!" We listened to the Sharing Shabbat CD in the car and she recognized the music, saying "go to the services" and singing along with her hearty "Amen!"

Jodie works hard every day to learn things that others learn without effort and take for granted. She struggles to communicate. She doesn't know how to make friends. Her body rarely seems at peace. But she seems to have found meaning and a sense of belonging at Sharing Shabbat. On Saturday mornings, when I'd say it was time for services, she would smile. Whether she enjoyed the service or just looked forward to the bagels and donuts afterwards, I'll never really know. But she happily went to services and participated with her robust "Amen." And for this we are so grateful to the entire Sharing Shabbat community.

On June 5, 2011 Jodie became a Bat Mitzvah. Once again, she exceeded our expectations. Her thirteenth birthday didn't just pass, unmarked, like any other day. Sure, she held a baby doll while she stood on the bimah in front of the family and friends who gathered for the occasion. In her other hand she held a box of Cheez-Its (I hope they are kosher). It wasn't her best behavior at a service. And when the rabbi presented her with a copy of the Torah as a gift from the community she looked right at him and shouted "No Book! No Book!" But she said the prayers and read her line of Torah and added many joyful "Amens." Afterwards our friends and family came back to our house for lunch and several raucous rounds of the hokey pokey. We were all there to welcome Jodie into the Jewish community as an adult. A great day. And I still cry every time I hear Ma Tovu. Amen.

~Alison Singer

When Ladybugs Roar

Hope is that thing with feathers that perches in the soul and sings the tune without the words and never stops... at all.
~Emily Dickinson

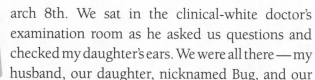

March 8th. We sat in the clinical-white doctor's examination room as he asked us questions and checked my daughter's ears. We were all there — my husband, our daughter, nicknamed Bug, and our infant son. I'd known for a while, as milestones slipped farther away, that we were headed toward that day. I'd prepared for the doctor to tell us it wasn't just hearing loss or poor parenting skills.

She was almost two years old and had never responded to her name. That wasn't something other parents had to teach their children.

Nothing can prepare you for that moment when a doctor first brings up autism. A load of bricks drops on you.

When I wrote in my journal that night, I said, "There are no words." I'd meant there were no words to describe the devastation we felt as parents as we sat in the doctor's office and heard those words that would change everything. It could have also described the loss Bug had gone through. One by one, the words she'd gained were lost to the quiet of autism.

By March 8th, she had no words.

My husband and I grieved on March 8th. On March 9th, we got to work.

Our lives became a maelstrom of movement. We made appointment after appointment. Therapists. Doctors. Specialists. Interventionists. I'm not sure we actually slept that first year.

And we read. My husband and I read everything we could get our hands on. From the clinical to the crackpot theories, we read it all. I had a migraine from that first March 8th to the next March 8th from staring at print and from stress.

Several well-meaning professionals told us it was okay to grieve because it was as if we'd lost a child. And, for a while, I believed that. They said Bug would never marry. They hoped she might someday hold down a job — a menial job. We should prepare ourselves for the possibility that she'd live with us forever.

In my mind, I packed away the prom dress, the wedding dress, and the business suit.

Then, we found out our odds of having another child with autism, and I mentally and physically packed away the baby clothes and prayed my son would be passed over.

Shortly after that, the interventionists sat in front of me, as Bug played in the corner and I rocked her brother, and they handed me a paper that said my almost two-year-old had the receptive language skill of a seven-month-old. Not only had we lost her, but she had lost us.

The impact of March 8th wasn't entirely negative. I will be forever grateful that our pediatrician listened to me on that day because we were given the priceless gift of time. Parents of young children on the spectrum can hear the tick-tocking of time in their mind. "Early intervention is key" is our mantra.

Another impact was the amazing joy of getting our child back and re-experiencing the milestones that had faded. The second "first word." The second "first time she says 'Mommy.'" The first time Bug made eye contact. The first time she put her feet in rice without screaming. Her joy in swinging and signing "more." These are moments that tick by unacknowledged by parents of typical children, or milestones they only experience once.

You count each tick-tock of the clock when it's this valuable.

Then there are the days that stick with you forever.

We were months into our new schedule. I'd started doing therapy at home. We were getting ready to move to a house so we could have a dedicated therapy room and hang swings and Lycra hammocks. I sat in Bug's room, picked up a cow plush toy, and showed it to Bug.

"What does the cow say?"

"Moo. Moo."

"What does a dog say?" The dog puppet didn't look much like a real dog, but Bug didn't seem to notice. We were making progress. Real progress. I was exhausted, but it felt worth it.

"Arf. Arf."

I held up the cat. I never got tired of Bug's few precious words. Animal sounds seemed easier than other words. She liked animal sounds. "What does a cat say?"

"Minnow. Minnow."

It was all the more adorable for sounding not quite right. Imperfection can be just as sweet as perfection.

I held up the ladybug puppet—intending to move on to things other than animal noises.

"RAWR." Bug made glancing eye contact with the puppet, not with me—though my face was right next to the ladybug's. If she saw my huge, ridiculous smile, she didn't react.

"What sound does a ladybug make?" I had to hear that again.

"RAWR."

That day was the day I learned bugs roar. And indeed they do. From that first miserable March 8th to its one-year anniversary, our progress with Bug was nothing less than astounding. The same professionals who'd given us dire predictions were struck dumb with all of Bug's words as she slowly stepped out of the quiet of autism.

There were struggles. There were illnesses where Bug seemed to regress, and we were terrified we were losing her again. There were days I spent two hours on the phone begging our insurance company for services that should have been covered. There was mind-numbing debt, debt we still struggle with a decade later. There were injuries—Bug didn't recognize pain the way a typical child would, and she couldn't tell us what hurt. But, beyond all that, there was the steady progress over time.

From my journal:

Words come now —
more and more.
Ladybugs — a lion's roar.
You were never going to be lost.
All that I have,
all that I am,
is yours.

Bug is now on the cusp of being a teenager. My son has been diagnosed with Asperger's — a diagnosis made easier because Bug came first. They are both mainstreamed in school. Most people don't know — they don't know we had our March 8th.

I think, I believe, I know that the quiet of autism can be overcome. My own ladybug has learned to roar. I'm slowly unpacking the prom dress, the wedding dress, and, given her math skills — a business suit.

She was never going to be lost. She was always meant to roar.

~Wendy Sparrow

The Poem in My Nightstand Drawer

Just like the butterfly, I too will awaken in my own time.
~Deborah Chaskin

M y husband of twenty years and I have two daughters, one of whom has autism. Parenting is hard if you are doing it right, no matter what kind of children you have. We simply refuse to give up. Our marriage has, at times, been held together by our secret fears of being responsible for the children alone. We've opted for sticking with the teamwork approach, despite our battered forces.

When Madison was a toddler, she had excruciating tantrums, night terrors, and everything in between. The tantrums were about nonsensical things, such as, "I want to go swimming, but I don't want to get wet." They were also about the tiniest details: a molecule of food on a shirt, the placement of common household items, the need to adhere strictly to routines. There was a cleansing ritual if her favorite stuffed animal made contact with the floor. The wind was a particular issue. If Madison saw a playground swing moved by the wind, or, worse yet, if the wind blew her skirt up against her legs, it would send her into a screaming fit as if she were being tortured.

When I think back on those days, I wonder how or why we ever left the house. But we did. I was sometimes accosted by misguided people from my parents' generation who blamed our child's behavior on my abysmal parenting skills. The unsolicited comments from those unfettered by age and poor manners really didn't help matters at all. There were many days when I privately sobbed for lack of knowing what else to do.

There were few answers for us back then. I read voraciously. I filled up a 100-page composition notebook with notes from no less than twenty-three parenting books, often while nursing our newborn daughter or pumping breast milk. I even added a crisp Table of Contents in the front and page numbers throughout. Nothing seemed to help.

The summer Madison was six and her little sister was three, Madison was given a butterfly habitat for her birthday. We received the Painted Lady larvae through the mail and watched as the larvae devoured their food, grew and grew and grew, and eventually formed chrysalises. We were amazed when four healthy butterflies emerged dazed and crumpled from these cocoons, and instinctively beat their wings for the first time.

We enjoyed watching the butterflies for several days. I knew they would live only a short time, and that it would be too dramatic to watch them die in the mesh cylinder that was their home, having never known freedom. One August day I talked the girls into releasing them. I took the easy way out and lied. I told them that the butterflies would come back to visit us. I envisioned myself pointing out "our butterfly" to them every time we saw a Painted Lady. Madison seemed to go along with this, and she even helped me convince her little sister, over whom she had considerable influence, that this was the right thing to do.

The butterflies were not mentioned again until I found the following poem in Madison's little flower-shaped spiral notebook that October:

Dear buterflys

when you lived in a cage I never wantid to let you go

enjoy liveing outside
I miss you
becous the werld is so long that you will go too far

love Madison

I'm ashamed to say I was astonished. Was this the same child who could have a forty-five-minute tantrum about which direction her juice cup was facing? This was our first indication that she was processing information other than some sensory detail like the fact that there was a wrinkle in her socks—that she was considering the perspectives of others, even if those "others" were just butterflies. The little poem proved that she had known all along that we would never see our butterflies again, and she also knew that her sister would not go along with my plan without her support. I gained respect for the intellectual gifts and compassion of a child who went along with my plan of liberating her brief pets, even though she could not go along with anything else.

We still have tough days, and Madison still argues about things that can't be easily changed. Her obsessions have progressed from the minutia of everyday life to issues so fundamental that she shouldn't be worrying about them at all, like her militant views on people who have large families, drink soda, or smoke cigarettes.

Autism has been an unexpected journey in our lives, a daily lesson that we cannot control everything. Yet, I live with a remarkable child who has taught me more than I've taught her. The day I found the butterfly poem, I learned that screaming, hysterical little girls are not always what they seem. And, I learned a universal fact: that people with autism are often having much more complex thoughts than they can easily express.

Are those brilliant pages from a flower-shaped spiral notebook laminated and tucked away in my nightstand drawer, to be used for inspiration during the tough days? You bet they are.

~Mary Roth

Two Worlds

*Happiness is an attitude. We either make ourselves miserable
or happy or strong. The amount of work is the same.*
~Francesca Reigler

Halloween. An exciting night for parents and children alike. Little ones dressed up as their favorite characters. Plastic pumpkins in hand ready to fill with treats. Spider webs, jack-o-lanterns, the scent of fall wafting through the air. And if you're my four-year-old son Joshua living with autism, a bottle of laundry detergent.

It was October 31st, the first year Joshua and his two-year-old sister, Shiloh, would get the chance to trick-or-treat together. I dressed Joshua up as a pirate and Shiloh as a cupcake. How cute they looked! I envisioned them skipping through the neighborhood, excitedly collecting goodies. So with pumpkins and camera in hand, we set off with a few family members and a friend.

The first house we went to had a dog that barked. Shiloh wasn't fazed at all. "Trick or treat!" she shouted, grabbing her candy and running off to the next house. Immediately I turned to Joshua. Panic mode had set in. Already nervous about this new and unusual adventure, he had covered his ears to muffle the sound of the barking dog. And he cried. And cried and cried. Sensory disorders are the most difficult differences to bear for the child living with autism and the most heartbreaking to see as a parent. My mom held Joshua tightly and tried to console him. I was doing my best to balance between my boy who needed my full attention and Shiloh who was excitedly running from house to house, grinning from ear to ear.

"Look Mommy, I got candy!"

"I know, baby. Good job!"

I desperately wanted to include Joshua. Despite trying to redirect him and show him what to do, nothing worked. He was experiencing total sensory overload.

We had chosen to go trick-or-treating in my good friend Rose's neighborhood. Rose has loved my son for many years and knows him well. I knew it was time to give in and bring Joshua to her house. There, he would be able to calm down and regroup and Shiloh would have my complete attention. As Rose took my sweet boy from my arms I could feel my heart break. I wanted him with me. I no longer cared if he went up to the houses; I just wanted him to be with the family. I didn't want to let him go. Rose looked at me the way she has done many times before. "Aspen," she said, "he's okay. He's going to be fine. It's going to be okay." I turned away from Joshua and walked towards my mom, who was holding back tears. I knew exactly how she was feeling. Those are the times when autism is hard. Really hard.

Later, Rose sent me a photo of Joshua eating a piece of candy while sitting on her washing machine. (Joshua has been fascinated by washing machines since he was eighteen months old.) He was calm and relaxed. At some point she decided to take him out and teach him how to trick or treat. She promised him they'd stay away from any home that had a dog. My heart broke when I saw the picture she texted me. There he was, just three feet tall, in his brown pirate pants that cupped the top of his sneakers to look like boots, his raggedy pirate shirt tucked under his black vest. The wig was gone (he didn't like it). His big green eyes and soft brown hair angled up towards the camera. And in his right hand was a giant, bright green bottle of laundry detergent. He was happy.

Joshua's first sentence as a toddler was, "I want the soap." At the time it was a bottle of children's shampoo. I praised him. Little did I know soap bottles would be among the objects that made him mysteriously happy for years to come. And now here he was, learning how to trick or treat, avoiding any homes with dogs or bright Halloween decorations or crowds of children in strange clothing, holding a bottle of detergent because it helped him feel safe. I cried, and smiled. I felt sad, and proud. My heart was grieving, but at the same time, relieved.

Eventually I met Rose and Joshua somewhere in the neighborhood and saw how he had learned the process... knock on the door, say "trick or treat," get a piece of candy and say "thank you." He did it so well! And it was something that was very hard for him to do. If holding that bright green bottle of detergent made him feel safe and happy, then I was happy too.

At some point during the evening Rose had called my husband, Ryan, and told him what a difficult night it was for me. I was bathing the kids later that evening when he came around the corner of the bathroom, gave me a look as if to say "I understand" and tightly wrapped his arms around me. Sometimes words aren't necessary.

Autism has taught me selflessness. It isn't about me and how my kids look or behave. It isn't about costumes or activities or even about gifts on Christmas morning—Joshua doesn't care about them. It's not about my agenda. With Joshua it's about trying to understand his world... seeing things from his perspective, hearing things the way he might hear them, tweaking my plans and adjusting my schedule to make life doable and fun for my boy. It's about time and love.

This year I gave up. I will never again dress up Joshua on Halloween unless he decides it's something he wants to do. I won't push traditional Christmas morning activities. On Easter we won't hunt for eggs—he doesn't care about eggs. I only want what every mother wants for her kids, but Joshua's different. And really, in the grand scheme of things... what will it matter? At times I have grieved over our differences and yet at other times I've celebrated them! I love the fact that Joshua notices detail. I love that he loves people and remembers their names and the memories he's made with them. I love his sweet smile and his quirky comments that make me laugh. I love that everything is literal with Joshua. It's black or it's white. He is straight to the point and he always tells the truth. I love my son. And true love is being willing to do whatever it takes to enter into another's world. It's unconditional love.

I believe that one day my boy will be able to tell me what it's like to live with autism, and I'll be able to tell him what it's like to be "neurotypical." And there at my kitchen table, with the sun setting behind the window and cups of coffee in our hands, we'll share our two worlds, and the dog that barked on Halloween won't be a blip on my radar (or his). Maybe we'll even share a bowl of candy corn. Yes... I think we will.

~Aspen Teresa Nolette

The Other Side of Hope

The human spirit is stronger than anything that can happen to it.
~C. C. Scott

t's not like there was an "aha" moment when I knew. It was a gradual realization that "normal" wasn't in the cards for us—the realization this wasn't a temporary situation. We would not be one of those families whose child "recovered."

Maybe the realization came after finally having time to think. The early years were a complete blur: a whirlwind of doctors, experts and therapists. It was an immediate immersion into a foreign culture with a new language and new concepts to learn.

A time when everyone had an answer; everyone had a program; there were countless anecdotal success stories. Six weeks of this therapy or maybe that. Have you tried a sensory diet? Auditory training? Restricting gluten? Neurofeedback? Interactive metronome? Vitamin B? The list was endless.

For a thousand or two, we will fix your child. Hope was on sale and I was buying. Some interventions helped a little, some not at all. At the end of each therapy, improvement was reported. Like the boy in *The Emperor's New Clothes*, I didn't see it. I didn't say that out loud, though. I wanted to be wrong. I didn't want to admit my hope was showing signs of tarnish.

Dozens of therapies later, I watched countless younger children acquire skills and pass us by. They did with ease what my child could not. I continued to hear stories of kids who bridged the gap and wondered, why not Sam? Were we doing something wrong? Kids develop at different times, I told myself. We'll blend by kindergarten. Well maybe by first grade… or will it be second? It will happen.

Or will it?

As Sam enters his seventeenth year, we are beginning the transition process into adulthood. That includes guardianship at eighteen. This legal act effectively proclaims Sam is incapable of managing his life alone; the unspoken words that this is forever.

With that legal document I will officially transfer to the other side of hope. And I ask myself, now what? What happens when hope is gone?

I will remember to breathe. Cry a little. Regroup. Rebuild expectations. Search again for a place to fit in. Maybe redefine the word "normal." Take another deep breath and move on. Find the joy in each moment and stretch it to a lifetime. Look for balance and hold tightly to my sense of humor. Find a new star to reach. I will look into Sam's eyes and know this is the same boy I have always loved, who has made me and countless others smile.

I will build new hope as I close the door on one dream and open the door to another.

~Janet Amorello

94

Softness in the Vast Blue Sky

Underneath the hardness there is fear
Underneath the fear there is sadness
In the sadness there is softness
In the softness is the vast blue sky
~Author Unknown

When my son James was a baby, he was so beautiful. Everything seemed possible. Over time, it was clear to everyone but me that something was different about him, something to be concerned about. But I saw only magical uniqueness. Even when he was diagnosed with autism, I failed to acknowledge or to accept the loss of my dreams. I failed to see him for, yes, the truly magically unique child he was.

After his diagnosis, I was suddenly in a new world, a world I did not want to be in. A world I didn't know how to navigate. A world I only wanted to escape from. I denied the impact on my heart and on my life, and set out to force happy normalcy on us all. The alternative was simply more than I could bear.

There were lots of people to meet that I never would have crossed paths with. Experts. Parents. Doctors. Teachers. Specialists. Support groups. I was flooded with way too much information. I couldn't begin to sort it out. I was numb. No time for feelings. I had to function. I was alone with a son I loved who had a problem. I had to fix the problem. That is what I knew how to do and I did it very well. Fix problems. Find a solution. Make everything all right.

Someone said I should talk to Sherry, a mom/expert. Sort of the mother superior for all the novitiate moms. I took James to her house. She was so friendly. I thought she was happy because she knew how to make this all go away. She was going to share the secret cure with me. She had this great big smile on her face as she exclaimed, "I love autism!" Wow, I thought, will I ever love autism? I was pretty sure I wouldn't.

Many families look forward to the summer. Family vacations. Trips to the beach. Sports. Picnics. Cooking out in the back yard. Enjoying time with the kids. I don't remember it that way. Summers were a stressful time. Without the structure of school, James's autistic behavior deteriorated. He had frequent tantrums. He did not like to do what other kids enjoyed, so he did not have friends. He did not like to do what families like to do together, so family vacations were not something I looked forward to. I saw summers as opportunities to focus on the autism therapy du jour—auditory training, sensory integration, behavior modification, diet changes, homeopathic treatments, and on and on. With each summer, he grew older and my hope for a cure grew more desperate.

One spring I was talking to the child psychologist who worked with James. I was going over several options for the summer. One option I dismissed quickly by saying, "This one would just be fun." The doctor leaned forward until he was sure I was paying attention and said slowly and deliberately, "Fun... is... good."

I guess all those years of training paid off for him, because that was one of the smartest things I ever heard. I think that is when the healing began. When I realized that life in all its uncontrollable messiness held the promise of joy along with pain. That my child was like any other child—he wanted to be safe and happy, to learn and grow and have fun. That I was like any other mother—loving my child with my whole being, wanting to shield him from harm, wanting to prepare him for a life beyond me.

James himself helped me. One day, as he was looking at himself in the mirror, I heard him shout, "It's great to be James!" What more could a mother ask? I learned to delight in him the way he delighted in himself.

Is there any mother whose heart has not been broken by her children? By loving them so much, by worrying about them, by losing them, by finding them again?

One mom I know has a child with leukemia. Another has a child on drugs. Another's child died in a fire. A friend's daughter has morphed into bridezilla. Another has a teenager who is, well, a teenager. I have a son with autism.

What were we thinking when we had these kids? I have never regretted for a moment having children, but I have marveled sometimes that I don't. Surely I would regret anything else in my life that had caused me such heartache. Would any of us, if we really knew what we were getting ourselves into, have knowingly walked into this soul pain?

Amazingly, the answer, I think, is yes. There will always be a raw tenderness in my heart for James, a place sensitive to touch. A place of quiet grieving. And that's okay. I breathe into the softness of it, trusting in the basic goodness of the universe, the perfection of it all, the sunny brightness of the vast blue sky.

~Galen Pearl

95

A Hug with No Arms

Millions and millions of years would still not give me half enough time to describe that tiny instant of all eternity when you put your arms around me and I put my arms around you.

~Jacques Prévert

When our boy was born, he didn't gaze at faces the way I'd seen other babies do with their mommies. He cried for hours. Being held close in a soft blanket did not soothe him. Neither did music, gentle bouncing, a clean diaper, or a bottle. He'd refused to nurse, struggling away from my skin. We were blessed with a baby who seemed not to love us. I had a constant fear that something was wrong.

Family advice didn't help. They insisted we were just nervous first-time parents and the baby was fine, or that he'd outgrow it when he could talk instead of fuss, or that it was my fault for painting the nursery when I was pregnant. I'd stenciled teddy bears around the baseboards to welcome him home.

Our boy had a cherub's face, big blue eyes and soft pudgy cheeks. He pronounced simple words, but my "Say mama…" brought silence. I gave him a dollhouse, hoping to interest him in playing family. The doll's plastic cradle had a battery-operated voice that called out, "Mama." Our boy imitated the high-pitched, strangely automated sound. It was better than nothing but not enough for me.

He caught the flu as a toddler. Small and feverish, he let me hold him on my lap for almost an hour. I breathed his precious smell while his warm weight lay against my heart.

At age four, our boy was diagnosed with Asperger syndrome. Though I'd suspected a problem, the autism spectrum wasn't the one I wanted to hear. I tried to love it out of him with sweet words and extra snuggling. He'd squirm away, shouting, "That's too much!"

He showed no sadness when our dog died, but wept huge rolling tears when I bought orange Jell-O. He preferred old T-shirts and sweat pants from the thrift store, clothes already worn thin by someone else's child. He chattered endlessly, but only about Legos and the tractors he made. Even after working with doctors and therapists, his heart seemed unreachable.

Instead of anticipating the joy a milestone gift would bring, my husband and I learned to cringe. Our boy threw screaming, red-faced fits at the sight of his new tricycle, the scooter he'd asked for, his birthday skates. Parenthood wasn't supposed to be like this.

Things got a little better in kindergarten. While he still didn't like faces, he looked at the hem of my dress one morning, and declared, "A good mom wears a skirt." It was high praise.

I worried, though, that he wouldn't sit close to me or smile when I smiled. He didn't show love. My deeper fear was that he didn't feel it either. When I'd drop him off at school, I'd hear kids call to their mothers, "Love you, Mom!" Our boy would slam the car door without looking back, no matter how many times I asked him for a quick wave. He didn't seem to have the cuddly kid gene.

Eventually, I resigned myself to his distance and odd preferences, the emptiness of the house.

As a young teenager, he suddenly asked for a "hug with no arms" meaning that we would stand next to each other without touching, without our eyes meeting, and silently agree we were hugging. I was stunned down to my toes. He wanted affection, but a glass prison window stood between us. I cherished anything he had to give.

One evening, after a stress-filled day at work, I sat at the kitchen table wiping my eyes with the back of my hand. My husband listened while I poured out the day. I spotted our boy lurking around the corner. He was an expert eavesdropper.

To unwind, I mixed up a batch of molasses cookies. The smell of cinnamon and the oven's warmth gave me a coziness I needed, but I began to dread our boy's reaction. He despised molasses cookies, the chewiness and the gritty sugar on his fingers. In the past, he'd yelled or stormed out when I made any cookie besides chocolate chip.

Tonight, however, he walked into the kitchen and picked up a stack of five cookies, wiping his sugary fingers on his jeans. He glanced into my eyes and looked away. Then he leaned near me in an armless hug.

"These are my favorite cookies, Mom."

He was lying. He hated molasses cookies. What he did with them, I'll never know. I'm sure he didn't eat them. But he must have planned to comfort me. His words were a hug.

He will likely never throw his arms around me, but I've come to understand what our boy must have known all along. A hug, even without arms, and a few carefully chosen words can fill a hole in the heart.

I leaned close and said, "I love you, too."

~Carrie Malinowski

Just Joey

If a man does not keep pace with his companions, perhaps it is because he hears a different drummer. Let him step to the music which he hears, however measured or far away.

~Henry David Thoreau

As Joey climbs into the driver's seat, buckles up, then backs the car onto the street, I am reminded of him as a little boy, fifty years ago, "driving" through our house and cruising the neighborhood, using the lid from my pasta kettle as a steering wheel. He was oblivious to other children, his sisters or the kids from next door playing hide-and-seek in the leaves or riding tricycles on the patio.

It was troubling to see him so absorbed in his own world, to the exclusion of anything else, but it was not out of the ordinary, not for Joey. It was just more of the perplexing behavior we had been aware of from the time he was eight months old, when I began to fear that he might be "different," maybe even "slow," certainly not developing as joyfully and remarkably as his sisters were or as predictably as Dr. Spock had taught us.

Despite my questions, throughout Joey's first four years our pediatricians routinely dismissed my concerns about him. "Stop comparing him to his sisters.... Boys do not develop as fast as girls do.... You're asking for trouble when there is none, Mother." At nine months, Joey could only occasionally turn over, could not sit without pillow props, did not attempt crawling. He stayed on his tummy in one spot on the floor where I put him, scratching intently on the carpet for long periods of time or just laughing at his hands. He did not grasp anything offered to him, never put anything in his mouth, not a thumb, not a Cheerio. My husband accepted whatever the doctors told me. "Just wait. He'll learn what he needs to do when he is ready."

I wanted to think they were right, and there were times when I almost did. Shortly before Joey's first birthday, he sat without props and made his first attempt to crawl. He eventually mastered a crawl, although a peculiar one, using only one knee and dragging the other. He made very good time. He discovered the joy of watching our front-loading laundry machine, incentive enough for him to pull himself to his feet to watch an entire cycle, screaming when it ended. I was as thrilled with his first tantrums as I was with his getting himself to a standing position. He had rarely cried before then, or expressed himself so effectively.

Eight months later, Joey was walking, holding onto furniture or someone's hand. His big sisters were thoroughly delighted when, with one on each side holding a hand, they could walk together. One of my favorite snapshots is of our first three children at ages three and a half, two and a half and one and a half, walking in the park holding hands.

Joey was twenty-six months old when he let go of my hand to take off by himself, walking as if determined to make up for lost time. In other ways as well, he was making up for lost time: learning to use a spoon, practicing a few words, making his "beaver face" on command from the girls, who responded with giggles as he knew and cared that they would. He started climbing onto the couch to look out the window; dropping toys in the toilet to see what would happen; writing on the walls with crayons while announcing "I scrivvling." He sprinkled baby powder throughout the house. He emptied the bookcases. He was no longer my placid little boy.

Joey was four when a new pediatrician joined the other doctors, who already knew us well. The new doctor recommended a comprehensive evaluation at a nearby university, to include observation and testing by a team of pediatric specialists. He insisted that my husband, Joe, attend at least the conference at the end of the three-month, once-weekly evaluation.

Joe did not feel as strongly as I did the need for the evaluation. He had not yet acknowledged that Joey's erratic development was a concern. Not only that, he would no longer be able to rely on my support in his own endeavors. Joe was a college teacher, dedicated to his profession and to independent research and writing. I had, initially, enjoyed being a part of that by typing correspondence and manuscripts and proofreading galleys, beginning even before we were married. But my enthusiasm for his work was dwindling, as was any confidence in myself as a mother. Worse yet, I had quietly begun to resent Joe's priorities, even though I realized their importance.

When Joe and I went to the clinic for the long-awaited evaluation conference, I thought I was somewhat prepared for whatever we might hear. I knew that Joe was not at all prepared to learn that Joey, his only son, was considered "retarded, unlikely to attend public school." (We did not know that only then, in 1963, the federal government had begun to write laws mandating free and appropriate public school education for children with disabilities.) We were stunned, hearing that Joey had intellectual limitations as well as visual-perceptual and neurological impairments that accounted for his coordination problems, difficulty chewing, and his unusual gait.

It was too much for us to grasp all at the same time. We were silent the entire trip home, except for one comment from Joe. "Joey will never want my books," he said. "The only legacy I can leave my son will have no meaning for him." The resentment I had been harboring toward Joe dissipated. My broken heart was for him, for myself, for all of us, on a day I will never forget.

Joe did not live long enough to know that Joey would be okay. He died unexpectedly at age fifty-two following a massive heart attack, when the kids were eighteen, seventeen, sixteen and thirteen. He did not know that by the time Joey left middle school, he was no longer classified as mentally retarded but as learning disabled. Currently the diagnosis is "Asperger syndrome, severe nonverbal learning disability, average verbal intelligence, significant deficit in performance."

Many years ago Joe saw his little boy driving an imaginary car, but he did not live long enough to see Joey as a young man driving his own car, purchased with money saved from his hotel housekeeping job. He saw Joey as a two-year-old taking his first walk, but did not see him walk across the stage at his high school graduation. He did not know that Joey took his place escorting each of the girls down the aisle on their wedding days. He did not see him walk to the podium in the hotel ballroom to accept a Lifetime Achievement award from his employer.

Joe would be gratified to know that, despite continuing hurdles, Joey is okay—working (more than twenty-five years without interruption), living quasi-independently in his own place, sharing in family events, enjoying a few close friends and his beloved cat. He thrives on church activities, involvement in historic train groups, filming videos, listening to bluegrass and classical music. He is an avid reader of non-fiction: transportation history, inspirational books, electronics catalogs, and cross-continent train schedules, which he has memorized.

Joey stops by weekly to take the trash out for me, and sometimes to eat pasta. He phones promptly at seven every morning with a cheery wake-up call, to make sure I am okay. At eighty, I am finally okay, knowing almost for certain that Joey is okay.

~Luisa R. Fortunato

97

Feeling Judged

Wellness is found not in isolation but in relationship.
~John Philip Newell

I saw a woman at the gym the other day who I really wanted to avoid. I used to see her a lot when my son Matthew, who has autism, was small. It seemed she was always there when he was bolting away from me at the grocery store, the swimming pool, the park. She watched me as I tackled Matthew before he wandered into the street, and while I tried to defuse a big bad meltdown. She was always sitting right behind us in church while Matthew flapped and tapped and giggled. Her pale blue eyes followed us everywhere and her frown was constant.

I wove my way around the exercise bikes and ducked behind the magazine rack to avoid the woman, and then ran smack into her in front of the drinking fountain. She was wearing that frown that I remembered well, and her eyes bored into me in such a way that I couldn't ignore her.

"You look familiar," she said, cocking her head. No kidding I look familiar. "Did our kids go to school together or something?"

"Maybe," I countered innocently. "I think we may have seen each other at the pool."

"Of course!" she said smiling, her frown softening ever so slightly. "You had that adorable boy. I remember he had... issues."

I laughed self-consciously and explained that Matthew had autism and that some years had been more challenging than others.

I told her that he was twenty-six now, living and working in this great community for people with disabilities near Santa Cruz called Camphill Communities California.

"I'll never forget the day he climbed to the top of the batting cage during a little league game," she said, shuddering. "He was teetering around and you climbed up like it was nothing and carried him down."

We burst out laughing and went on to talk about how her children were doing, the ones I never got to know because I was so sure their mother was evil. What a waste! Here was this really nice and compassionate woman who I assumed was judging me when in reality she was just curious. And concerned. Even now when she was laughing with me she was frowning. She was a frowner, not a judger! And who knew why she was a frowner? She may have been coping with "issues" of her own.

As we parted ways, I thought about all of the other people over the years that I had judged—and avoided—because I assumed they were judging me.

I thought back to the day I climbed to the top of the batting cage to retrieve Matthew. And to the day I ran into the surf in Carmel fully clothed to pull him from the surf. And to the day I sprinted down my street in red high heels and a black cocktail dress as Matthew rolled away precariously on a skateboard. We were stare-worthy in those days, and people still look at us sideways from time to time.

I hope we were giving our audience something to talk about at the dinner table.

~Laura Shumaker

98

Bedtime Routine

We do not remember days, we remember moments.
~Cesare Pavese

A kiss goodnight from your child is a privilege most parents take for granted.

For some of us with children on the autism spectrum, it is the elusive gold ring we reach for every night—and getting it makes everything—all the hard work, all the therapy, all the bills we pay—worth it, for that one brief moment when those soft lips touch our exhausted cheeks. If you're really lucky, you'll get an "I love you" along with it.

I've been putting James to bed for over eight years, and our interaction in those final minutes before he drifts off to sleep has evolved over time. Pre-diagnosis, I thought nothing of it—I'd give James a big kiss, put him in his crib, whisper goodnight, and walk out of the room. Post-diagnosis, the silence that I received in return was deafening. It had never occurred to me before to be concerned that when I said "Goodnight, James, I love you," my toddler said nothing in response. Suddenly, I needed to hear him say something. So, my husband and I began prompting James to say goodnight back to us. "Say goodnight, Mommy" we'd tell him. And from the crib, this is what we would hear: "Say goodnight, Mommy."

For over a year, this was the parting salutation of the day. Every night, it made me cry. I never got used to it, and I never gave up hope that one night, I'd hear something more organic come out of James's mouth.

Finally, when James turned four, he dropped the "say"—and his response became "Goodnight, Mommy." It was fantastic—but it was still prompted.

At six, I got my first unprompted, "Goodnight, Mommy. I love you." Next to my wedding, and births of my children, this was the most exciting night of my life.

A year later, my husband and I were putting James to bed, and we were treated to this little gem: "Mommy, how come when someone says I love you, you say I love you, too—not just I love you?" Given James's fixation with numbers, my husband sought to clarify. "Well, you know, buddy, it's T-O-O, like, also, not T-W-O," Linguist James stepped up. "There's three different kinds of too—there's T-O-O, also, and there's T-W-O, the number, and then there's T-O—like, you know to go TO someplace!"

James, now eight, routinely kisses us goodnight and tells us he loves us. The other evening, he came out with a classic, quirky, comment—pure James. After giving me a big hug and kiss, James told me, "You're a great mom! You're not a mom with feathers, or a mom with colors and markers. I'm glad you're a… a person!" I don't know if he had the book *Are You My Mother?* on his mind, or if this was just one of the many random thoughts that cross my son's brain on a daily basis. I do know it was music to my ears… and one more gold ring that I grasped tightly in my hand.

~Nancy Burrows

We're All a Little Spectrum

Faith is a passionate intuition.
~William Wordsworth

I remember March 2002. My son was almost three and the state's largest autism clinic, after a six-hour drive, an all-day evaluation and an expensive overnight hotel stay, had just offered me their professional opinion and advice. He had low-functioning autism and was moderately mentally retarded. His IQ was in the low 60's. I had anticipated the diagnosis, but not the dire picture that they painted.

That was more than ten years ago and a lot has changed since then. My son has blown every dire prediction right out of the water. With a lot of hard work from a small army of therapists, consultants, and educators, he is at present mainstreamed in a middle school classroom, earning high-honor-roll grades, and speaking without the use of his communication device. He still prefers to be a loner, but he has established friendly relationships with kids at school and in the community. We're still working hard on behaviors, but his peers accept him just the way he is.

It's been a long journey. On the way we spent a lot of time in the waiting room of the outpatient therapy center and I've met dozens of amazing moms and dads and kids with lots of different diagnoses. Every single family I have met has left me with a profound and lasting impression about how life goes on, love happens naturally, families adapt to their new realities, and finding your blessings to count them isn't so hard.

Getting to know these families showed me over time that no matter the diagnosis, there were similarities. The kid with Down syndrome flaps his hands when he's excited, too! The kid with the G-tube avoids eye contact, too! The hearing-impaired kiddo perseverates on topics that interest him, too! The kid with a traumatic brain injury lines up his crayons, too!

Eventually, my son was dismissed from outpatient therapy because he had met his goals. He continued to receive speech and OT in school, but we had to say goodbye to our outpatient-therapy extended family.

Volunteering at school allowed me to see my son and his peers in their natural setting and again, I realized that even kids without IEPs were stimming. Even the neurotypical kids had sensory issues. My son wasn't the only kid who didn't want to touch the putty or use glue or eat "wet" food at lunch. My son wasn't the only one who didn't really want to play in a group or didn't like the echo in the gym. My son wasn't the only one who had meltdowns and completely lost it for reasons that were never fully known.

So as the years have passed, as I have watched my son, now twelve, and my neurotypical daughter, now seven, both blast their way through school and exhibit their own wonderfully unique and amazing personalities, I have reached two important conclusions.

One is that sometimes mother's intuition really does trump years of medical training and scientific testing. To the team of students and doctors and psychiatrists and mental health professionals and social workers from 2002, I emphatically say, "You were wrong." They were really arrogant to think that the best of 2002 was all that the future had to offer us, and they were wrong to hold out so little hope. The last decade has brought us a ton of new information, new therapies, new technology, new resources, and new opportunities. I am so glad that I listened to my instincts when every fiber in my body rebelled against their professional opinions!

My other conclusion is that we all, every single one of us, have a little spectrum in us. If you look at all the criteria that define the spectrum diagnosis, every single person on the planet could identify with something on that list. They make us unique, individual, charismatic, maddening, dysfunctional, determined, joyous, anxious and everything else in between. You don't need to have the autism or Asperger's diagnosis to be obsessed with details or topics that might not interest anybody else, or to have a fantastic memory or a sensory dysfunction, or to prefer quiet time at home to a boisterous crowd, or to find eye contact a little too intense. We all have a little spectrum in us, and it's part of what makes each of us a beautiful person.

I thank God for both of my children and our friends and all of their unique positions on the spectrum for giving me the chance to realize this facet of humanity, and to appreciate that we are all extraordinary beings. I look forward to seeing how my introverted, technology- and history-obsessed son (who still hates "wet" food and flaps his hands when he's excited but is a pro at a proper social introduction), and my exuberant, fearless, creative and thoughtful daughter (who sometimes avoids eye contact), continue to mature into amazing adults, each with their own degree of spectrum perfection.

~Laura Cichoracki

Traditions

Perhaps all the dragons in our life are princesses
who are only waiting to see us act, just once, with beauty and courage.
~Rainer Maria Rilke

parked the car and stared at the Walmart entrance for a minute, not wanting to go in. I avoided Walmart as much as I could these days. It was the second week of November, and we were in full-fledged holiday territory. But I couldn't even consider Thanksgiving or Christmas, because this year I didn't know how to celebrate either of them.

My two-year-old son had been diagnosed with autism only a month earlier, although we'd known for a long time what the diagnosis would be. And, as many in the autism community are painfully aware, sometimes autism comes with peripheral issues — digestive sickness, seizures, allergies, and the like. Our diagnosis came with celiac disease and a host of food sensitivities. Any exposure to gluten, dairy, soy, or corn (even a single bite) would cause copious amounts of vomiting and an otherwise miserable little boy for the next week.

Once I finally made my way inside, I grabbed the dish detergent we needed and made my way across the store to the shampoo aisle. I paused by the newsstand. I saw cover after magazine cover, each heralding holiday tradition and cheer. How to make the perfect Thanksgiving stuffing. How to make the best Christmas cookies. That reminded me of the neighborhood Christmas cookie exchange party. Half-eaten cookies lying around everywhere, cups of cider waiting to be spilled, plus crowds, tons of noisy children, a grabby gluten-allergic two-year-old, and the probability of epic autistic tantrums. What a logistical nightmare! Probably better not to go. Another thing to avoid.

But it wasn't the lack of cookies, parties, or stuffing themselves that bothered me — it was the lack of tradition. As a kid, I had things I looked forward to every year. Things that were the same every holiday season, even when I came home from college. If it couldn't be extra church services (the crowds are a problem around high holidays), or cookies, or parties, or travel, then what could I give my children? What were Thanksgiving and Christmas going to look like for our family?

By the time I got back to my car, it had started snowing. First snow of the season. I can't say I cared. These magical holiday bits and pieces felt like they would just float by us this year, maybe forever. I cried my way home.

My three-and-a-half-year-old daughter was shouting when I walked in the door.

"Mama, look at the snow. It's snowing outside. There's snow falling out of the sky. The snow is on the ground and on the car and on the stones and on the driveway and on my rock collection and in my room!"

"It's in your room?"

"No. It's outside on the grass and on the roof and on the cat and doggy!"

"Really, you see a dog outside?"

"No. I see the snow. It's snowing outside and everywhere."

Her excitement spilled over until we had her and her brother bundled up and ready to play in the inch of snow on the ground. My husband took them out while I made dinner.

I watched them tumble around and scrounge up enough snow to make a snowman, which they showed me through the kitchen window. They were all rosy-cheeked and runny-nosed, and even my little guy ran back and forth in the snow, tentatively bending over to touch it every five or six paces.

And that's when a sudden inspiration came to me.

My mom had recently made mashed potatoes with almond milk,

and I remembered thinking they tasted normal. Maybe that would work for hot chocolate. Did we have any almond milk?

Check.

Did we still have those allergen-free chocolate chips Grandma got for us?

A third of a bag. Check.

Voila! I poured almond milk in a pan and slowly melted chocolate chips into it. I'd expected them to lump up in a goofy way like most every food substitute seemed to do, but they dissolved like butter. "Ha!" I yelled. My first victory.

My family came tumbling in through the kitchen door, snow flying off scarves and boots, chattering and shouting about how it should snow forever. I triumphantly raised my chocolate spoon and cried out, "Hot chocolate! Who wants hot chocolate?"

The kids paid no attention, but my husband looked at me, shocked.

"You made hot chocolate? Can he have any?"

"Yes, dear. It's safe."

He laughed and started pouring while I began pulling off coats and hats. That's when I realized my daughter was shouting about getting the Christmas tree out.

I looked at my husband. He smiled, and set to work with the kids.

Our boy was running in circles in the light of the Christmas tree, stopping to glance at it every so often and take a swig of hot chocolate from his Sippy cup. He picked up an ornament with bells on it and resumed his running, jingling. My husband and our little girl were clinking their mugs together in a toast to the first snow, Christmas lights glowing off their faces.

There it was. I thought it was completely impossible, but here, I was witnessing our first holiday tradition, everyone participating in his or her own way. And it was beautiful.

~Maura Klopfenstein-Oprisko

Learning to Iron

A ship is safest in the harbor, but that is not what ships are built for.
~John Shedd

All of a sudden, Will has left the safety of the family harbor. His ship has launched and he has moved into his own apartment in another city seventy miles away. His job is the beginning of his true career. He worked hard for this chance. All the years of therapy, special services, study and encouragement have resulted in this giant step toward independence, despite the giant challenge of autism.

During the interview with a huge corporation, they told him that if he were hired, he would start on April 16. On April 12, his father and I suggested that he probably wasn't going to get the job. Whew! We had dodged that bullet. He would not be moving away from home. The very next day, the human resources department contacted him, offering him a position as an entry-level web developer. He would start on April 25. He was excited and nervous.

We were happy for him and dreadfully nervous. But we had stepped boldly forth into the risk that he might move away. We were the ones who encouraged him to go to the interview, and his dad actually drove him seventy miles for it, 140 miles round trip.

Anxiety plagued me. Had I prepared him enough? Had I taught him what he needed to know to live on his own, to navigate life outside the harbor? I wouldn't have many more chances to teach him what he needed to know.

A week after we moved him, his sister Mary and I went to visit him for the weekend and bring another load of his furniture and possessions. I wanted to see how he was doing on his own. His apartment was still very sparsely furnished, with an air mattress in his bedroom and lawn chairs in the living room. He was camping in his own apartment. He would buy real furniture when he could afford it.

I got another chance to teach Will how to grab his dress clothes out of the dryer so that he would not have to iron them. However, the clothes didn't come out of the apartment dryers as wrinkle-free as I had hoped. So we went shopping and he bought an ironing board and an iron.

Then we went back to his apartment and took all of his dress clothes out of the closet. I gave him and Mary ironing lessons. At home, my method of grabbing clothes quickly out of the dryer is an effective wrinkle deterrent, so my ironing lessons in the past were halfhearted. But this time, both my children paid close attention. Both Will and Mary picked it up quickly. Will told me he has ironed his clothes every week since.

I am shocked that this is so hard. Letting go is harder than I thought it would be, but other parents, parents of typical kids, tell me that they found it difficult as well. When my kids were little, they had separation anxiety. Now I am feeling that anxiety on the other end of parenthood.

My chances to prepare my son for his future are diminishing quickly. He is learning his own lessons, and he is enjoying it for the most part. I love the John Shedd quote: "A ship is safest in the harbor, but that is not what ships are built for." I have this saying in the signature line of my e-mails both at home and at work, to remind myself daily that my kids cannot stay in the harbor. In the end, keeping them in the harbor is not safe.

~Ann Kilter

Afterword
Real Look Autism

*If we are to achieve a richer culture, we must weave one
in which each diverse human gift will find a fitting place.*
~Margaret Meade

For more than twenty years, I was a local TV news anchor in Baltimore. Here are some of the facts as I would have read them on the six o'clock news:

Good evening, I'm Mary Beth Marsden and I'm married with three children. Our youngest and only girl was diagnosed with autism spectrum disorder at age three and a half. She's now a fifth grader in a public school, included in regular classes with support. She is strong-willed, innocent, and wildly creative. She's slow at processing information, struggles with social dynamics, and sometimes her emotions get the better of her. Those are the facts... but here's my story.

When I left the small screen I wanted to do "something" in the world of autism. After talking it over with some friends, I developed an idea for a reality show. I called it *On The Spec.* For months, I pitched the idea to production houses and a few well-known cable networks until I finally got a nibble, from a channel you probably know well. The *On The Spec* concept, along with some episode ideas, made it to a producers meeting where they were looking at possibilities for new programming. It didn't take long to get an e-mail that read "Thanks but no thanks." What? I didn't get it. In my mind, autism was everywhere. The mainstream media couldn't get enough.

Autism stories were frequently in the news and each year it seemed the CDC was raising the prevalence numbers. Why wouldn't a show about autism be popular?

I called the producer and he was kind enough to call me back. He gave me some standard line about how this wasn't their focus and they were moving in another direction... blah blah. I finally said, "Look, off the record, can you give me a little more than that?"

He said, "Fine. Off the record, we find the whole subject matter too depressing."

For a second I didn't say anything except maybe a very low and soft "wow." I then thanked him and told him very sincerely, "On the record, I just want you to know that the people I know touched by autism are some of the warmest, most empathetic, funny, loving people I know, and they would never want you to look at them and feel depressed." He said he understood. Then I said, "What if I found an autistic hoarder?" I couldn't help myself.

Now I make my own videos. They are videos of children on the spectrum who are making progress with the help of certain therapies or strategies. The videos are not seen by millions of people, but many thousands. They are not appearing on cable, but on YouTube. They have a purpose and they are filled with hope.

I wasn't always so optimistic about autism... in fact I think while I made sure my daughter was getting help, I never fully accepted the diagnosis. Maybe I was afraid if I acknowledged it by name it would be permanent. There were times I didn't know what to call it or how to talk about it. (We still don't spend time with labels when we are talking with our daughter and for now she is fine with that.) But, as time passed, something changed. I began embracing this huge and dynamic autism spectrum. I started owning it and I'll tell you—it freed me. I feel empowered now when I talk with others about autism. I feel eager to share my story if it will help someone else and I am always open to another person's point of view. This is an amazing community of people who have different approaches and circumstances. We have, in some cases, wide-ranging viewpoints about research and treatment. But I believe if we listen and respect each other we are "one" and as "one" we have a huge voice.

Awareness is not a slogan, but a necessity if we are to help create communities that will welcome and include our children. If others see us as "depressing" we need to fix that, and I believe education, understanding and acceptance is the key.

And I still think autism would make for a great reality show.

~Mary Beth Marsden

Glossary

Applied Behavior Analysis (ABA): A set of principles used in therapy, intervention, or education that are based on research about how people learn. There are many principles in ABA, and they may be used in highly structured (usually known as Discrete Trial Training) or more naturalistic teaching situations (such as Pivotal Response Training). Some of the main ABA principles guide the presentation of teachers' cues to the learner about expected responses as well as how teachers should present rewards or reinforcement to give feedback to the learner and increase their motivation for correct responses.

Autism Spectrum Disorders (ASDs): An umbrella term used to refer to a group of similar developmental disabilities, including autistic disorder, Asperger syndrome (AS), pervasive developmental disorder not otherwise specified (PDD-NOS), childhood disintegrative disorder (CDD), and Rett's disorder, as defined by the psychiatric manual, DSM IV (*Diagnostic and Statistical Manual of Mental Disorders, Fourth Edition*). The hallmark of all of these conditions is a marked impairment in social interaction and language/communication skills, as well as the presence of restricted, repetitive behaviors and interests.

Asperger syndrome: Historically, ASD was a broad label for individuals diagnosed with autism, pervasive developmental disorder not otherwise specified (PDD-NOS), or Asperger syndrome. Autism and PDD-NOS differed primarily in the number of symptoms present. To be diagnosed with Asperger syndrome, an individual had to meet additional criteria: demonstrate no delay in language development and have intellectual abilities of at least average levels. With recent changes in professional diagnostic guidelines, these labels will no longer be used. Rather, the diagnosis that will be given to all who qualify will be "autism spectrum disorder." To receive a diagnosis of ASD, an individual must show impairment in social and communication learning and behavior.

Aspie: Slang term for a person with Asperger syndrome; sometimes used by people with AS to refer to themselves, but may be considered offensive when used by others.

Autism: A complex neurobiological disorder that typically lasts throughout a person's lifetime. Autism impairs a person's ability to communicate and relate to others. It is also associated with rigid routines and repetitive behaviors, such as obsessively arranging objects or following very specific routines. Symptoms can range from very mild to quite severe.

DSM IV: This acronym refers to the *Diagnostic and Statistical Manual of Mental Disorders, Fourth Edition*. The DSM IV is published by the American Psychiatric Association to provide clinicians with guidelines for diagnosing a wide range of disorders.

Expressive Language: Refers to a person's ability to use language, usually in the form of speech.

Floortime: A treatment method as well as a philosophy for interaction that involves meeting children at their current developmental level and building upon their particular set of interests and strengths.

Hand Flapping: One of the repetitive and possibly self-stimulatory behaviors performed by people with ASD or other neurodevelopmental disorders.

High-functioning autism (HFA): Term used to refer to those on the autism spectrum who have minimal impairment in IQ. Severity of problems with social interaction, restricted interests, or preference for sameness may range from severe to mild across individuals. Sometimes the label HFA is used interchangeably with Asperger syndrome. Other times it may be used instead of Asperger syndrome because there was an early language delay or cognitive delay, which disqualifies a diagnosis of Asperger syndrome according to the diagnostic guidelines used by most professionals.

Hyperlexia: The ability to read the text in a book but not understand what is read. It is not uncommon to hear about children with ASD who teach themselves to read before they start school, but who have great difficulty getting the gist of stories.

Inclusion: In education, a placement in which the student with a disability attends a general education classroom with typically-developing peers.

Individualized Education Program (IEP): In the United States, the official and legal document negotiated between parents, teachers, school administrators, and others that sets down the educational plan for a special needs student. According to the United States Department of Education, the IEP "is the major mechanism for ensuring a child receives a free appropriate public education (FAPE). The IEP serves as a blueprint for the child's special education needs and any related services."

Low-functioning autism: Term used to refer to those on the autism spectrum who suffer relatively more impairment due to their disability compared to others.

Mainstream: In education, a placement in which the student with a disability is placed in the special education classroom but visits the general education classroom for instruction and social activities.

Meltdown: A term for the loss of control experienced by a person with an autism spectrum disorder who is overwhelmed by social, emotional, sensory, or other stressful stimuli. May include screaming, kicking, hitting, throwing objects, biting, banging head into the wall or floor, collapsing to the floor, etc.; a tantrum.

Occupational Therapy: A treatment that focuses on using productive or creative activity to maximize the functioning of physically or emotionally disabled people. Occupational therapists help an individual develop mental or physical skills that aid in daily living activities. They assess fine motor skills, age-appropriate self-help skills (like dressing), and sensory issues (like hypersensitivity to touch).

Pervasive Developmental Disorder Not Otherwise Specified (PDD-NOS): Historically, ASD was a broad label for individuals diagnosed with autism, pervasive developmental disorder not otherwise specified (PDD-NOS), or Asperger syndrome. Autism and PDD-NOS differed primarily in the number of symptoms present. With recent changes in professional diagnostic guidelines, these labels will no longer be used. Rather, the diagnosis that will be given to all who qualify will be "autism spectrum disorder." To receive a diagnosis of ASD, an individual must show impairment in social and communication learning and behavior.

Picture Exchange Communication System (PECS): An augmented communication program intended to help children and adults with autism to acquire functional communication skills. It uses ABA-based methods to teach children to exchange a picture for something they want—an item or activity.

Pragmatic Language: Refers to the "art of conversation": taking turns speaking, staying on a topic for a polite number of turns (even if it's not your favorite topic), showing interest in someone else's comments, etc. Individuals with ASDs, and particularly those with Asperger syndrome, are known to have difficulty with pragmatic language. Helping them to learn pragmatic language skills is often a part of speech therapy.

Receptive Language: Refers to a person's ability to understand spoken language.

Sensory Integration Therapy: A treatment used to help children, including those with autism spectrum disorders, who have motor, sensory, and perceptual difficulties. It is based on the belief that you can change the brain by changing experience. If a person has poor sensory integration—which then impacts the ability to function and learn—you can provide sensory experiences that will improve not only sensory integration itself, but overall functioning. Providers of Sensory Integration Therapy are most often occupational therapists.

Social Skills Training: Encompasses different approaches to teaching the building blocks of social behavior and interaction. Strategies for addressing the social deficits that characterize autism are varied, ranging from role-playing desirable and undesirable social behavior, to social stories, to social skills groups including children with ASD and typical peers.

Speech and Language Therapy: The assessment and treatment of issues in communication which may include articulation (pronunciation of sounds), receptive language (understanding and processing what is communicated by others), expressive language (the ability to communicate to others), fluency (including stuttering), voice problems (including pitch and intonation), and pragmatics (the social use of language).

Stimming: Short for "self-stimulation," a term for behaviors which stimulate one's own senses, such as rocking, spinning, or hand-flapping.

The preceding ASD glossary was provided courtesy of the Interactive Autism Network at Kennedy Krieger Institute. For a comprehensive listing of terms, therapies, and treatments, as well as evidence-based research findings, visit www.iancommunity.org.

Meet Our Contributors

Jessica Adam is happily married to the love of her life. She is blessed to be the mother of the sweetest boy on the planet. She enjoys writing, reading, and hiking on the family's forty acres. She hopes to write many more stories about her favorite things.

Janet Amorello received her BFA degree from Emmanuel College. Janet is Vice President, Director of Marketing for a community bank. Her son, 17, has autism. She enjoys art, writing, reading and taking life a day at a time with her husband and son. Follow her on Facebook at www.facebook.com/BlendingWithAutism.

Douglas Baker is a rarely practicing attorney, sometime writer, and full-time legal editor in Madison, WI, as well as parent to Daniel, a remarkable child who has taught his father, mother, and twin sister Anna much about life and value. E-mail him at debaker50@gmail.com.

Christine Bakter has two sons with autism. She is the 2007 Autism Speaks Founder's Award recipient for excellence in volunteer leadership and political advocacy, and in 2009 helped pass autism insurance reform in New Jersey. She advocates as a member of the Special Needs Advisory Commission in Hamilton, NJ. E-mail her at mom2aspies@gmail.com.

Angela Benam lives in Baltimore, MD with her husband and two young sons. She works both at home to focus on her family, and also at a Baltimore City public school. Angela is interested in traditional foods and in conscientious, respectful treatment of children. E-mail her at A.Sciarretta.Benam@gmail.com.

Lorri Benedik has been freelancing for twelve years. Her stories and articles have appeared in numerous publications including *Reader's Digest* and *Canadian Living*. Lorri devotes her time to biography writing, living in Montreal with her husband Manny, their awesome son Zach, and mini-schnauzer. E-mail her at lorri@lorribenedik.com.

Jennifer Berger currently resides in Queens, NY with her husband Aaron and their 5-year-old son Josh. A former editor and freelance writer who loves to read and write, Jennifer is now a stay-at-home wife, mother and full-time advocate for her child.

Writer, speaker, spiritual director, and mother of an adult son with autism, **Kathleen Bolduc's** passion is helping parents find God in a child's disability. Her books include *Autism & Alleluias* and *His Name Is Joel: Searching for God in a Son's Disability*. She is hard at work on a new book.

Katherine Briccetti, author of *Blood Strangers: A Memoir*, a Lambda Literary Award Finalist, holds an MFA degree in creative writing and a PhD in clinical psychology. She is a school psychologist in California and is writing a memoir about raising a son with Asperger's and working with children on the autism spectrum.

Jean McAllister Brooks trained in anthropology and is a mother and advocate. She is currently wondering how the Common Core State Standards and related new assessments will affect students with significant intellectual disabilities and their noble teachers. Send interesting information her way via e-mail at mcallisterbrooks@msn. com.

Trey Brown earned degrees from the U.S. Naval Academy and St.

John's College, Annapolis, flew tactical Navy helicopters, taught English at USNA, was an official Navy-Pentagon spokesman, and is now speechwriter for the Principal Deputy Director of National Intelligence. His son Ben was diagnosed with autism in 2004. E-mail him at benandcoopersdad@gmail.com.

Anne Moore Burnett is the author of the Mom's Choice Award Gold Recipient-winning book, *Step Ahead of Autism*. She currently holds the position of State Director for Best Buddies International. Anne enjoys writing about many topics including her two children, Joey and Mattie; running; nature; and everyday life.

Jennifer Bush is a blogger with degrees from UC Berkeley and Yale. She spent several years working in the high tech trenches of Silicon Valley. Jennifer lives in San Jose, CA with her husband, 3-year-old daughter, and 5-year-old son, who is on the autism spectrum. E-mail her at wantapeanutblog@gmail.com.

Stephanie Carmel graduated from Boston College in 1989. She is the mother of two boys, one on the spectrum and one neurotypical. She writes for a disability advocacy company, and hopes to publish both children's books and the novel that has been swimming about in her head for many years.

Liane Kupferberg Carter is a journalist whose articles and essays have appeared in many publications, including *The New York Times*, the *Chicago Tribune* and The Huffington Post. She writes a monthly column for *Autism After 16*. Contact her at www.facebook.com/ LianeKupferbergCarter.

Beth Cato is an active member of the Science Fiction and Fantasy Writers of America, and a frequent contributor to the *Chicken Soup for the Soul* series. She's originally from Hanford, CA, but now resides in Buckeye, AZ with her husband and son.

Laura Cichoracki is an ordinary mother to two amazing children and wife to a wonderful husband. She believes strongly that every child, without exception, has a gift that must be discovered and developed. She works for a local special education cooperative and enjoys reading.

Lana Clifton holds a degree in English. She is a freelance writer who is also a wife and a homeschool teacher to her two children. She loves reading, writing, photography, bike riding and spending time with her family in their North Texas home. E-mail her at lana@lclifton.com.

Christine Coleman is your typical suburban stay-at-home hockey mom who enjoys writing, knitting and photography. She navigates the trials, tribulations and triumphs in the world of autism (and parenting in general!) as she raises her two boys and little girl with her husband in the Greater Toronto Area of Ontario, Canada.

Melinda Coppola has been writing since she was ten. A yoga teacher and Reiki master, she enjoys infusing her work of heart with her voice as a poet. Melinda lives happily in a quiet Massachusetts town with her husband Nick, her daughter Emily, and a couple of well-loved pets. E-mail het at Melinda@SpectrumYoga.net.

Allison Hermann Craigie received her B.S. degree in journalism from the University of Maryland. She promotes Asperger's awareness, most notably as Sam's national tour manager. She is a former member of the Princeton Child Development Institute's Board of Trustees, and resides in South Florida with her son and daughter. E-mail her at SamGelfandSpeaks@gmail.com.

Tina Dula's son Myles was diagnosed with autism in 2003. She founded the Myles-A-Part Foundation in 2007 to provide financial and emotional support for families living with autism. The Dulas' journey with autism has been featured on Headline News, NPR, *The Montel Williams Show*, and other media outlets.

Alison Dyer received a Bachelor of Arts degree from the State University of New York College at Cortland. Her older brother Jeffrey has autism and has shaped her life in every way. She works at Autism Speaks as the Social Media Manager and resides in New York City.

Jean Ferratier has a passion to share life experiences through inspirational stories. She is a heart-centered awareness coach, linking synchronicity with life purpose.

Shari Cohen Forsythe received a B.A. degree from the University of Illinois and a J.D. degree from Suffolk University Law School. She loves singing, writing, traveling, tennis and dance. Shari lives in Northbrook, IL, with her husband Duncan and sons Alex and Noah. E-mail her at cohenforsythe@sbcglobal.net.

Growing up in Oregon, **Luisa R. Fortunato** earned a B.A. degree in arts and letters followed by an M.S. in counseling psychology. With her college-professor husband, they raised four children in Ohio. After twenty-five years counseling in vocational rehabilitation, she retired to enjoy grandchildren and pursue creative writing.

Seth Fowler's son, William, was diagnosed with autism at the age of two and a half. His wife, Melanie, wrote the book *Look At My Eyes* to help other families navigate the autism spectrum. Seth and Melanie continue to help other parents through speaking engagements and outreach initiatives. Learn more at www.lookatmyeyes.com.

Jennifer Froelich is a novelist living in Idaho with her husband and two children. Her first novel, *Dream of Me*, was published in 2011. Her second, *A Place Between Breaths*, is due for publication in 2013. Jennifer is a graduate of Arizona State University's Cronkite School of Journalism.

Sharon Fuentes is a freelance writer, autism advocate and proud mom of two who has mastered the art of run-on sentences and writing between the hours of 7:50 a.m. and 2:35 p.m. Monday through Friday; unless of course there is a snow day... then just forget about it! E-mail Sharon at MamasTurnNow@hotmail.com.

Amy Giles received her B.A. degree in English Literature from the State University of New York at Oneonta. She is a freelance copywriter. Amy is also a parent member for her school district's Committee of Special Education. She lives in Long Island, NY. E-mail her at amygiles1066@verizon.net.

Michael Gingerich has co-founded Someone To Tell It To (someonetotellitto.org), a non-profit counseling service. He is a graduated of Indiana University of Pennsylvania and Lancaster Theological Seminary. Michael and his wife Kathy live in Hershey, PA. They have three sons and two granddaughters.

Kym Grosso has a 16-year-old son on the spectrum and a 6-year-old daughter. She has a B.S. degree in speech therapy and an MBA degree in health care administration. She belongs to several autism organizations, and has published autism articles on AutismInRealLife.com and PsychologyToday.com. She also writes paranormal romance novels.

Dawn Hentrich is a stay-at-home mom, freelance writer and Jill of All Trades. She spends her day chasing after her "Au-some" son, writing for her blog, preparing for the zombie apocalypse and introducing her son to the finer points of rock and roll. Visit her blog at thissideoftypical.com.

Kate Coveny Hood is mother to one fantastic son with special needs and equally fabulous boy/girl twins (all born within eighteen months). Before parenthood, she and her husband traveled the world. New adventures include writing (www.thebigpieceofcake.com) and producing a national stage show (www.listentoyourmothershow.com) in Washington, D.C.

Peggy Janousky received her Masters of Education degree from Hofstra University. She is a freelance children's author. Peggy also maintains a private practice where she supports and guides other families with special needs children. She is happily married and the proud mother of two amazing young men. E-mail her at pjanousky@gmail.com.

Sue Jeantheau is a full-time wife and mother of two daughters. She directs two senior handbell ensembles in the greater Richmond, VA area, and enjoys sewing and cooking. Sue would like to encourage you in your journey at sjeantheau@gmail.com.

Ann Kilter graduated from Michigan State University in 1984. She has spent twenty-six years preparing her autistic children for the day when they would leave the harbor. She works full-time as a legal secretary, but writes a blog about transition. Learn more at www.annkilter.com.

Maura Klopfenstein-Oprisko and her husband are proud parents to a 4-year-old autistic son and a 6-year-old gifted daughter. She has a B.A. degree in professional writing and writes a restricted diets column for Crawfordsville's *Journal Review*. Unsolicited hugs from her kids bring her indescribable joy.

Karen Krejcha is Executive Director and Co-Founder of Autism Empowerment, a non-profit promoting acceptance, enrichment, inspiration and empowerment within the autism and Asperger's communities. She is a 2012 GRASP Distinguished Spectrumite Medal honoree, enjoys writing, public speaking and is a former professional bowler. E-mail her at karen@autismempowerment.org.

Kathy Labosh is the mother of two boys with autism and the author of several books on autism: *The Child with Autism at Home and in the Community*, *The Child with Autism Goes to Florida* and *The Child with Autism Learns About Faith*. Learn more at www.fhautism.com or e-mail Kathy at labosh@msn.com.

Michelle Landrum is a former journalist who changed careers to work with autism researchers. She lives in Baltimore with her husband Michael Bayer, two sons, and their Pitbull mix. She enjoys a wide circle of friends who have children on the spectrum—and other great friends who are kind and supportive. E-mail her at michellelandrum2010@gmail.com.

Kathleen Leopold is the mother of four children—three of whom are on the spectrum. Her personal blog is Autismherd.blogspot.com. She also co-runs the Autism Blogs Directory and is one of the producers and co-hosts of "The Blog Ladies" on The Autism Channel.

Sarah Darer Littman is an award-winning author of books for young people and a columnist for CTNewsJunkie.com. She and her son Joshua are the blue-haired stars of the StoryCorps animation *Q & A*, which has given people around the world insight into Asperger syndrome, parenting, and love. Visit her at sarahdarerlittman.com and Twitter @sarahdarerlitt.

Sarah Maizes is a parenting humorist, author, blogger and founder of MommyLiteOnline.com, a parenting website. She is a regular contributor to TODAYMoms.com, The Huffington Post, and CBS Los Angeles, and is the author of several humor books and books for children. Visit her at www.MommyLiteonline.com.

Carrie Malinowski is a first grade teacher and reading tutor. She is a previous contributor to the *Chicken Soup for the Soul* series and the author of *Hand-Me-Down Bear*, a picture book for children ages four to seven. Ms. Malinowski lives in Arizona with her husband, son, and her dog, Chester. Visit her at www.carriemalinowski.com.

Terri Manzione graduated St. John's University School of Law. After seventeen years of practicing law, she began working with families raising children on the spectrum, and the agencies who care for them. She loves writing about the journey of raising Stuey, and the road toward making Joseph's Wish come true.

Jean Marino lives on an island in upstate New York, where she tolerates the harsh winters and relishes rare sunny days. As a mother of five, she's proficient at gluten-free cooking, embarrassing antics, and juggling time between work, play and writing. Though days can be hectic, and her schedule is full, her family is her everything and life is good.

Sharon Martin received her Bachelor of Applied Arts degree from Central Michigan University in 1989. After working in magazine publishing, she now works in marketing at Purdue University. Sharon enjoys spending time with her three children and finding the humor that accompanies life on the spectrum. E-mail her at fullmoondesign@gmail.com.

Hope Maven is the mother of two boys with autism. She holds a master's degree and post-graduate certificate in autism spectrum disorders from the University of St. Thomas in Minnesota. Guidance from other parents of children with autism fast-tracked her sons to intensive early intervention. Now, she pays it forward.

Leigh Merryday is a school media specialist, wife and mother to two young children—one typical and one autistic. In addition to authoring her award-winning blog, Flappiness Is, she has been published in other print and online parenting publications. E-mail her at flappinessis@gmail.com.

Sally Meyer resides in Utah. She is an award-winning screenwriter. Her poems on autism are displayed at trainland.tripod.com/poems1.htm. Sally has eight children and ten grandchildren. She's producing

Rain Child, a documentary about children on the autism spectrum. E-mail her at Rainmom2000@aol.com.

Sarah Mitchell believes in living life to the fullest. As a mother of three, she divides her passion between her family, her farm and writing. Sarah is revising her novel-length manuscript to submit for publication with the hope that when her children are young adults, they'll read it and be proud.

Bonnie Monroe, a parent of two, teaches high-functioning autistic children how to sail independently, in Clearwater, FL. Bonnie enjoys spending time with her 13-year-old high-functioning autistic son sailing. Check out the Facebook site Camp Awesome of Clearwater Community Sailing Center or e-mail her at bonniemonroe55@gmail. com.

Lava Mueller lives in Vermont where she teaches writing at a community college. When she checked with her son about publishing this story he said it was fine with him as long as he got half the cut. E-mail Lava at lavamueller@yahoo.com.

Gwen Navarrete is a Training and Development Specialist who received her B.S. degree in hotel administration from Cornell University. She actively volunteers and teaches CPR/First Aid for the American Red Cross. Originally from New York, New Jersey, and Manila, Philippines, Gwen currently resides in Las Vegas, NV with her family.

Aspen Nolette is a stay-at-home mom and resides with her husband Ryan and two children, Joshua and Shiloh, in Chesapeake, VA. She enjoys spending time at the beach, taking photographs and writing. Aspen plans to continue to share her sons' beautiful story through future published works. E-mail her at aspennolette@gmail.com.

Lori Odhner and her husband John have nine children. Raising a child on the spectrum has impacted them all for the better. His siblings wear T-shirts printed with a $100 bill, a photo of him instead of Ben Franklin and the caption "It's All about the Benjamin."

Adrienne Paradis recently left the workforce to be a stay-at-home mom, and enjoys living in beautiful Roxborough, CO with her husband and son. This is her first story submitted for publication, but Adrienne looks forward to becoming an accomplished writer that benefits other parents of special-needs children.

Phil Parham, entrepreneur, speaker, author, and dad to three wonderful boys. He was a contestant on *The Biggest Loser*. Phil co-authored *The 90-Day Fitness Challenge* and *The Amazing Fitness Adventure for Your Kids*. He's an advocate for the autism community. Learn more about the program his son attended at learningrx.com or e-mail Phil at PhillipParham7@gmail.com.

Cynthia J. Patton is a special-needs attorney, founder of the nonprofit Autism A to Z, and an award-winning writer and speaker. Her work has appeared in ten anthologies, including the *Chicken Soup for the Soul* series. Cynthia is completing a memoir on her unconventional journey to motherhood. Learn more at CynthiaJPatton.com.

Faith Paulsen's poetry and prose have appeared in journals and collections including philly.com, *Apiary*, *Wild River Review*, *Literary Mama*, three *Cup of Comfort* collections, *What Canst Thou Say?*, and three in the *Chicken Soup for the Soul* series (four now!). She is the mother of three amazing sons and lives with her husband in Norristown, PA.

Galen Pearl leads retreats and discussion groups based on her program to develop habits to grow a joyful spirit. She writes a blog and has published a book about her program, titled *10 Steps to Finding Your Happy Place (and Staying There)*. E-mail her at galenpearl@gmail.com.

D'Ann Renner, author of *Dancing from the Shadows*, is a writer and speaker with a passion for helping disadvantaged children. D'Ann enjoys reading, writing, rafting, traveling, and volunteering. She and her husband are the proud parents of two third-world children, one of whom has autism. Contact D'Ann at dannrenner.com.

Michele Bissonnette Robbins is a mother, author, songwriter and social change catalyst. She is Managing Director of YES! (www.yesworld.org), which connects and inspires visionary young leaders worldwide. She lives with her beloved husband of nineteen years, Ocean, and their autistic twins, River and Bodhi, in California. Contact her through raisingautistictwins.com.

Alisa Rock received her Bachelor of Arts degree from Western Maryland College in 1991 and her MBA degree from Johns Hopkins University in 2000. Having fled finance, survived publishing, and clawed through the nonprofit world, Rock now sits and eats truffles as a stay-at-home mom/unemployed blogger. Learn more at www.rockautismexperience.com.

Joyce Rohe is the stay-at-home mother of two beautiful children and is expecting her third child soon. Married to her wonderful husband, Nick, she is the blogger for Spectrum of Blessings, and draws her inspiration for writing through her experiences raising a child with autism. E-mail Joyce or visit her blog at www.spectrumofblessings.com.

D.M. Rosner's publications include *The China Doll* (K-3 picture book about autism), and *Welcome to My World: Adventures in Raising a Child with Autism* (parenting humor). She lives in Florida with her two boys, and runs AutismGear.com, for which she designs autism awareness shirts, handout cards, and other items.

Julie Casper Roth is an award-winning video artist and filmmaker living in upstate New York. She received her Bachelor of Arts degree, with honors, from Smith College and an MFA degree from the University at Albany, where she currently teaches. E-mail her at julie.casper.roth@gmail.com.

Mary Roth and her husband are the proud parents of two extraordinary and delightful daughters. Mary graduated from Purdue University with a B.A. degree in mechanical engineering and has done some technical writing. This story is dedicated to Mary's mother, Marilyn, who loves this poem as much as Mary does.

Tyann Sheldon Rouw is a mother of twin boys with autism. She earned a B.A. degree from the University of Northern Iowa and a MSE from Drake University. She enjoys reading, cleaning up messes, and driving a minivan. She is writing a book about her three sons and their adventures.

Michelle Rubin is the mother of three wonderful sons, ages 20, 16 and 11. She is the founder and director of Autism After 21, which provides education, recreational activities and support for individuals on the spectrum who have aged out of the school system. Michelle is an avid runner and tennis player.

Jeneil Palmer Russell blogs at rhemashope.wordpress.com about life with her Army husband Brandon and their daughters Rhema, who is 9, autistic, epileptic, beautiful, brilliant, funny and gentle-hearted, and Hope, who is 6, silly, joyful, imaginative, kind, and full of all the best of childhood. Jeneil is the author of *Sunburned Faces*.

Caroline Saul received her Social Science degree from the University of Birmingham, England in 1996. She immigrated to Israel in 1999 where she lives with her husband and four children. Caroline writes about raising children on the autism spectrum and is currently building a collection of her work. E-mail her at caroline.saul203@gmail.com.

Amy McMunn Schindler, educated in journalism and law, has studied autism from the School of Hard Knocks for over a decade. The mother of two autistic sons, she is a native West Virginian living in Rochester, NY with her husband and kids, the dog, fish, gecko and some crickets. Visit her at www.fromthemomcave.blogspot.com.

Carol Schmidt has served as an educational consultant to an early autism project at Colorado State University as well as for schools and families in Colorado. She is co- author of *Autism in the School-Aged Child: Expanding Behavioral Strategies and Promoting Success*. She has a son on the autism spectrum.

Shelley Stolaroff Segal is a playwright, composer, and essayist living in Greensboro, NC. She earned her English Literature and theater degrees at UNC Chapel Hill and the Drama Studio London. Her latest play, *My Son*, was recently produced at the International Civil Rights Center & Museum. E-mail her at shelleys@iquest.net.

Laura Shumaker is the author of *A Regular Guy: Growing Up With Autism* and of a popular autism blog for the *San Francisco Chronicle*. She is the proud mother of three sons. The oldest, Matthew, has autism. Laura lives in Northern California with her husband, Peter.

Former journalist **Robin J. Silverman** loves to write creative nonfiction. Part of the Kansas City Writer's Group, she's been published in the *St. Louis Post-Dispatch*, *Ingram's* magazine, *Canyon Voices*, *Mayo Clinic Guide to Women's Cancers* and *Voices of Autism*. She's writing a book about parenting a daughter with Asperger syndrome.

Alison Singer is co-founder and president of the Autism Science Foundation, a non-profit organization dedicated to funding autism research and supporting families raising children with autism. Her daughter, Jodie, is diagnosed with autism. Alison also has an older brother with autism. Learn more at www.autismsciencefoundation. org.

At home in the Pacific Northwest, **Wendy Sparrow** writes for adults and young adults. She has two wonderfully quirky kids, a supportive husband, and a perpetually messy house because everything is more fun than cleaning. Most days she can be found goofing off on Twitter @WendySparrow.

Steve Spilde is a full-time parent and works part-time as a spiritual director at the Franciscan Spirituality Center of La Crosse, WI. Prior to that, he severed as a Lutheran pastor at parishes in Wisconsin, Texas, and Minnesota. E-mail him at stevespilde@charter.net.

F. Lewis "Big Daddy" Stark brings his unique view of fatherhood to life in his books and blog. His tales from the lighter side of raising a child with autism show that raising a kid with special needs is not all doom and gloom. Rather, it can be quite humorous and inspirational.

Amy Stout is a wife, mommy, and freelance writer, who, together with her family, is exploring the land of "Autism." She dreams of having a spotlessly clean castle but she tends to "nest" and snuggle with her family more than clean. She loves to travel and has a weakness for coffee and coffee houses! Learn more at histreasuredprincess. blogspot.com.

Florence Strang is a Registered Psychologist and Horticultural Therapist who lives in scenic Lewin's Cove, Newfoundland with her three children. Her book, *100 Perks of Having Cancer Plus 100 Health Tips for Surviving It*, co-written with Susan Gonzalez, will be released in 2013 (Basic Health Publications). She blogs at www.perksofcancer. com.

René Thompson lives with her editor husband, son and grouchy cat. She's working on a book concerning African Americans in southeastern Kentucky. Her son David is a sophomore and scored in the 99% on the PSAT, and continues to want to be a math teacher. E-mail her at naithom@aol.com.

Jayne Thurber-Smith is an award-winning writer for various publications including *Faith & Friends*, *Floral Business* magazine and *The Buffalo News*, and is a sports contributor to CBN.com. Her and her husband's favorite activity is being included in whatever their four adult children have going on. E-mail her at jthurbersmith@cox.net.

Eric Tor received his B.A. degree in economics from Brown University in 2009. He now works as a derivatives trader in Chicago, and by night is a music director and performer for various improv comedy troupes and bands. His brother, Charlie, will be starting college next fall. E-mail him at erictormusic@gmail.com.

J. Vetter received a Bachelor of Arts degree in computer science/information systems. She is a stay-at-home mom to two children. She enjoys running, writing, counted cross stitch, and stand-up paddle boarding. She is currently working on her first novel.

D. Alison Watt is the author of *Hurricane Dancing*, a book of poetry about life's experiences with a child who is severely affected by autism. Ali enjoys spreading awareness through speaking and writing. She has recently completed a work about her daughter turning eighteen. E-mail her at dalisonwatt@comcast.net.

Janoah White is a freelance writer living in Chicago, IL. She holds a Master of Arts degree in journalism and a Bachelor of Arts degree in television, both from Columbia College Chicago. Janoah truly has a heart for individuals with special needs, as well as their loved ones.

Jean Winegardner is a writer who lives in Maryland with her husband and three neurodiverse sons. She blogs as Stimey at www.Stimeyland.com. Jean was diagnosed with Asperger syndrome in

2012. She believes that if you have a choice between laughing and crying, you should always try to laugh.

Jennifer Doelle Young lives in Toronto, Ontario, where she writes software documentation and blogs about her life. She enjoys running, photography and *Whack-a-Mole*, but it's her family that is the chicken soup for her soul. She dreams of co-authoring a book about autism with her son. E-mail her at jendoelle@gmail.com.

René Zimbelman is finishing her first novel, *Mizerably Happy*. She graduated with a degree in marketing and she returned to school for further instruction in early childhood education. René loves to write, hike, travel and be with family and friends. Visit her blog at renezimbe.blogspot.com.

Meet Our Authors

Rebecca Landa, PhD, CCC-SLP, is the founder and director of the Center for Autism and Related Disorders at Kennedy Krieger Institute in Baltimore, Maryland. She is also a professor of psychiatry at the Johns Hopkins University School of Medicine.

Dr. Landa earned her master's degree at the Pennsylvania State University and her doctorate at the University of Washington. She completed post-doctoral training in psychiatric genetics at Johns Hopkins. She is the recipient of the NIMH Shannon Award for excellent and innovative research, as well as the Rita Rudel Prize for Developmental Neuropsychology.

Dr. Landa is a both a researcher and speech-language pathologist. She has practiced in the public schools, university clinics and hospital settings. Dr. Landa has consulted with schools and families on an international level to establish state-of-the-science educational programming for children with autism spectrum disorders. Her research focuses on neuropsychological, learning and communication process in autism across the lifespan, with a special interest in early detection and intervention.

Dr. Landa and her husband have two grown children. Learn more about her work by visiting www.kennedykrieger.org.

Mary Beth Marsden is a local Emmy Award-winning broadcast journalist who graduated from the University of Maryland with a Bachelor of Arts in Communications. She started her career at WJLA-TV in Washington, D.C. as a television news producer and after a couple of stops at TV stations on the East Coast, moved back to Maryland. Mary Beth spent twenty-one years as a reporter and the evening news anchor at WMAR-TV, in Baltimore. Today, she is the host of an afternoon news program on WBAL-Radio and is often interviewed or asked to speak on topics involving television, radio, social media, education and autism.

Mary Beth and her husband Mark have two boys and a girl who, at the age of three and a half, was diagnosed with an autism spectrum disorder. Several years after her daughter's diagnosis, Mary Beth wanted to do something to help others facing some of the same challenges. In 2011, she started producing videos that offer "solutions" for families affected by autism.

Mary Beth believes awareness and understanding are the keys to making this world a more welcoming place for people on the spectrum. Her enlightening videos can be found on her website RealLookAutism.com, on the Real Look Autism YouTube channel, as part of Disney Family's video library and on The Autism Channel.

You can contact Mary Beth at reallookautism@gmail.com or on Twitter @marybmarsden or on Facebook at Real Look Autism.

Nancy Burrows is a freelance writer who graduated Phi Beta Kappa from the University of Pennsylvania, with a Bachelor of Arts degree in English. Nancy spent years writing and producing for advertising agencies and television networks such as PBS, Nickelodeon, and TV Land. She married her high school sweetheart in 1995. His surgical training led them from New York to Missouri to Minnesota—and finally to Maryland. They currently live in Baltimore, with their fourteen-year-old daughter, Allie, and eleven-year-old son, James.

When James was diagnosed with an autism spectrum disorder at two and a half, Nancy put her career on hold to focus on researching and implementing an early intervention plan. Raising Allie and James, and acting as mom/therapist/advocate was a full-time job for eight all-consuming years. Now, Nancy is thrilled to be a part of this book, putting her creative skills to work on a project that has tremendous personal meaning for her family. In her stories, "James 101" and "Bedtime Routine," she hopes readers will get a sense of James's quirky charm.

Please contact Nancy at nancyburrows813@gmail.com and share your thoughts about *Chicken Soup for the Soul: Raising Kids on the Spectrum*.

Amy Newmark is Chicken Soup for the Soul's publisher and editor-in-chief, after a thirty-year career as a writer, speaker, financial analyst, and business executive in the worlds of finance and telecommunications. Amy is a *magna cum laude* graduate of Harvard College, where she majored in Portuguese, minored in French, and traveled extensively. She and her husband have four grown children.

After a long career writing books on telecommunications, voluminous financial reports, business plans, and corporate press releases, Chicken Soup for the Soul is a breath of fresh air for Amy. She has fallen in love with Chicken Soup for the Soul and its life-changing books, and really enjoys putting these books together for Chicken Soup for the Soul's wonderful readers. She has co-authored more than five dozen *Chicken Soup for the Soul* books and has edited another three dozen.

You can reach Amy with any questions or comments through webmaster@chickensoupforthesoul.com and you can follow her on Twitter @amynewmark.

www.chickensoup.com

Thank You

We owe huge thanks to all of our contributors. We know that you poured your hearts and souls into the thousands of stories and poems that you shared with us. We appreciate your willingness to open up your lives to other parents of children with ASD and share your own experiences, no matter how personal.

We could only publish a small percentage of the stories that were submitted, but every single one was read and even the ones that do not appear in the book had an influence on us and on the final manuscript.

We couldn't have created this book without the help of Bryan Stark at the Kennedy Krieger Institute. He helped to shepherd this project through for all of us. We are also indebted to D'ette Corona, the assistant publisher of Chicken Soup for the Soul, who managed this complex process from soup to nuts, working with the four coauthors and all the contributors.

We also owe a very special thanks to our creative director and book producer, Brian Taylor at Pneuma Books, for his brilliant and sensitive vision for the cover and interior of this special collection.